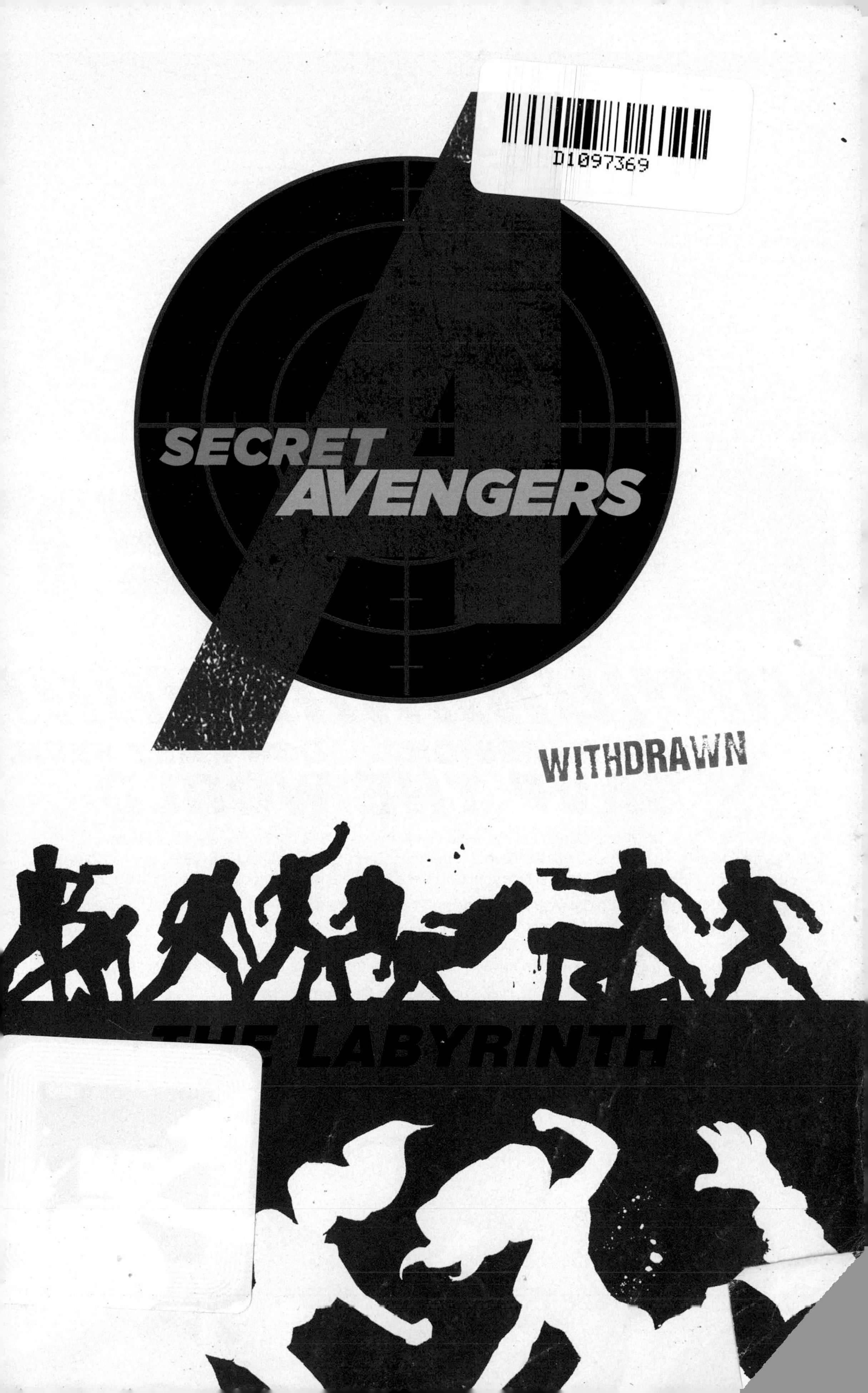
SECRET
AVENGERS
THE LABYRINTH

COLLECTION EDITOR: **JENNIFER GRÜNWALD**
ASSISTANT EDITOR: **SARAH BRUNSTAD**
ASSOCIATE MANAGING EDITOR: **ALEX STARBUCK**
EDITOR, SPECIAL PROJECTS: **MARK D. BEAZLEY**
SENIOR EDITOR, SPECIAL PROJECTS: **JEFF YOUNGQUIST**
SVP PRINT, SALES & MARKETING: **DAVID GABRIEL**
BOOK DESIGNER: **RODOLFO MURAGUCHI**

EDITOR IN CHIEF: **AXEL ALONSO**
CHIEF CREATIVE OFFICER: **JOE QUESADA**
PUBLISHER: **DAN BUCKLEY**
EXECUTIVE PRODUCER: **ALAN FINE**

10 9 8 7 6 5 4 3 2 1

SECRET

RUN THE MISSION. DON'T GET SEEN.
SAVE THE WORLD.

S.H.I.E.L.D. Director Maria Hill has assembled a covert squad of heroes she calls the Secret Avengers — Black Widow, Spider-Woman, Hawkeye, S.H.I.E.L.D. agents Nick Fury and Phil Coulson, and M.O.D.O.K., a (former?) terrorist Hill hired to create new technologies for S.H.I.E.L.D.

Recently, Black Widow, Spider-Woman and Agent Coulson were sent to Sokotra to recover a sentient black hole bomb that calls itself Vladimir. Spider-Woman was able to develop a friendship with the bomb and calm him down while Black Widow took down Lady Bullseye. On that mission, they discovered Coulson is suffereing from PTSD. But before anyone could do anything about it, he took off without saying why.

In an effort to help his friend out, Nick Fury looked in Coulson's locker for a clue as to where he'd gone — but was greeted with a face full of acid instead. Who is responsible for the acid? And who killed the captive Hitman? Director Hill thinks everything might lead back to M.O.D.O.K.

To complicate matters further, M.O.D.O.K. discovered a startling secret about the Fury — a cybiote programmed to exterminate all life that S.H.I.E.L.D. had taken prisoner. It had recently been pregnant.

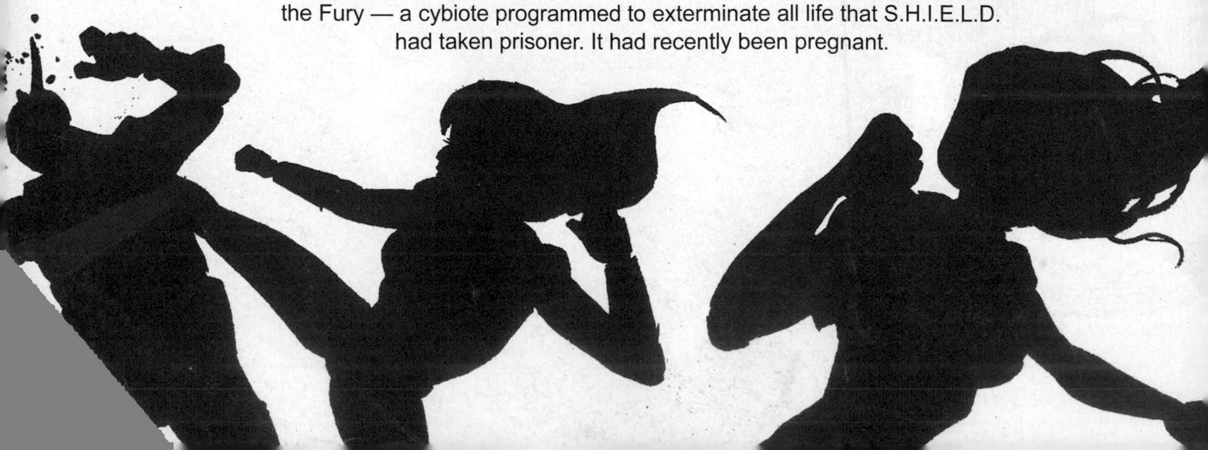

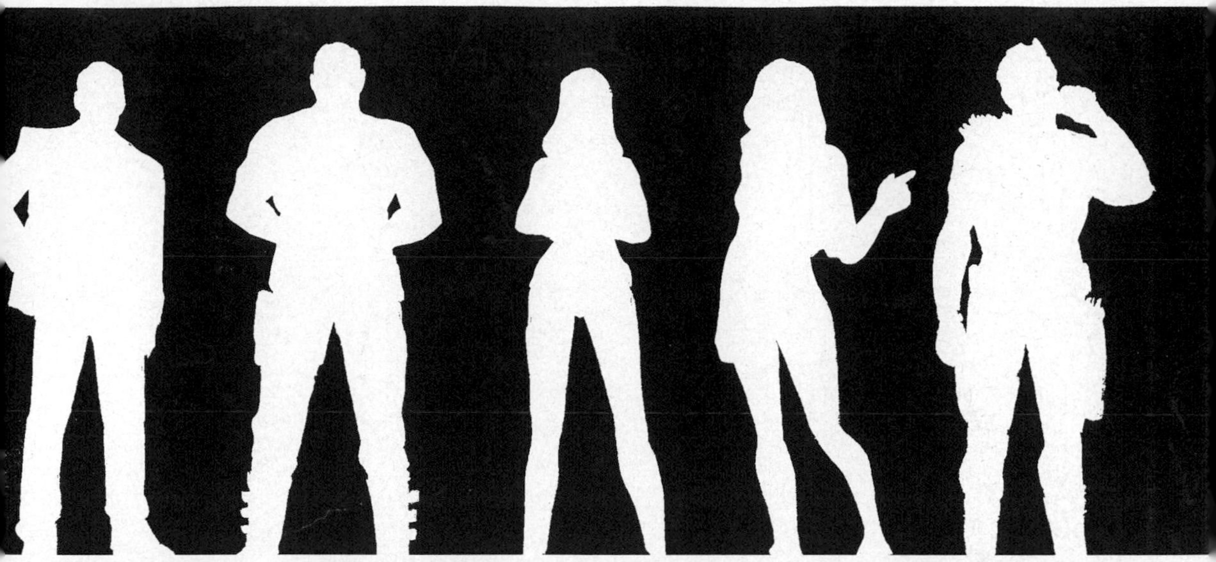

AVENGERS

WRITER:
ALES KOT

ARTIST:
MICHAEL WALSH

COLORIST:
MATTHEW WILSON

LETTERER:
VC'S CLAYTON COWLES

COVER ART:
TRADD MOORE & MATTHEW WILSON

ASSISTANT EDITOR:
JON MOISAN

EDITOR:
WIL MOSS

EXECUTIVE EDITOR:
TOM BREVOORT

AVENGERS CREATED BY STAN LEE & JACK KIRBY

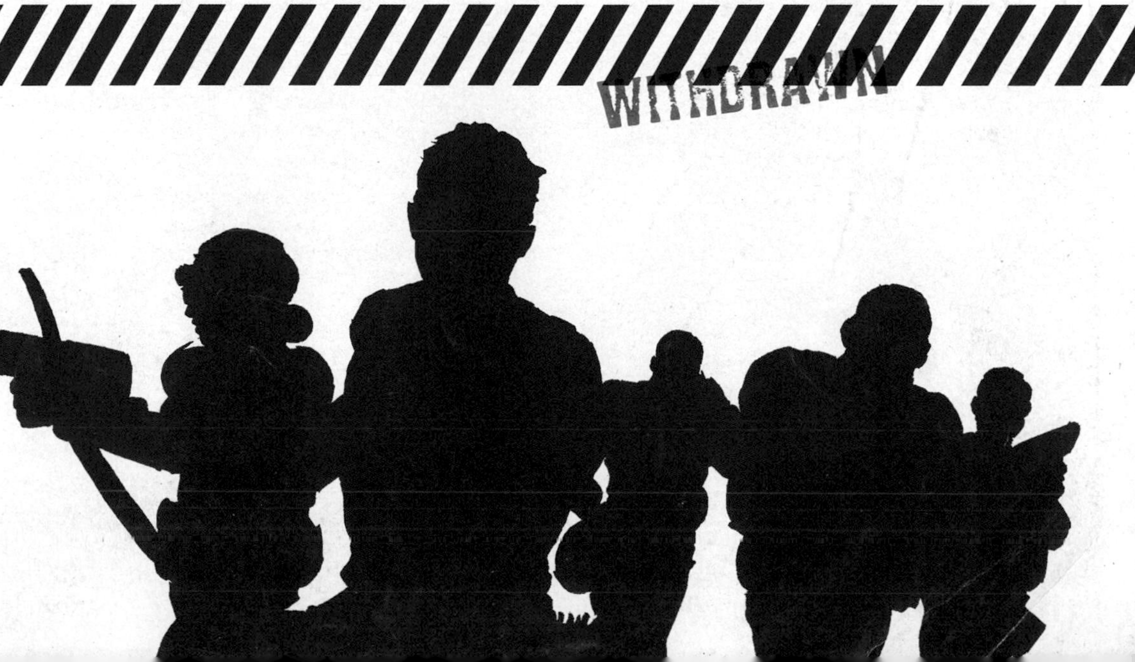

6

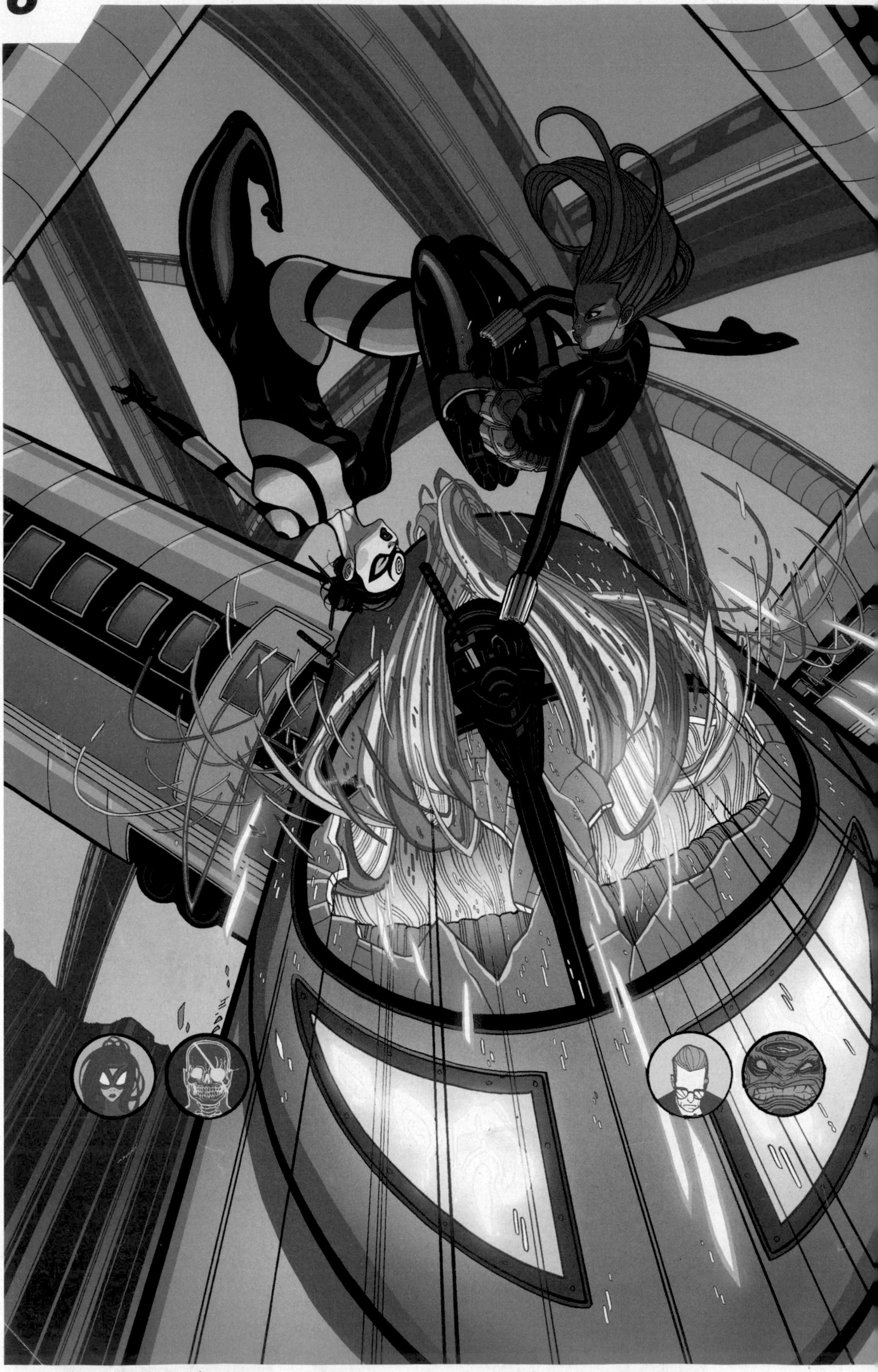

NOTHING STOPS THIS TRAIN

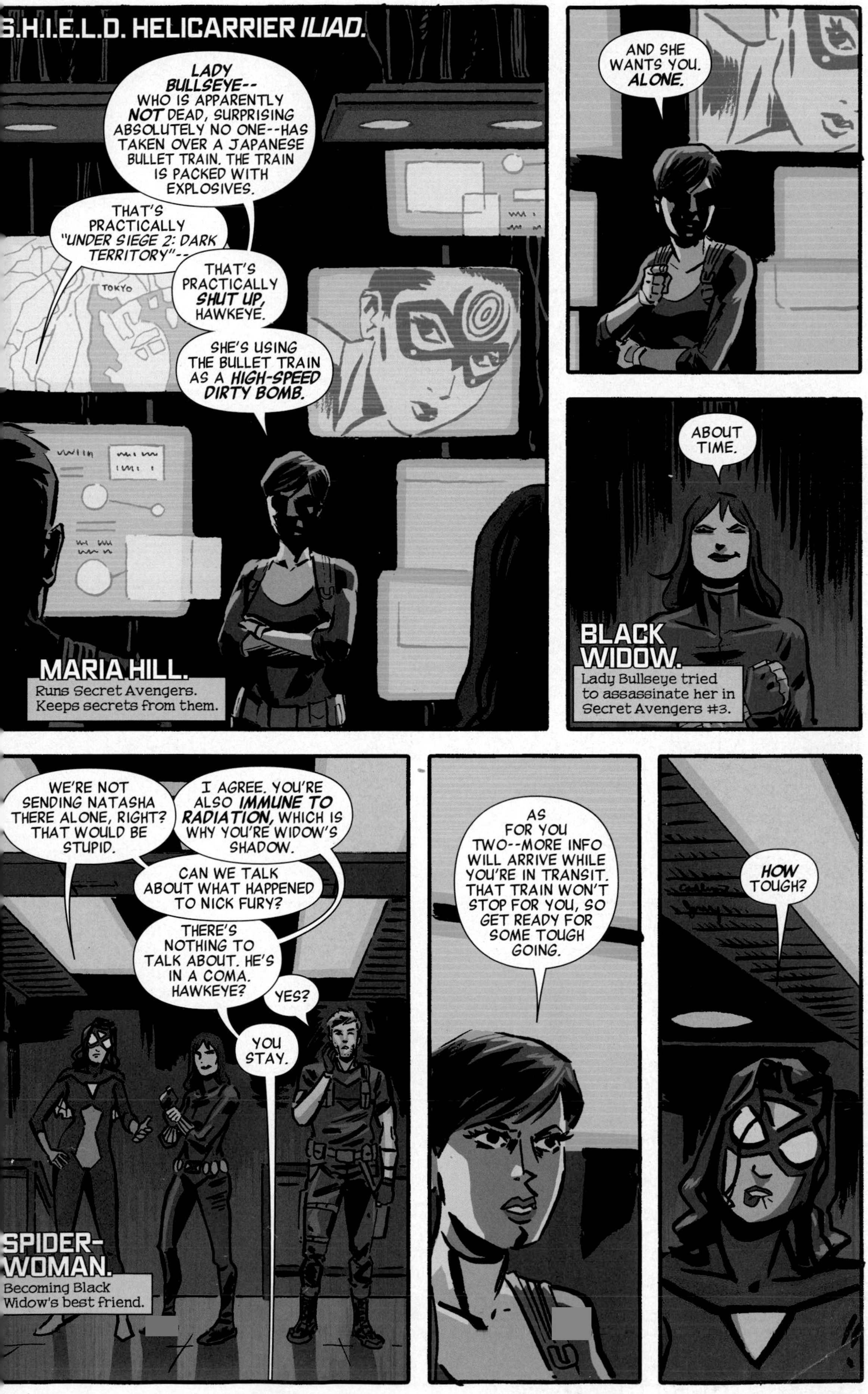
S.H.I.E.L.D. HELICARRIER ILIAD.
LADY BULLSEYE--WHO IS APPARENTLY NOT DEAD, SURPRISING ABSOLUTELY NO ONE--HAS TAKEN OVER A JAPANESE BULLET TRAIN. THE TRAIN IS PACKED WITH EXPLOSIVES.
THAT'S PRACTICALLY "UNDER SIEGE 2: DARK TERRITORY"--
THAT'S PRACTICALLY SHUT UP, HAWKEYE.
SHE'S USING THE BULLET TRAIN AS A HIGH-SPEED DIRTY BOMB.
TOKYO
MARIA HILL.
Runs Secret Avengers. Keeps secrets from them.
AND SHE WANTS YOU. ALONE.
ABOUT TIME.
BLACK WIDOW.
Lady Bullseye tried to assassinate her in Secret Avengers #3.
WE'RE NOT SENDING NATASHA THERE ALONE, RIGHT? THAT WOULD BE STUPID.
I AGREE. YOU'RE ALSO IMMUNE TO RADIATION, WHICH IS WHY YOU'RE WIDOW'S SHADOW.
CAN WE TALK ABOUT WHAT HAPPENED TO NICK FURY?
THERE'S NOTHING TO TALK ABOUT. HE'S IN A COMA. HAWKEYE?
YES?
YOU STAY.
SPIDER-WOMAN.
Becoming Black Widow's best friend.
AS FOR YOU TWO--MORE INFO WILL ARRIVE WHILE YOU'RE IN TRANSIT. THAT TRAIN WON'T STOP FOR YOU, SO GET READY FOR SOME TOUGH GOING.
HOW TOUGH?

"VERY."

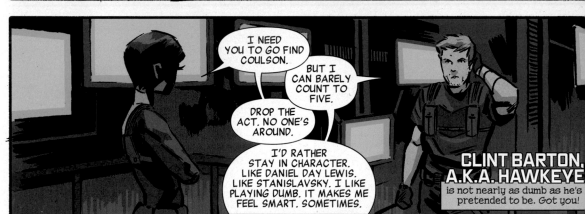

I NEED YOU TO GO FIND COULSON.

BUT I CAN BARELY COUNT TO FIVE.

DROP THE ACT. NO ONE'S AROUND.

I'D RATHER STAY IN CHARACTER. LIKE DANIEL DAY LEWIS. LIKE STANISLAVSKY. I LIKE PLAYING DUMB. IT MAKES ME FEEL SMART. SOMETIMES.

CLINT BARTON, A.K.A. HAWKEYE
is not nearly as dumb as he's pretended to be. Got you!

LADY BULLSEYE.
Mysterious international assassin. Has mysterious grudge against Black Widow.*

*SERIOUSLY. WE DON'T KNOW WHAT THIS IS ABOUT. BUT SHE'S COOL, RIGHT? READ THE *DAREDEVIL: LADY BULLSEYE* TPB TO FIND OUT MORE ABOUT HER.

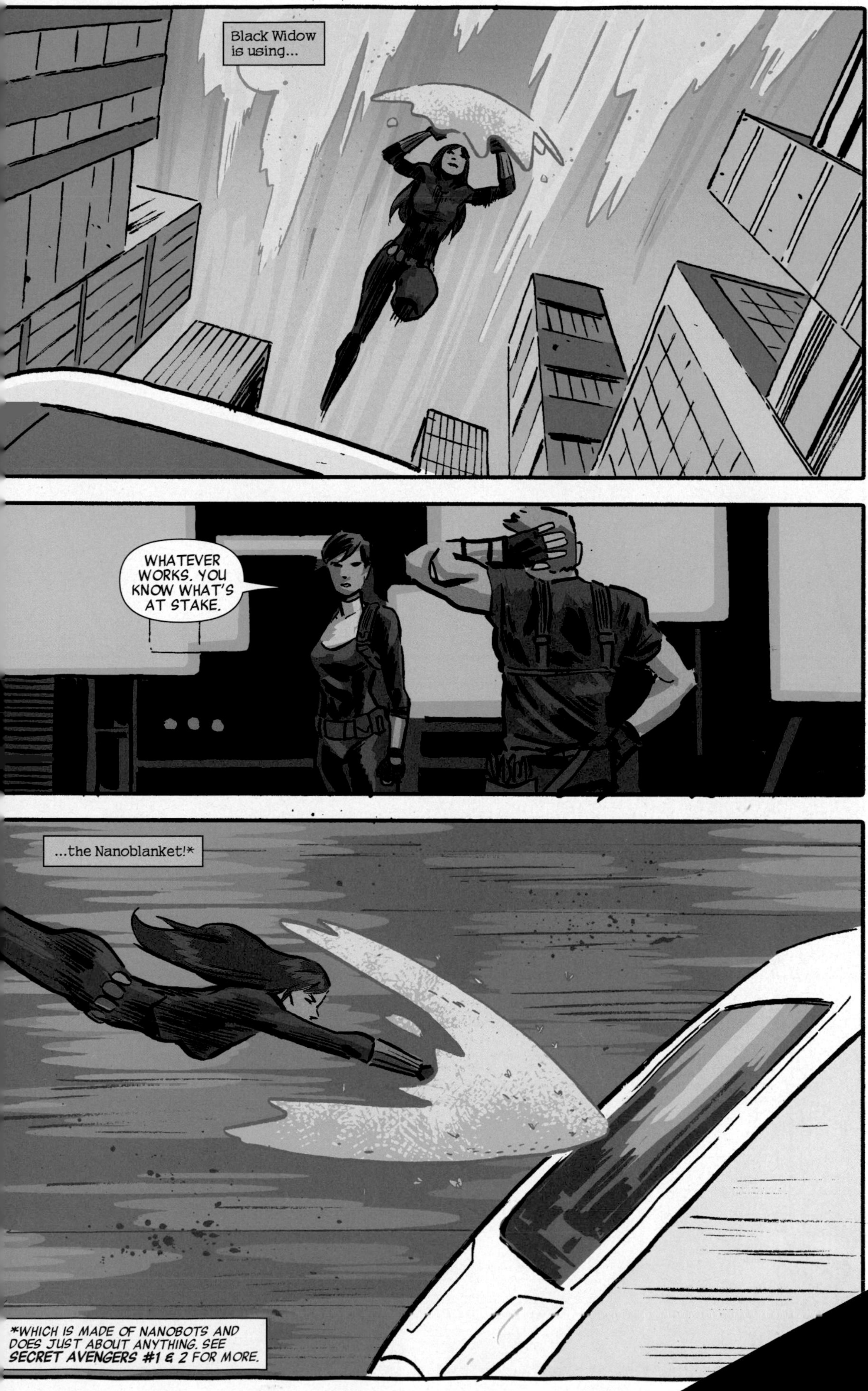
Black Widow is using...
WHATEVER WORKS. YOU KNOW WHAT'S AT STAKE.
...the Nanoblanket!*
*WHICH IS MADE OF NANOBOTS AND DOES JUST ABOUT ANYTHING. SEE SECRET AVENGERS #1 & 2 FOR MORE.

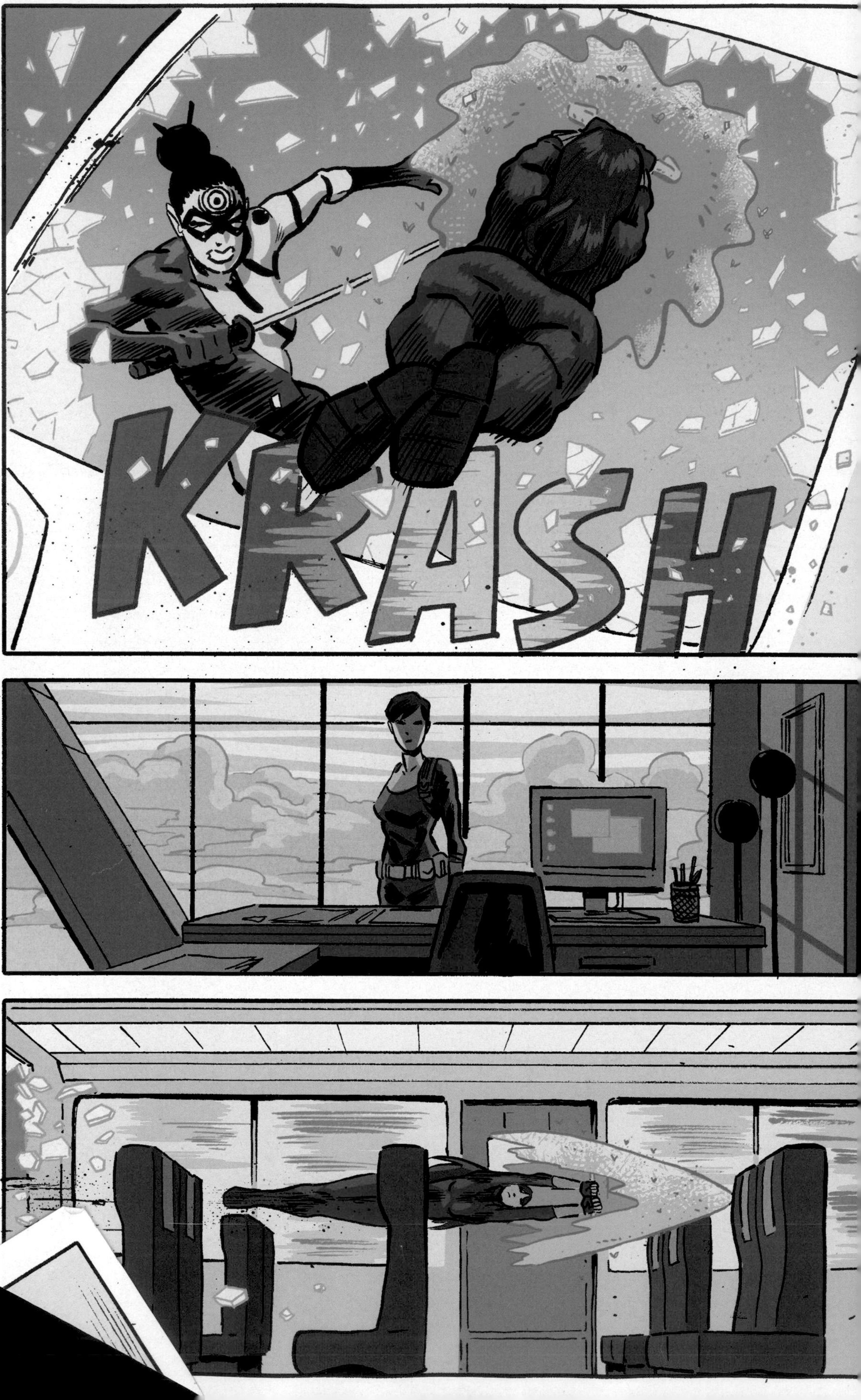
KRASH

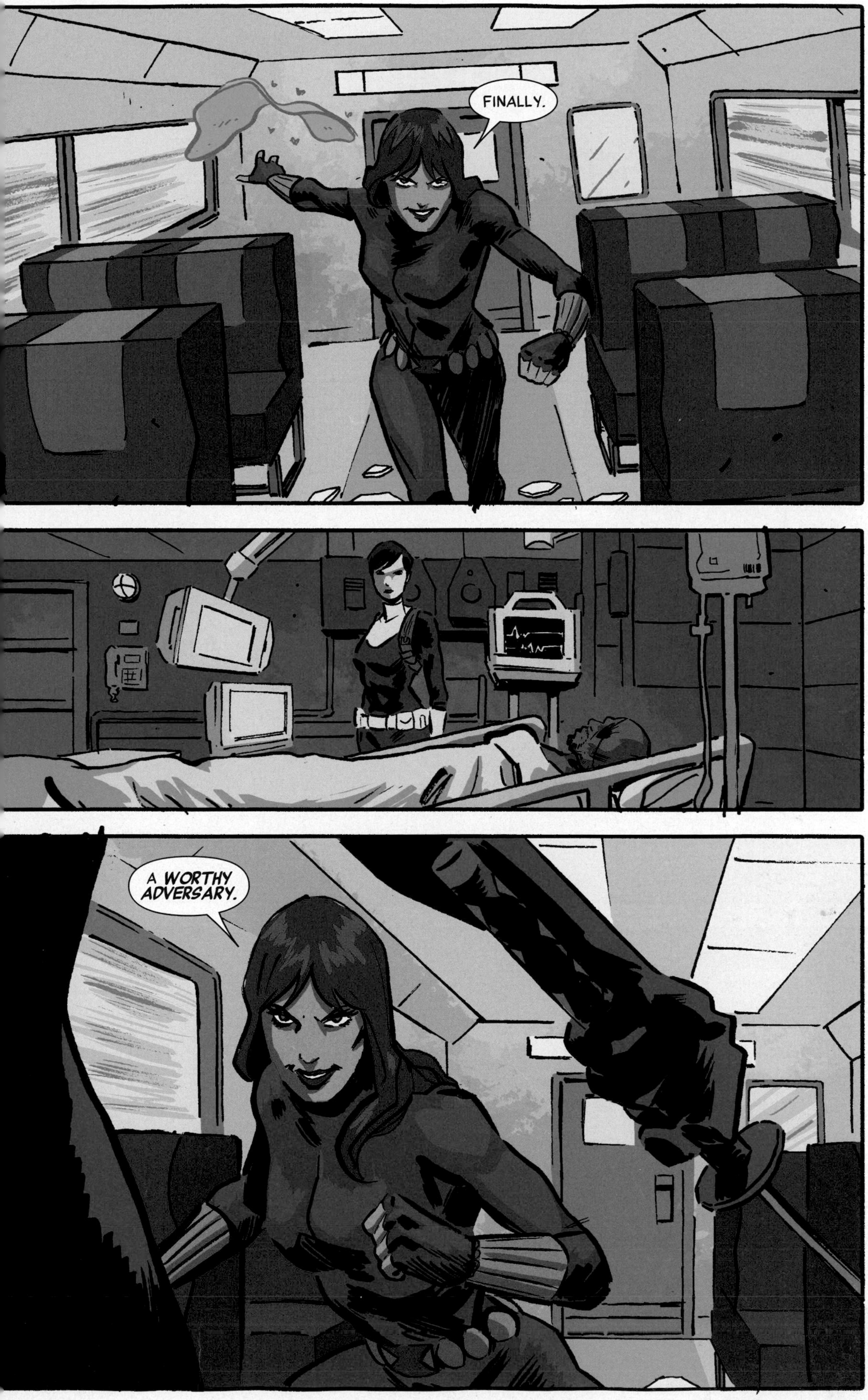
FINALLY.
A WORTHY ADVERSARY.

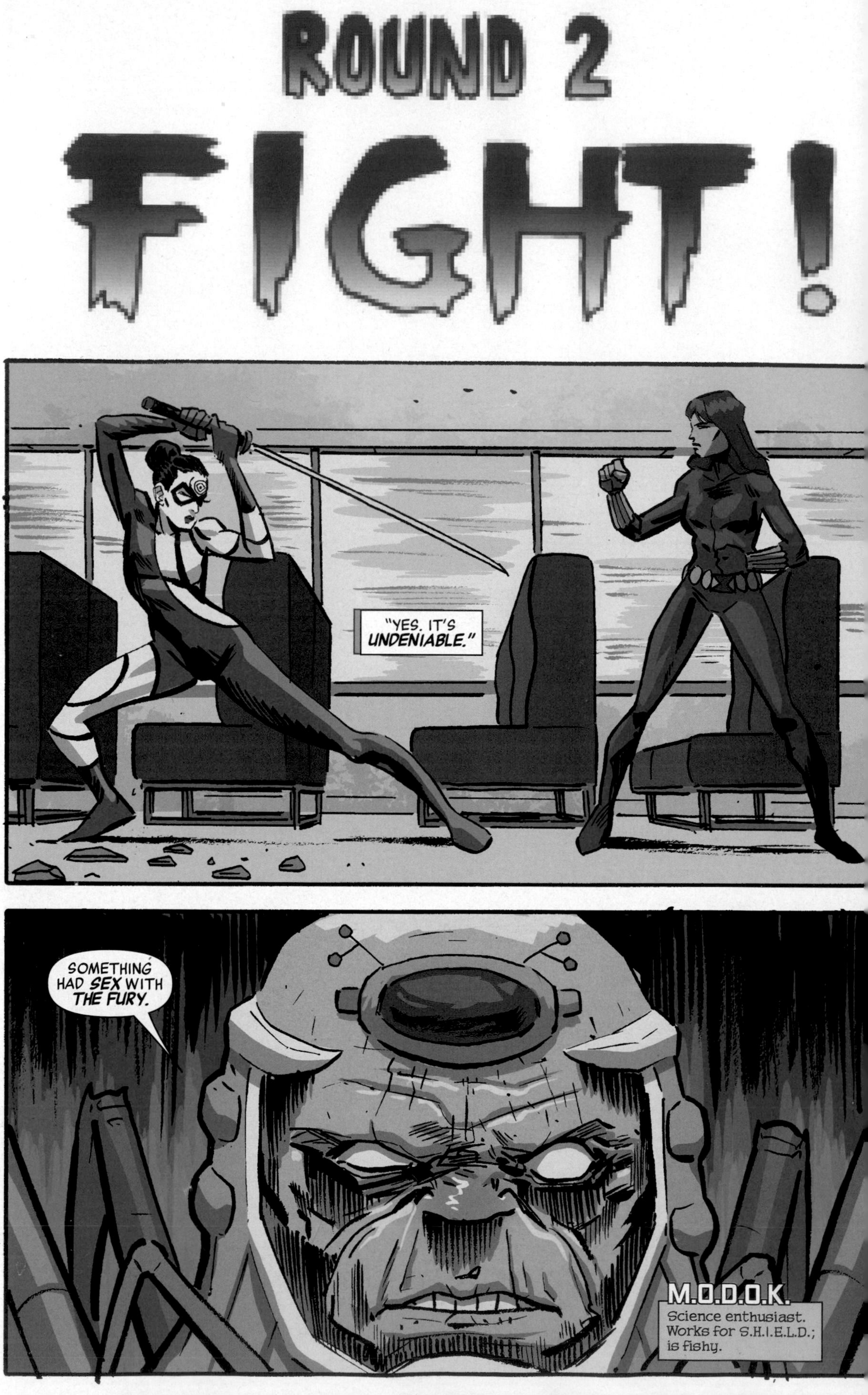
ROUND 2
FIGHT!
"YES. IT'S UNDENIABLE."
SOMETHING HAD SEX WITH THE FURY.
M.O.D.O.K.
Science enthusiast. Works for S.H.I.E.L.D.; is fishy.

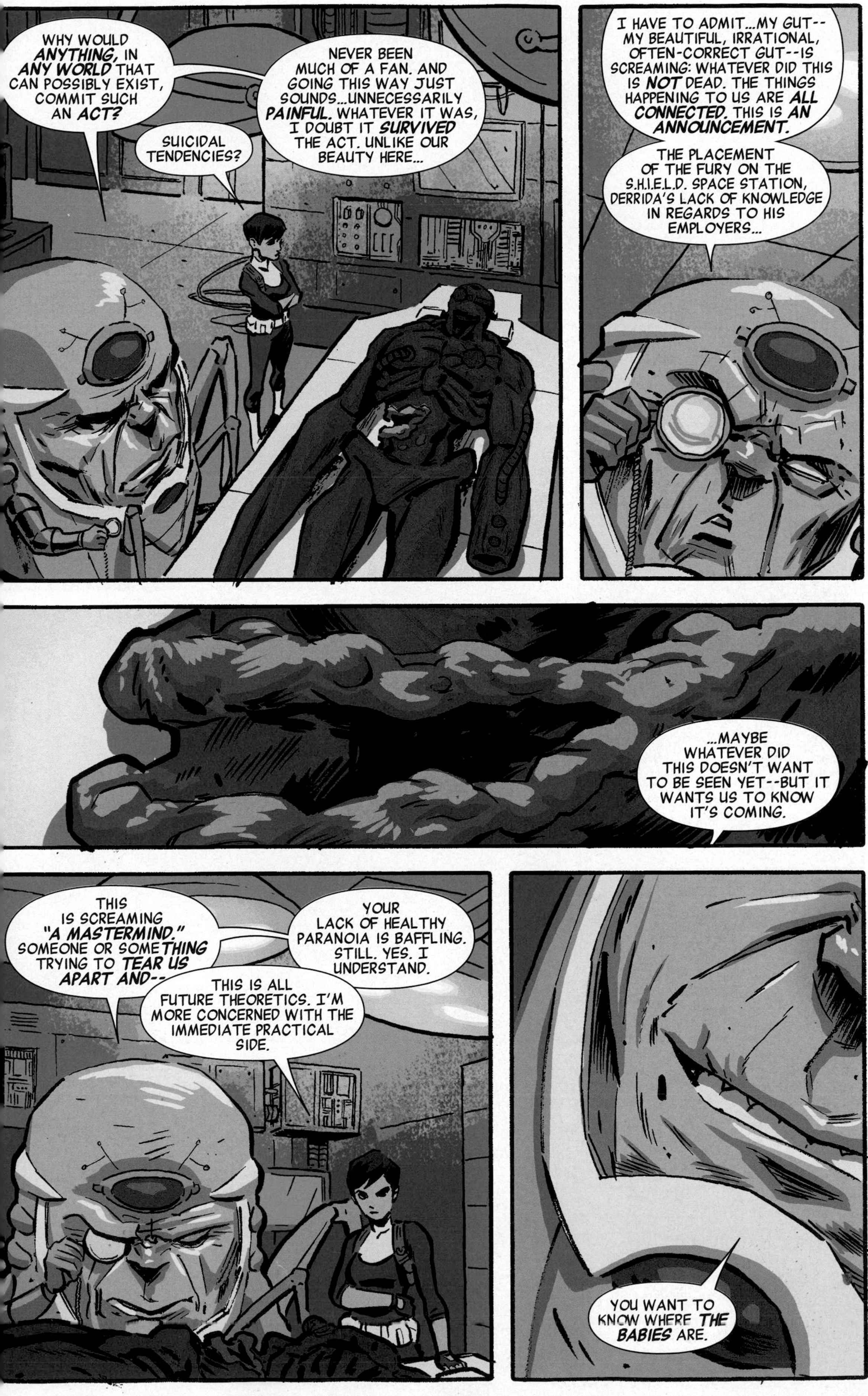
WHY WOULD ANYTHING, IN ANY WORLD THAT CAN POSSIBLY EXIST, COMMIT SUCH AN ACT?
SUICIDAL TENDENCIES?
NEVER BEEN MUCH OF A FAN. AND GOING THIS WAY JUST SOUNDS...UNNECESSARILY PAINFUL. WHATEVER IT WAS, I DOUBT IT SURVIVED THE ACT. UNLIKE OUR BEAUTY HERE...
I HAVE TO ADMIT...MY GUT--MY BEAUTIFUL, IRRATIONAL, OFTEN-CORRECT GUT--IS SCREAMING: WHATEVER DID THIS IS NOT DEAD. THE THINGS HAPPENING TO US ARE ALL CONNECTED. THIS IS AN ANNOUNCEMENT.
THE PLACEMENT OF THE FURY ON THE S.H.I.E.L.D. SPACE STATION, DERRIDA'S LACK OF KNOWLEDGE IN REGARDS TO HIS EMPLOYERS...
...MAYBE WHATEVER DID THIS DOESN'T WANT TO BE SEEN YET--BUT IT WANTS US TO KNOW IT'S COMING.
THIS IS SCREAMING "A MASTERMIND." SOMEONE OR SOMETHING TRYING TO TEAR US APART AND--
YOUR LACK OF HEALTHY PARANOIA IS BAFFLING. STILL. YES. I UNDERSTAND.
THIS IS ALL FUTURE THEORETICS. I'M MORE CONCERNED WITH THE IMMEDIATE PRACTICAL SIDE.
YOU WANT TO KNOW WHERE THE BABIES ARE.

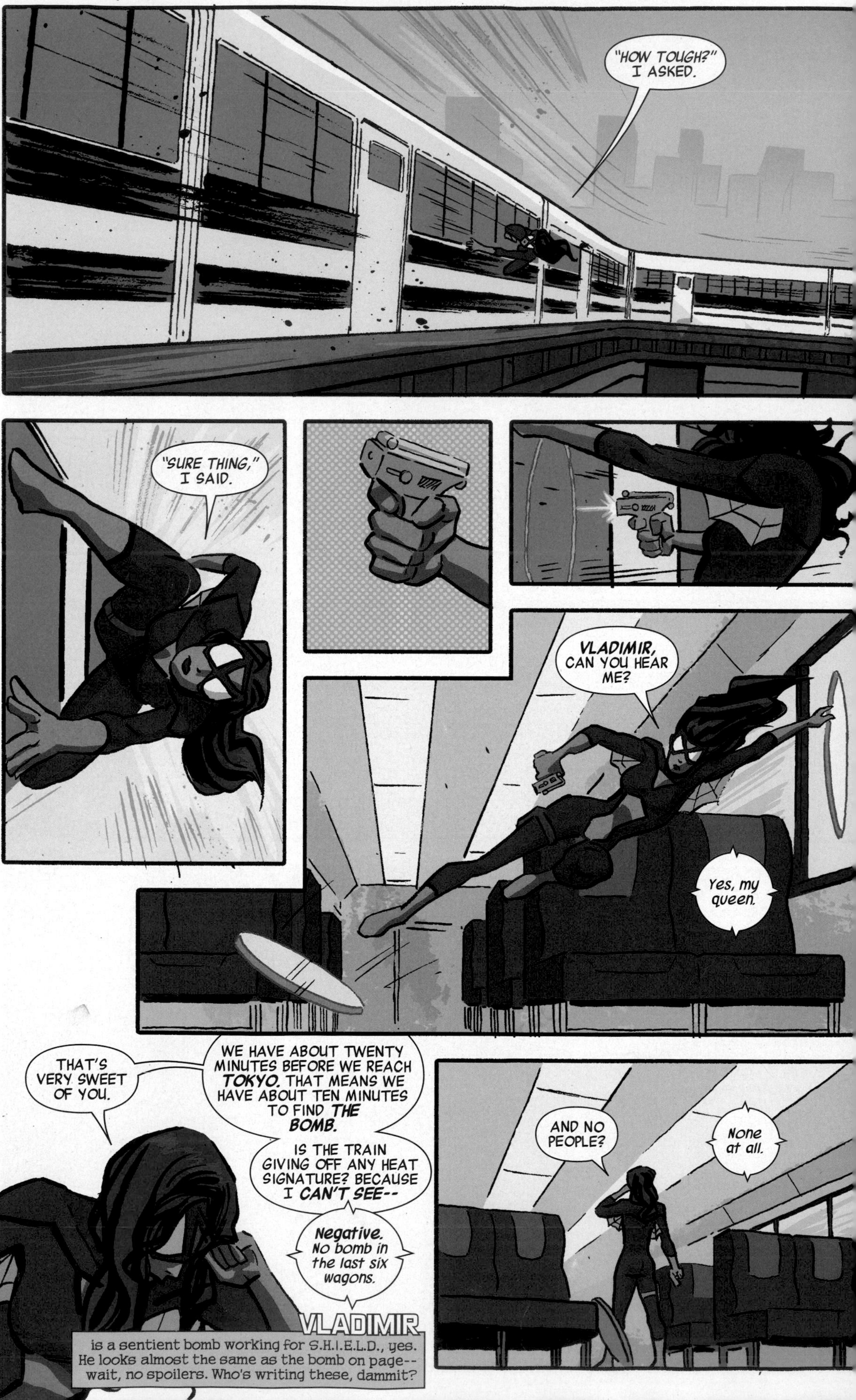
"HOW TOUGH?" I ASKED.
"SURE THING," I SAID.
VLADIMIR, CAN YOU HEAR ME?
Yes, my queen.
THAT'S VERY SWEET OF YOU.
WE HAVE ABOUT TWENTY MINUTES BEFORE WE REACH TOKYO. THAT MEANS WE HAVE ABOUT TEN MINUTES TO FIND THE BOMB.
IS THE TRAIN GIVING OFF ANY HEAT SIGNATURE? BECAUSE I CAN'T SEE--
Negative. No bomb in the last six wagons.
VLADIMIR
is a sentient bomb working for S.H.I.E.L.D., yes. He looks almost the same as the bomb on page--wait, no spoilers. Who's writing these, dammit?
AND NO PEOPLE?
None at all.

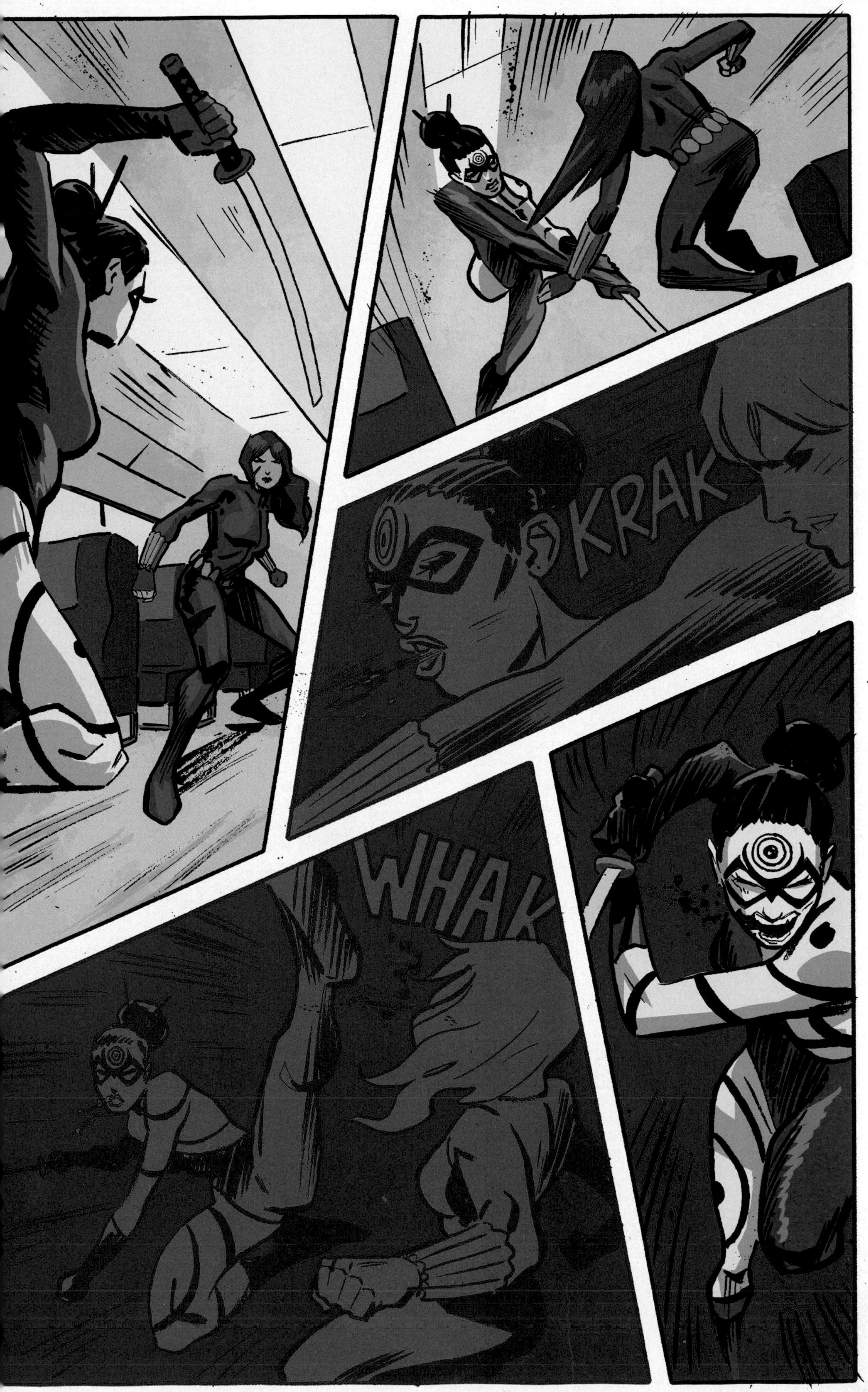
KRAK
WHAK

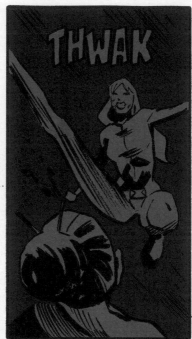

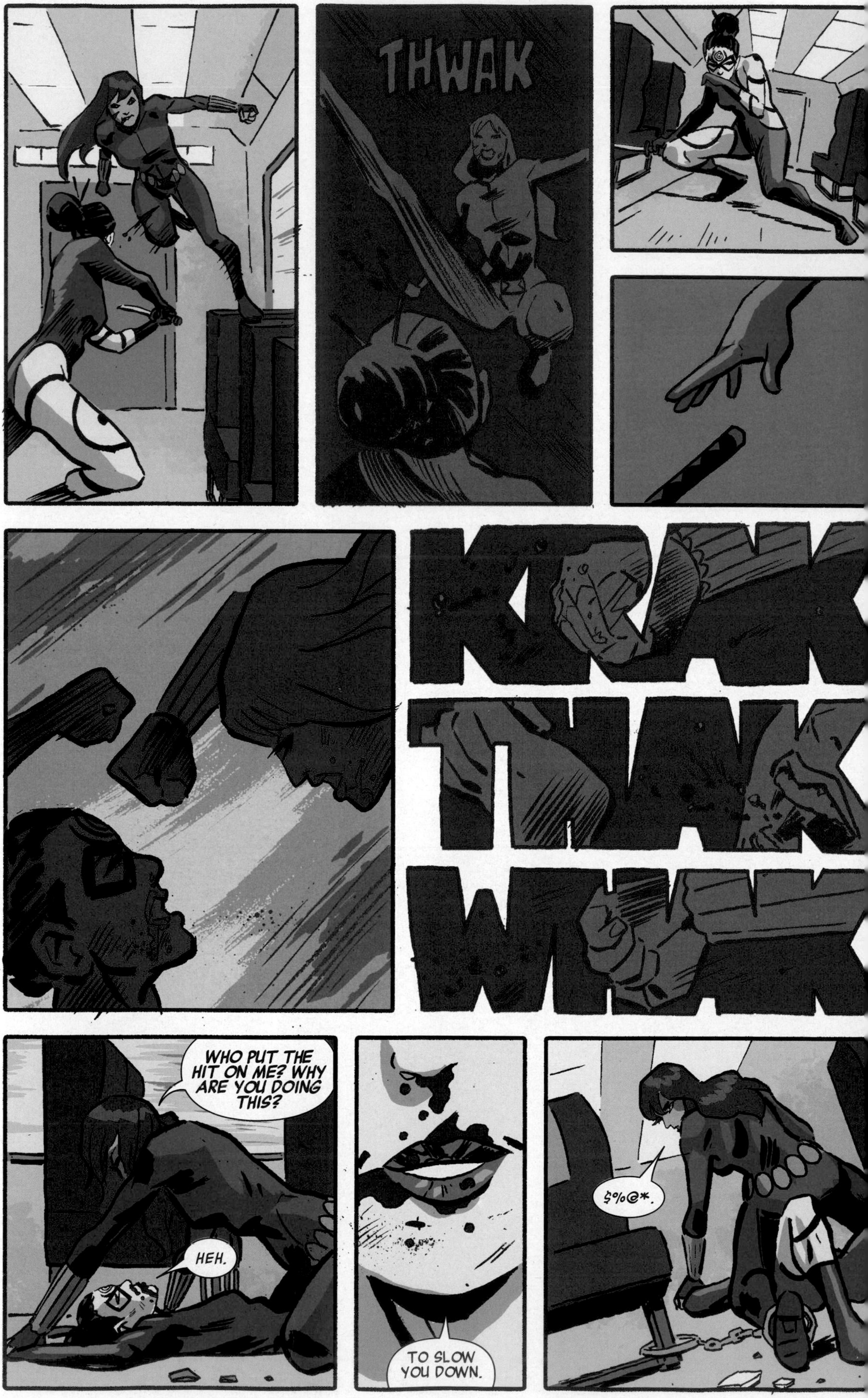
THWAK
KRAK
THAK
WHAK
WHO PUT THE HIT ON ME? WHY ARE YOU DOING THIS?
HEH.
TO SLOW YOU DOWN.
$%@*.

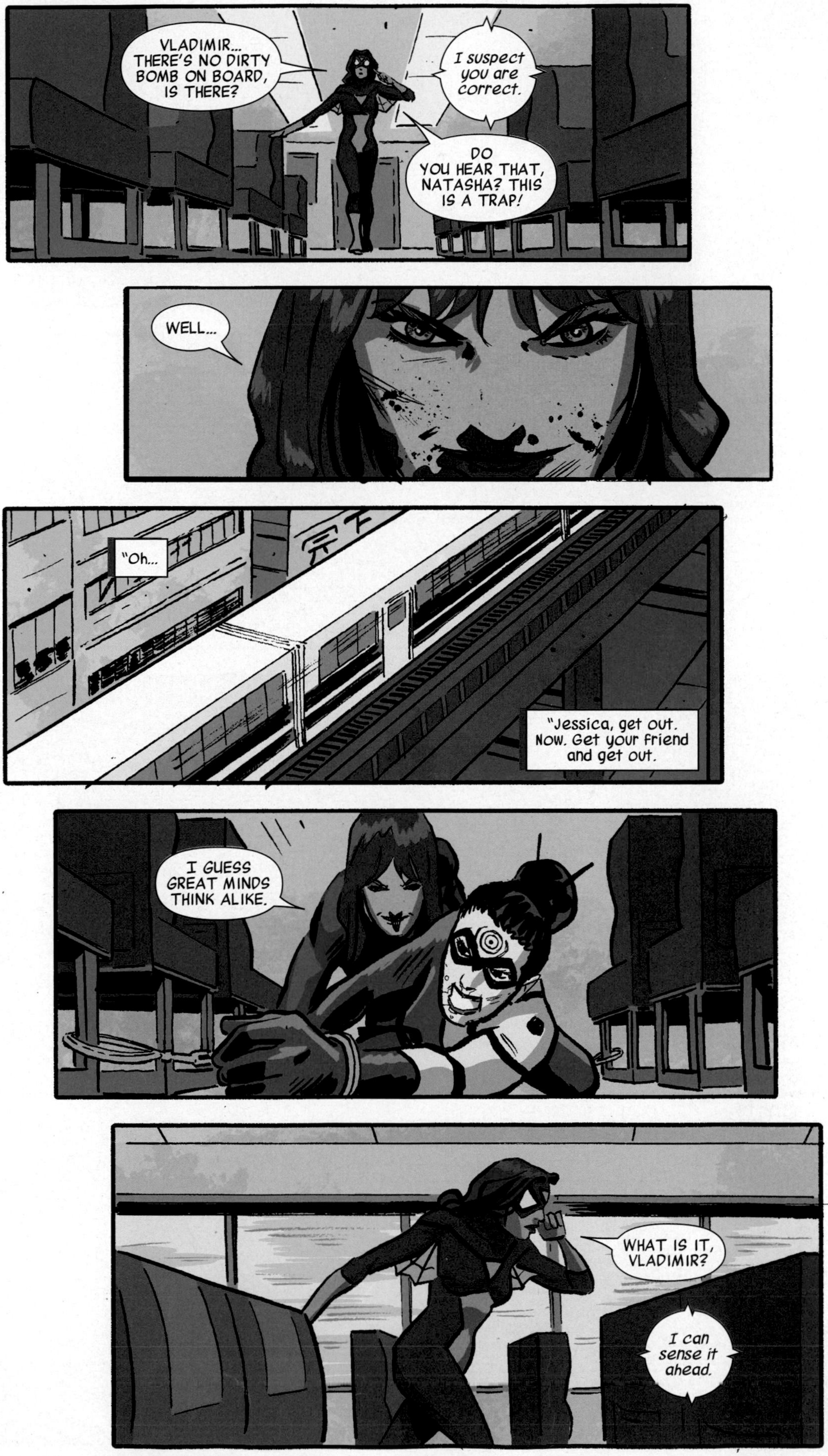
VLADIMIR... THERE'S NO DIRTY BOMB ON BOARD, IS THERE?
I suspect you are correct.
DO YOU HEAR THAT, NATASHA? THIS IS A TRAP!
WELL...
"Oh...
"Jessica, get out. Now. Get your friend and get out.
I GUESS GREAT MINDS THINK ALIKE.
WHAT IS IT, VLADIMIR?
I can sense it ahead.

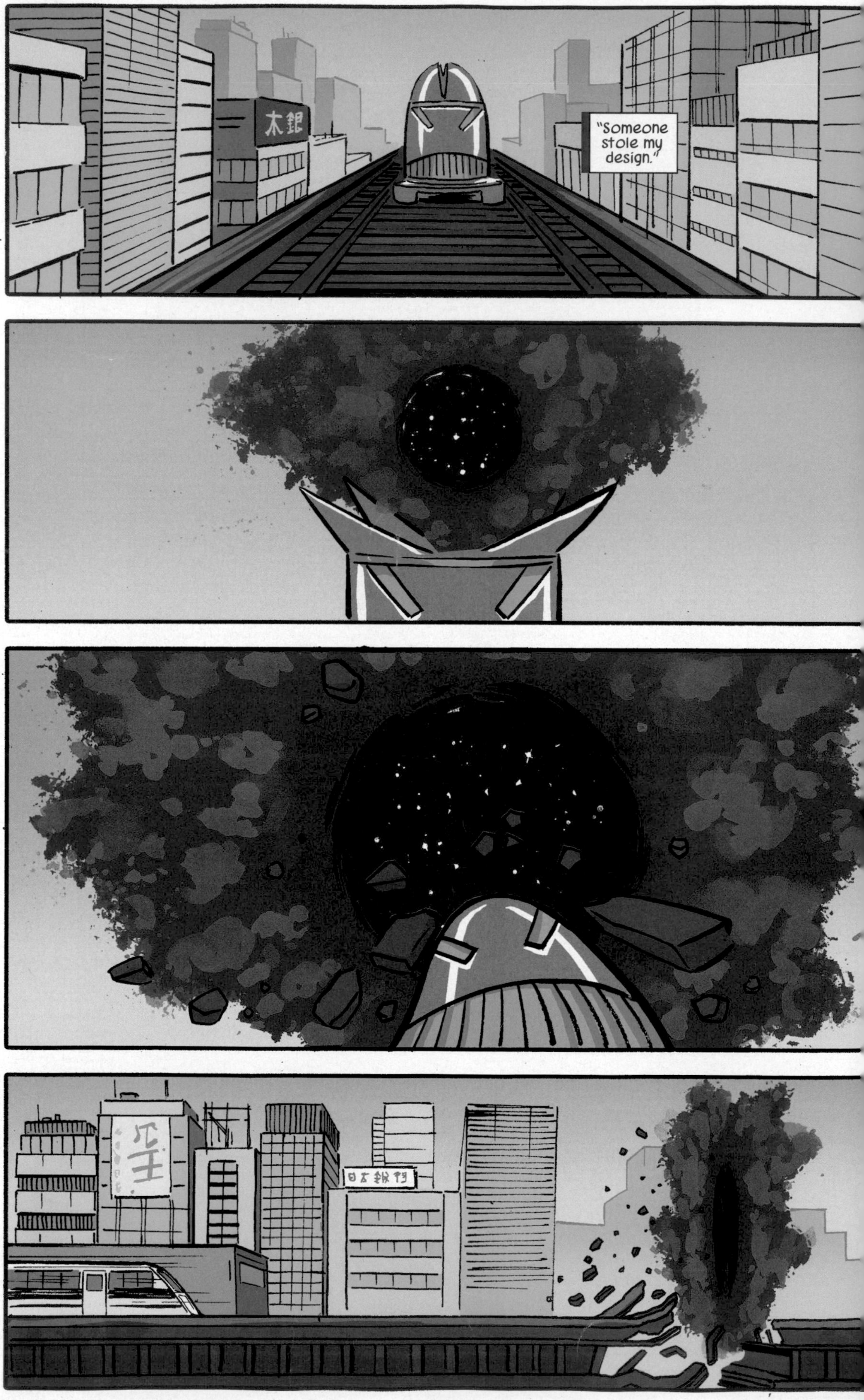
"Someone stole my design."

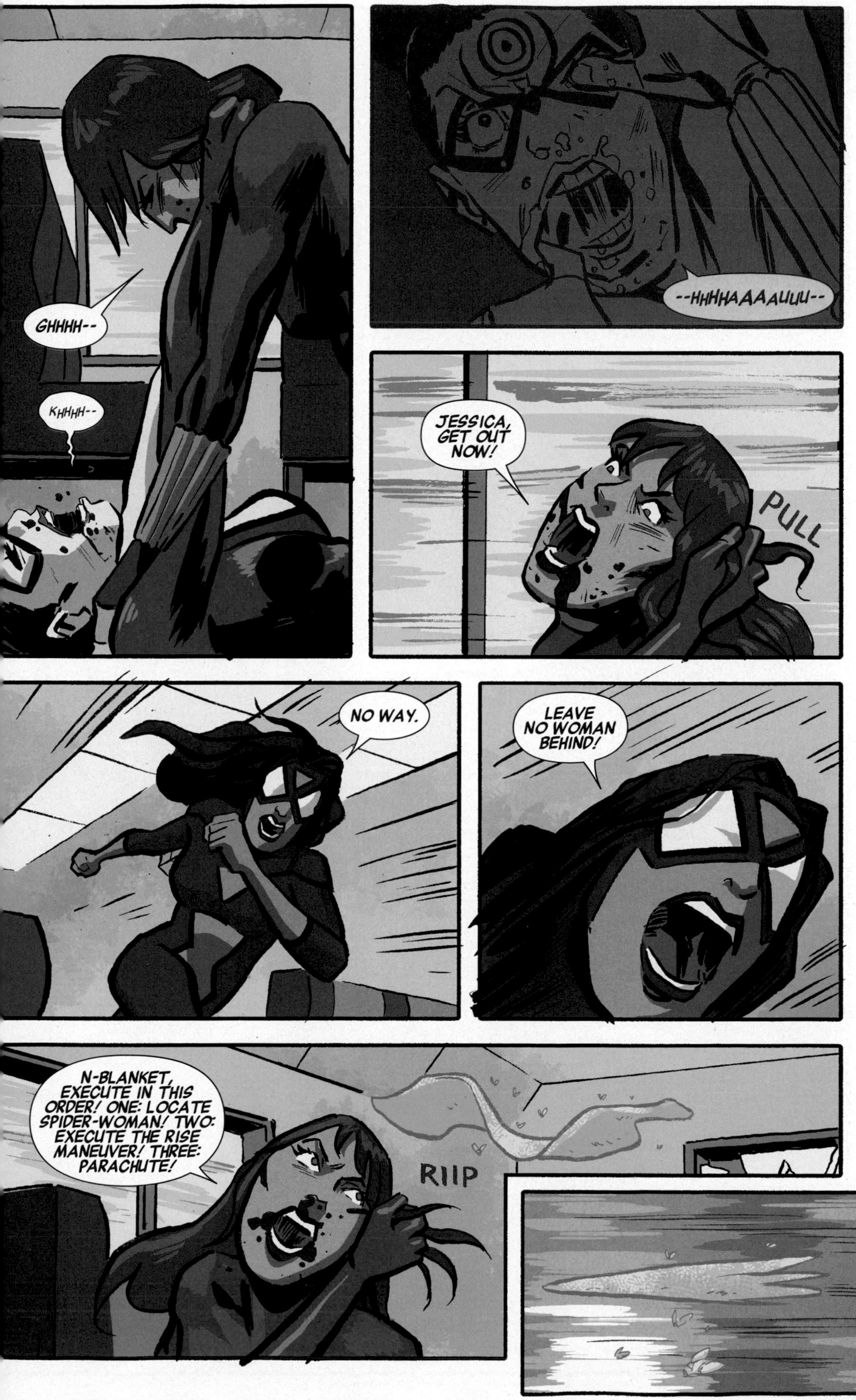
GHHHH--
KHHHH--
--HHHHAAAAUUU--
JESSICA, GET OUT NOW!
PULL
NO WAY.
LEAVE NO WOMAN BEHIND!
N-BLANKET, EXECUTE IN THIS ORDER! ONE: LOCATE SPIDER-WOMAN! TWO: EXECUTE THE RISE MANEUVER! THREE: PARACHUTE!
RIIP

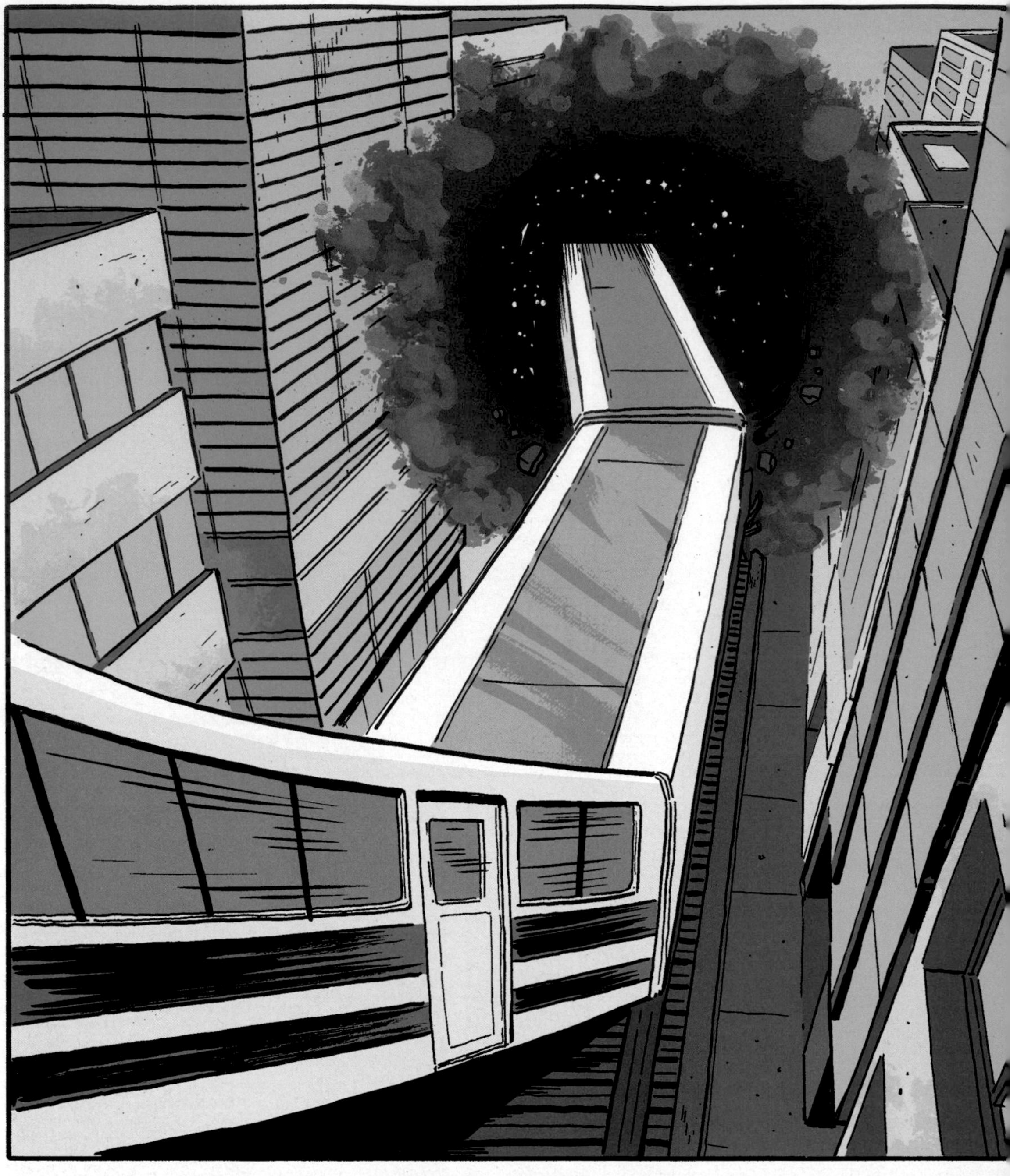

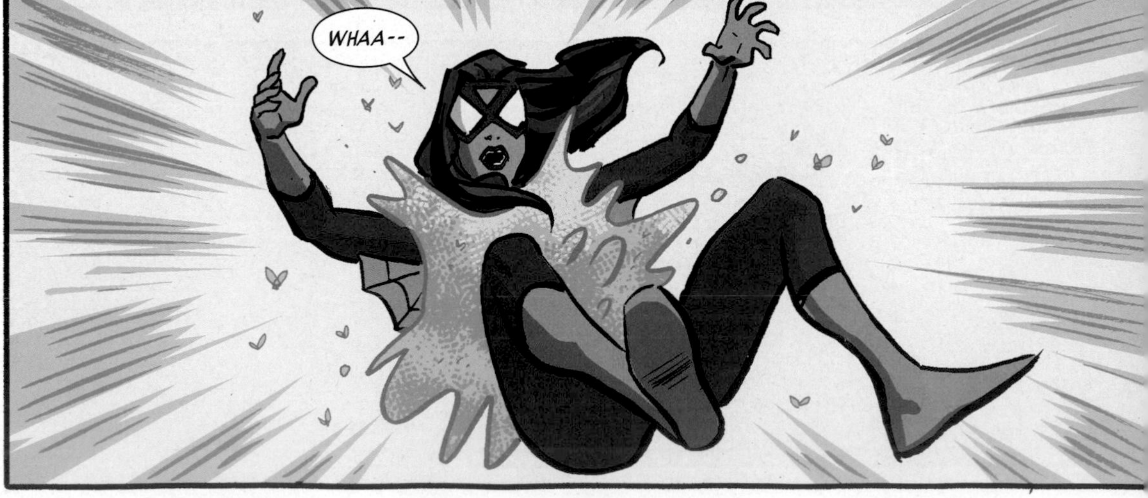
WHAA--

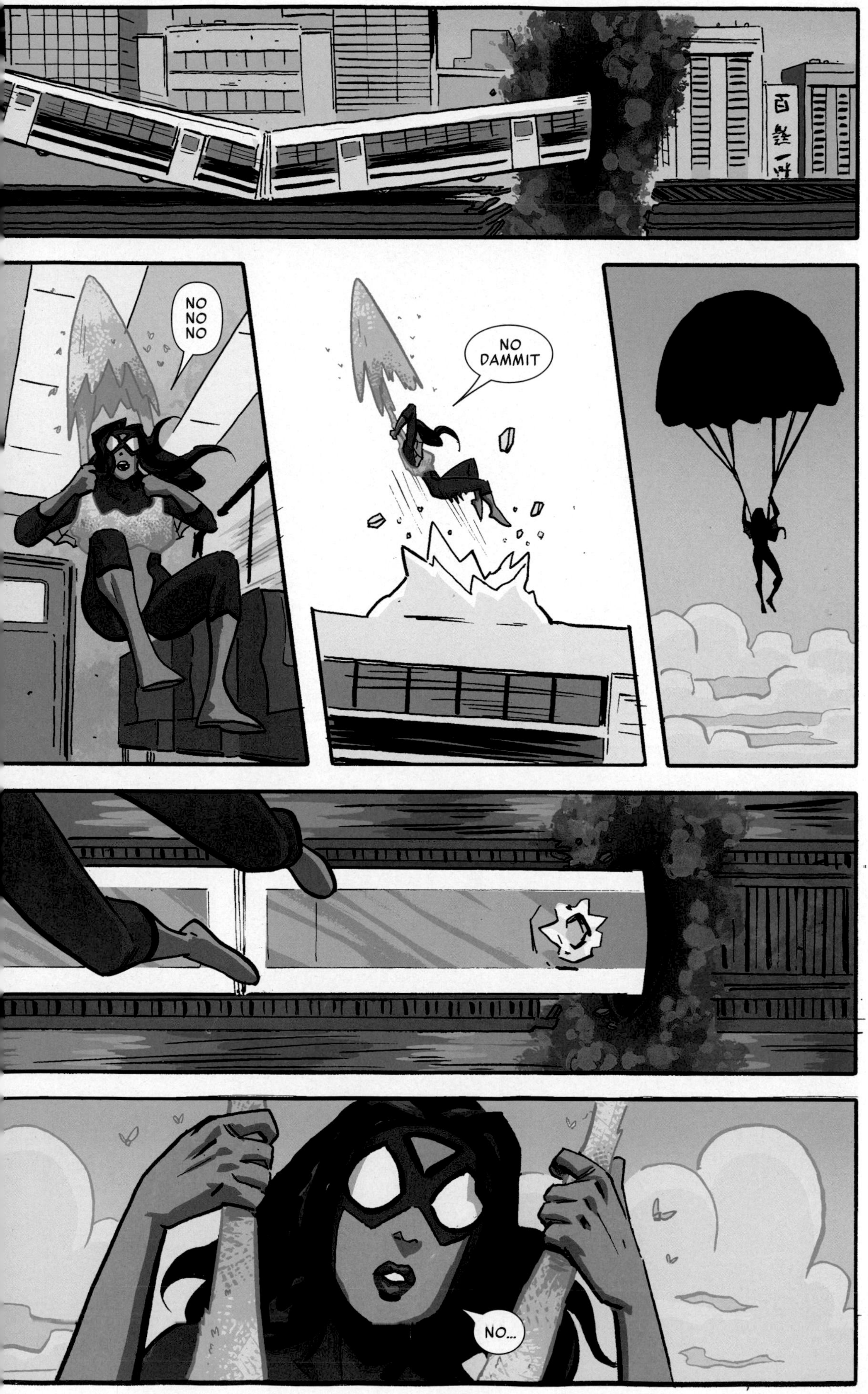

NO NO NO
NO DAMMIT
NO...

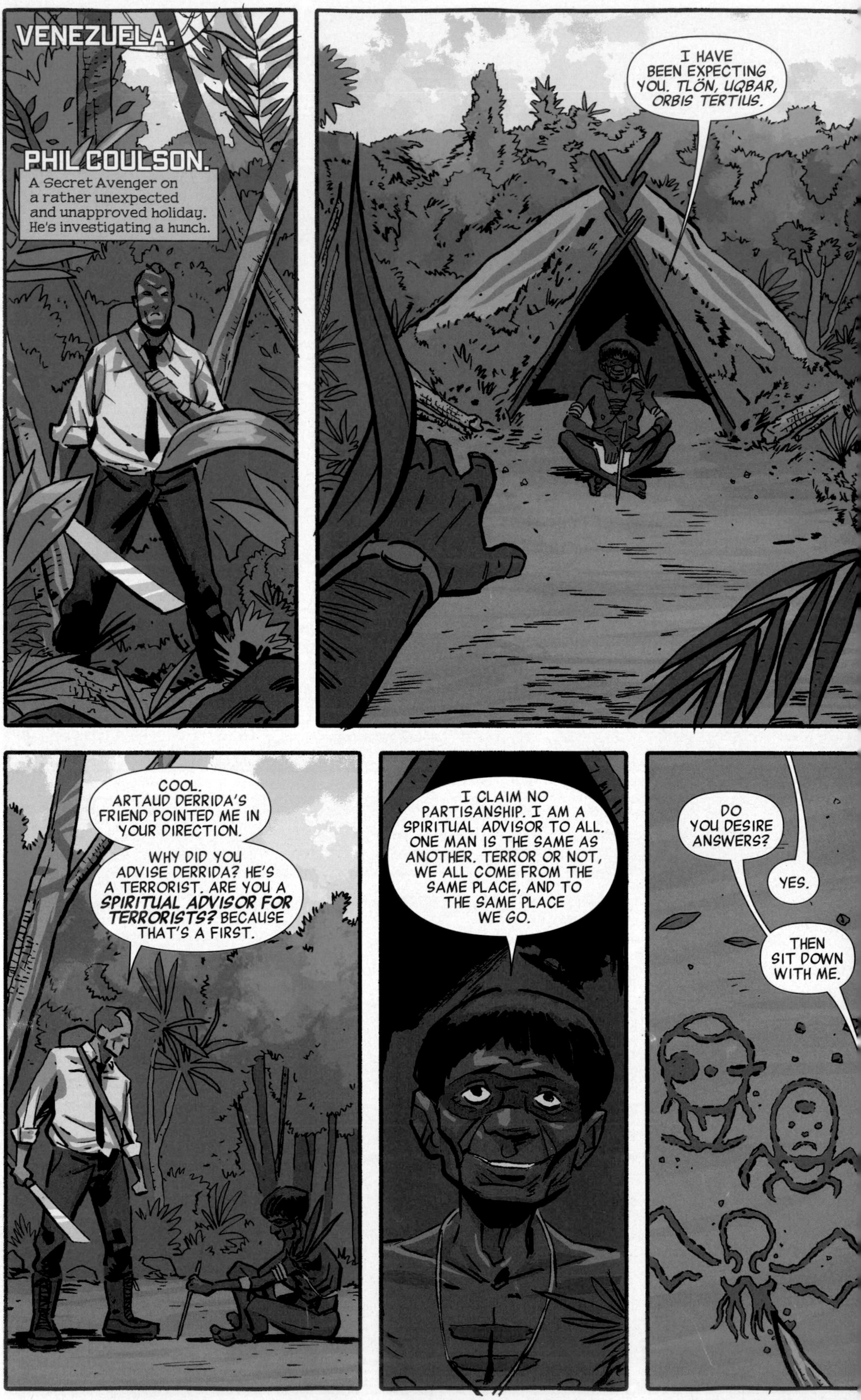
VENEZUELA.
PHIL COULSON.
A Secret Avenger on a rather unexpected and unapproved holiday. He's investigating a hunch.
I HAVE BEEN EXPECTING YOU. TLÖN, UQBAR, ORBIS TERTIUS.
COOL. ARTAUD DERRIDA'S FRIEND POINTED ME IN YOUR DIRECTION.
WHY DID YOU ADVISE DERRIDA? HE'S A TERRORIST. ARE YOU A SPIRITUAL ADVISOR FOR TERRORISTS? BECAUSE THAT'S A FIRST.
I CLAIM NO PARTISANSHIP. I AM A SPIRITUAL ADVISOR TO ALL. ONE MAN IS THE SAME AS ANOTHER. TERROR OR NOT, WE ALL COME FROM THE SAME PLACE, AND TO THE SAME PLACE WE GO.
DO YOU DESIRE ANSWERS?
YES.
THEN SIT DOWN WITH ME.

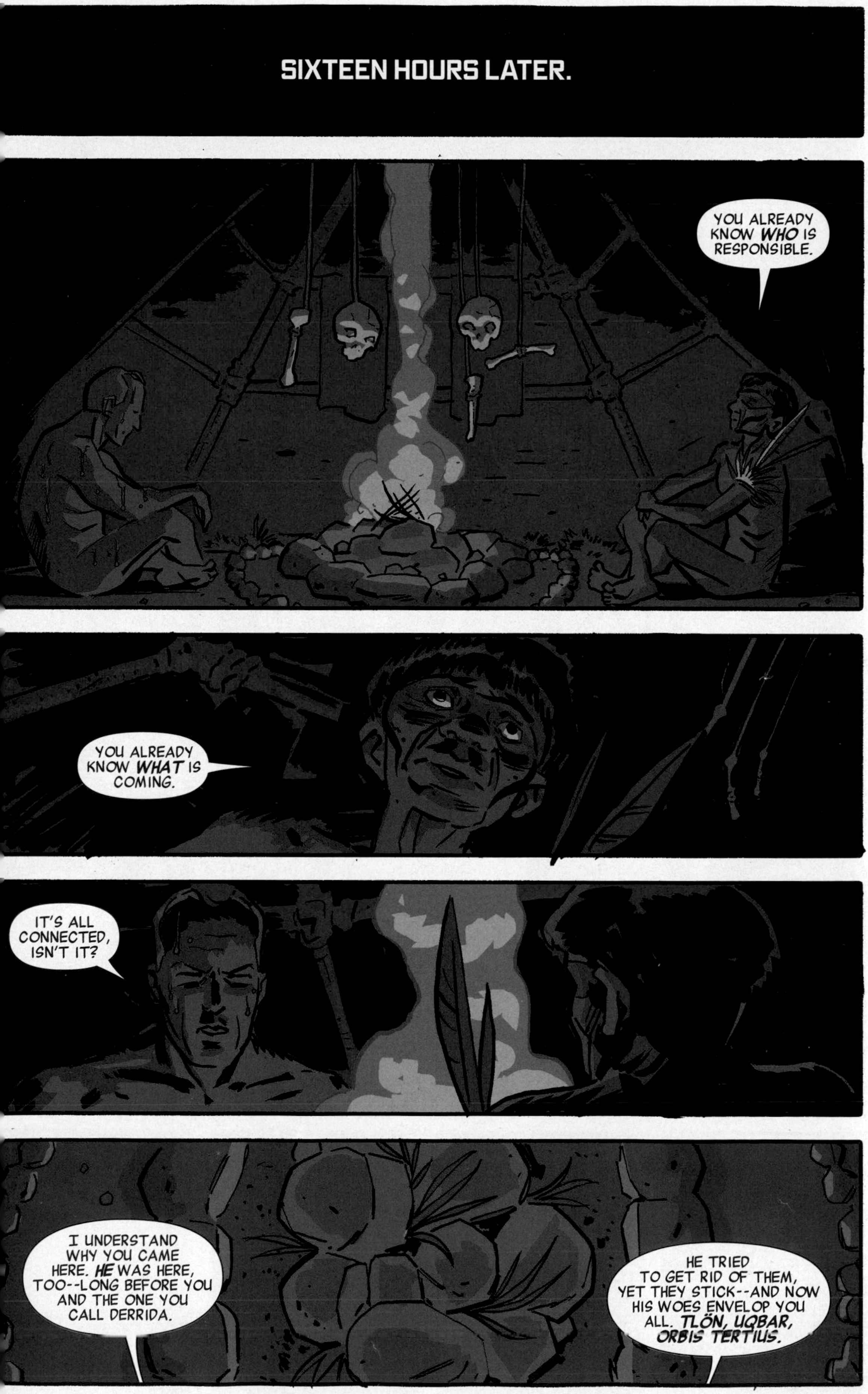
SIXTEEN HOURS LATER.
YOU ALREADY KNOW WHO IS RESPONSIBLE.
YOU ALREADY KNOW WHAT IS COMING.
IT'S ALL CONNECTED, ISN'T IT?
I UNDERSTAND WHY YOU CAME HERE. HE WAS HERE, TOO--LONG BEFORE YOU AND THE ONE YOU CALL DERRIDA.
HE TRIED TO GET RID OF THEM, YET THEY STICK--AND NOW HIS WOES ENVELOP YOU ALL. TLÖN, UQBAR, ORBIS TERTIUS.

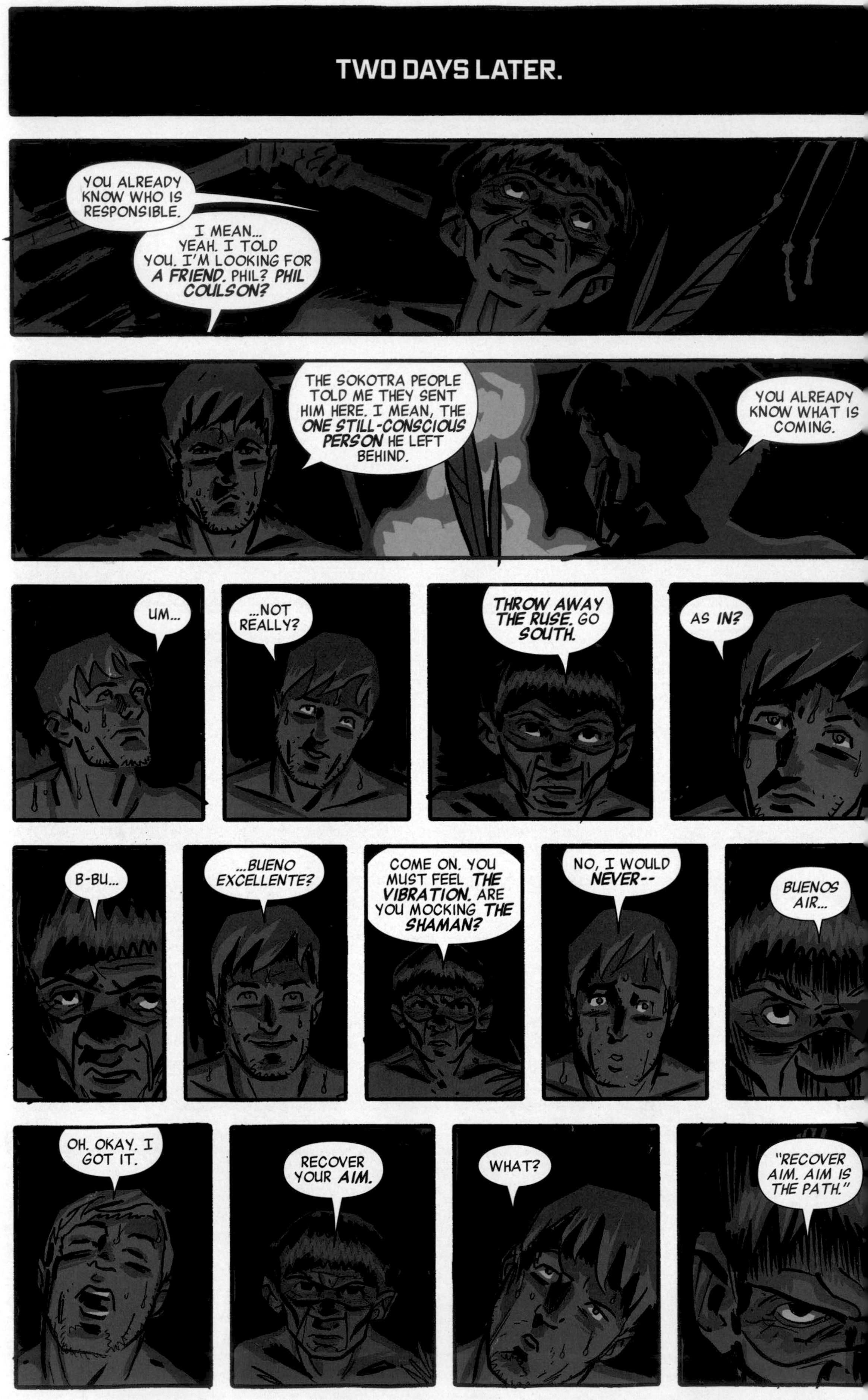
TWO DAYS LATER.
YOU ALREADY KNOW WHO IS RESPONSIBLE.
I MEAN... YEAH. I TOLD YOU. I'M LOOKING FOR A FRIEND. PHIL? PHIL COULSON?
THE SOKOTRA PEOPLE TOLD ME THEY SENT HIM HERE. I MEAN, THE ONE STILL-CONSCIOUS PERSON HE LEFT BEHIND.
YOU ALREADY KNOW WHAT IS COMING.
UM...
...NOT REALLY?
THROW AWAY THE RUSE. GO SOUTH.
AS IN?
B-BU...
...BUENO EXCELLENTE?
COME ON. YOU MUST FEEL THE VIBRATION. ARE YOU MOCKING THE SHAMAN?
NO, I WOULD NEVER--
BUENOS AIR...
OH. OKAY. I GOT IT.
RECOVER YOUR AIM.
WHAT?
"RECOVER AIM. AIM IS THE PATH."

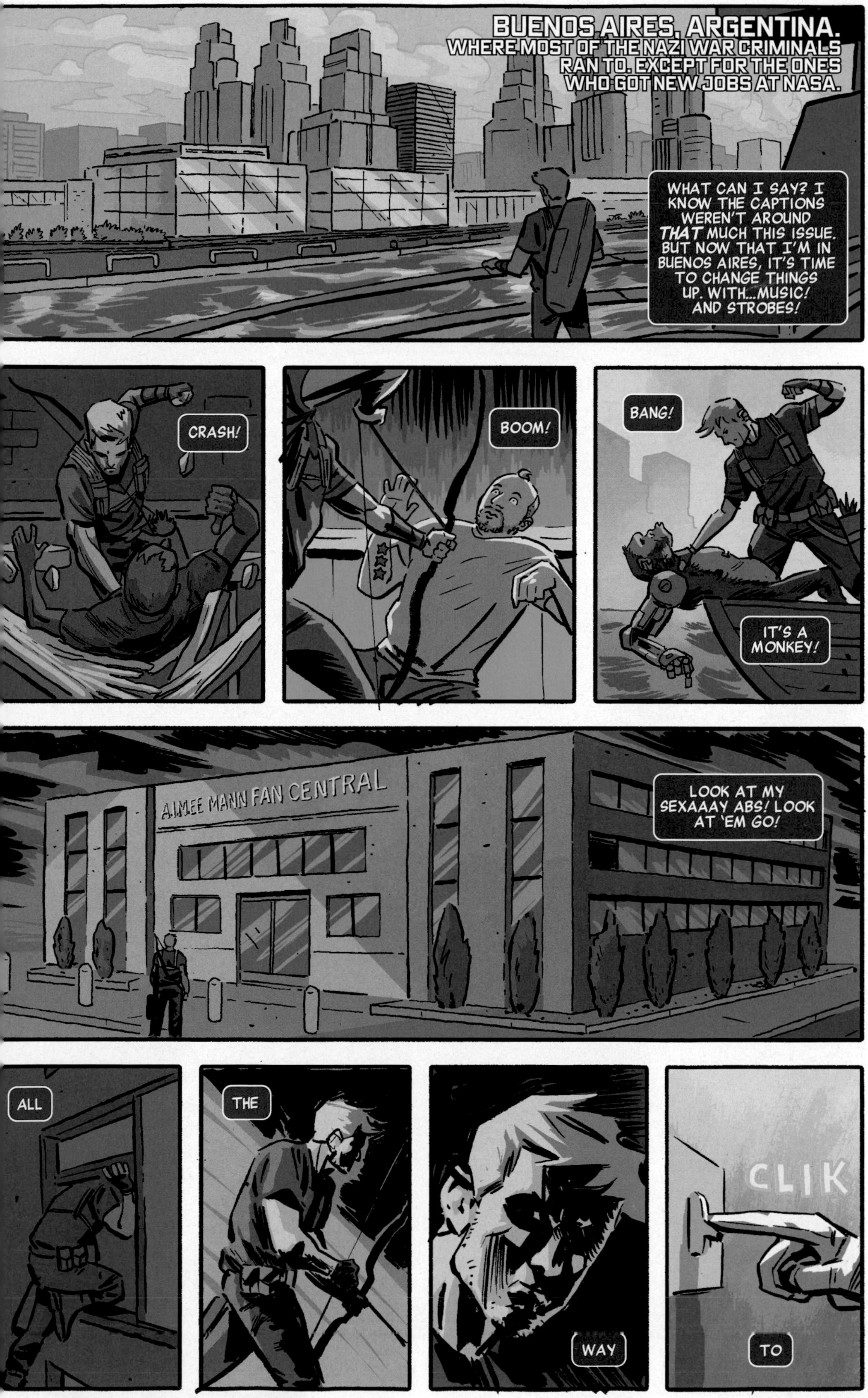
BUENOS AIRES, ARGENTINA.
WHERE MOST OF THE NAZI WAR CRIMINALS RAN TO. EXCEPT FOR THE ONES WHO GOT NEW JOBS AT NASA.
WHAT CAN I SAY? I KNOW THE CAPTIONS WEREN'T AROUND THAT MUCH THIS ISSUE. BUT NOW THAT I'M IN BUENOS AIRES, IT'S TIME TO CHANGE THINGS UP. WITH...MUSIC! AND STROBES!
CRASH!
BOOM!
BANG!
IT'S A MONKEY!
AIMEE MANN FAN CENTRAL
LOOK AT MY SEXAAAY ABS! LOOK AT 'EM GO!
ALL
THE
WAY
CLIK
TO

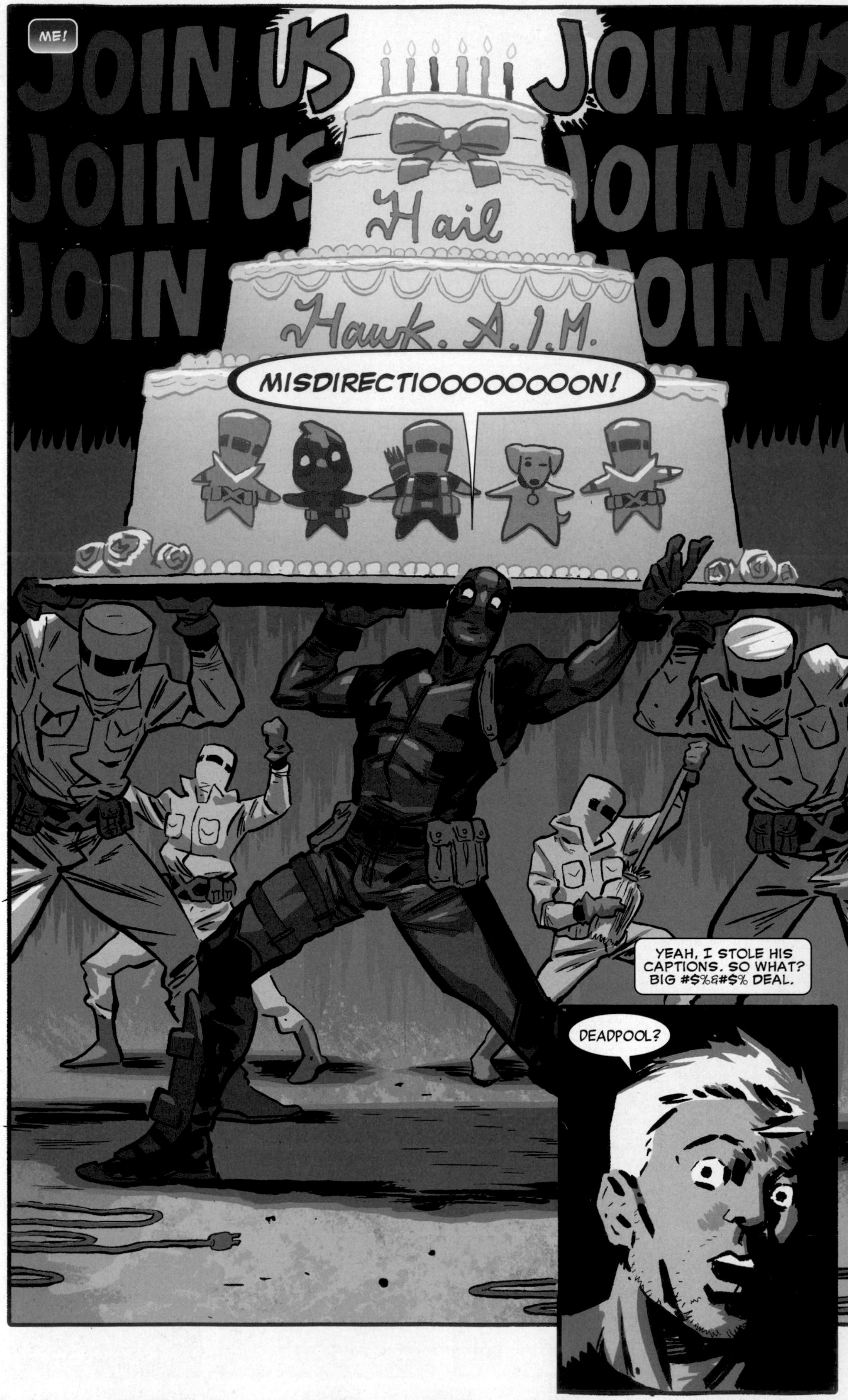
ME!
JOIN US
JOIN US
JOIN US
JOIN US
JOIN
JOIN US
Hail
Hawk. A.I.M.
MISDIRECTIOOOOOOOON!
YEAH, I STOLE HIS CAPTIONS. SO WHAT? BIG #$%&#$% DEAL.
DEADPOOL?

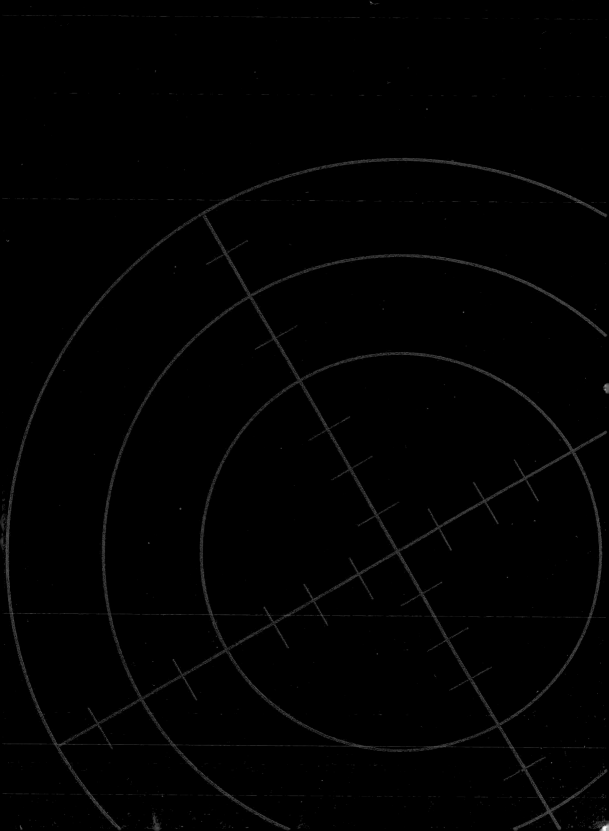

7

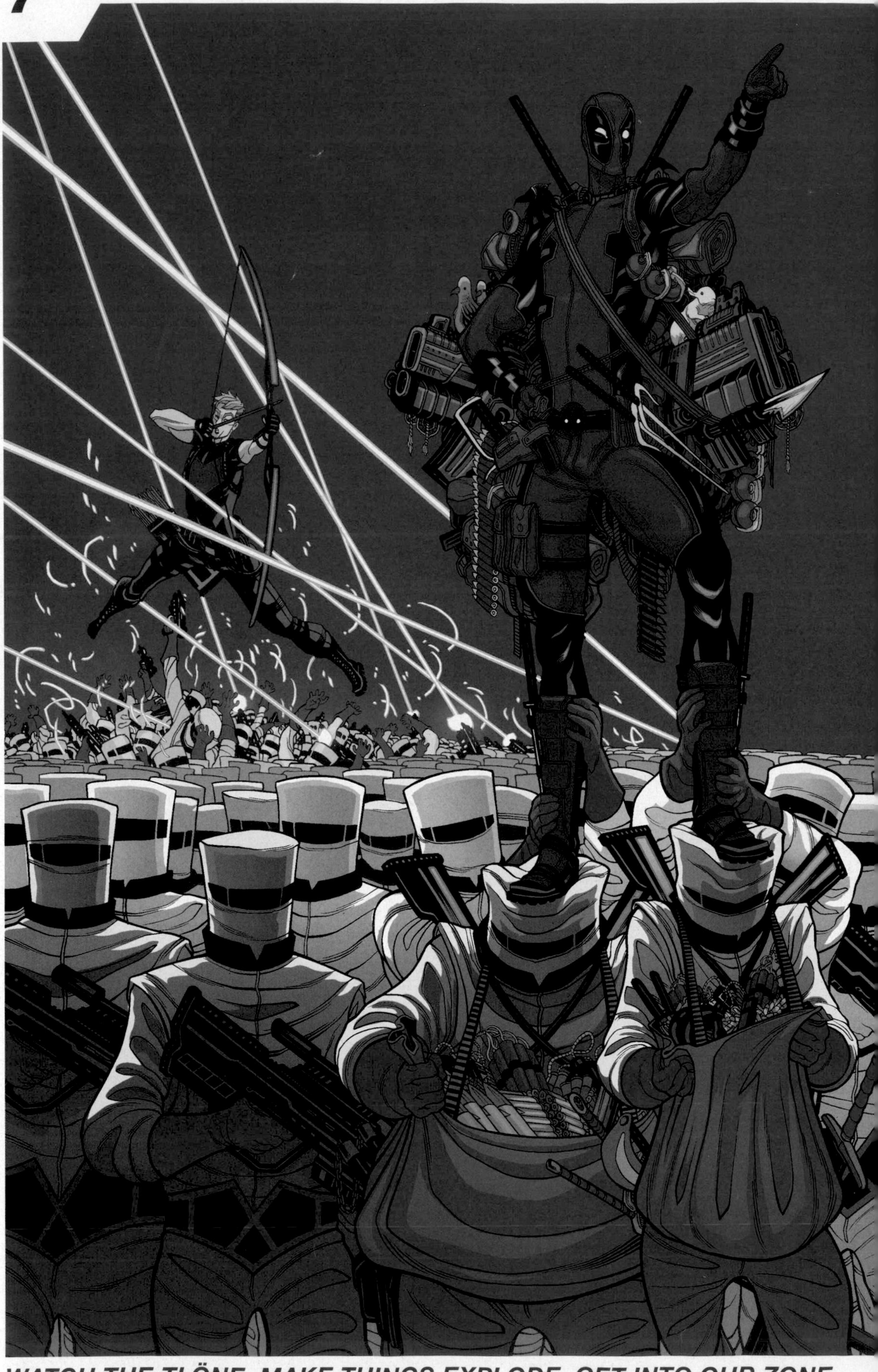

WATCH THE TLÖNE, MAKE THINGS EXPLODE, GET INTO OUR ZONE

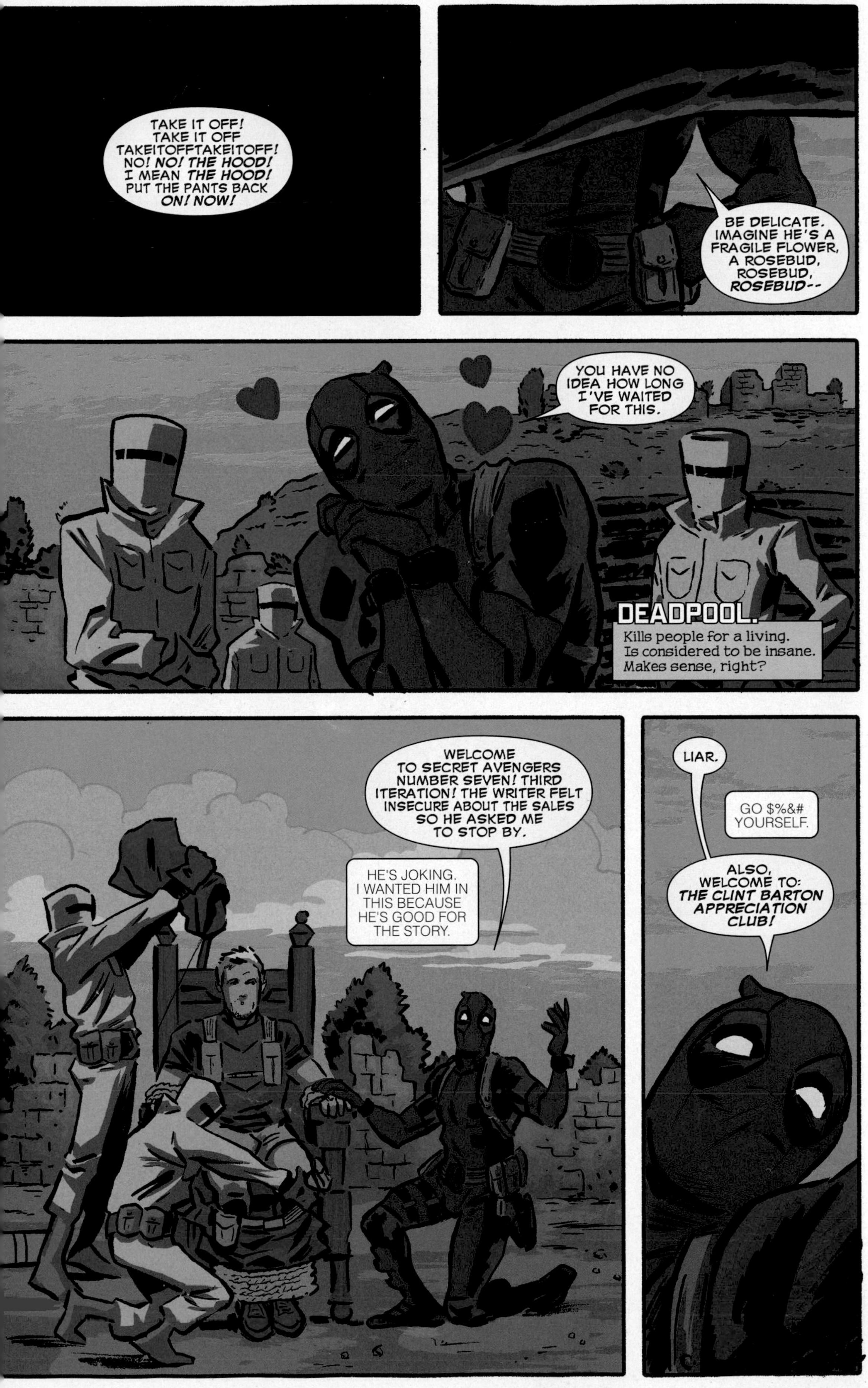

TAKE IT OFF! TAKE IT OFF TAKEITOFFTAKEITOFF! NO! NO! THE HOOD! I MEAN THE HOOD! PUT THE PANTS BACK ON! NOW!
BE DELICATE. IMAGINE HE'S A FRAGILE FLOWER, A ROSEBUD, ROSEBUD, ROSEBUD--
YOU HAVE NO IDEA HOW LONG I'VE WAITED FOR THIS.
DEADPOOL.
Kills people for a living. Is considered to be insane. Makes sense, right?
WELCOME TO SECRET AVENGERS NUMBER SEVEN! THIRD ITERATION! THE WRITER FELT INSECURE ABOUT THE SALES SO HE ASKED ME TO STOP BY.
HE'S JOKING. I WANTED HIM IN THIS BECAUSE HE'S GOOD FOR THE STORY.
LIAR.
GO $%&# YOURSELF.
ALSO, WELCOME TO: THE CLINT BARTON APPRECIATION CLUB!

S[illegible]T AVENGERS #7

WATCH THE TLÖNE, MAKE THINGS EXPLODE, GET INTO OUR ZONE

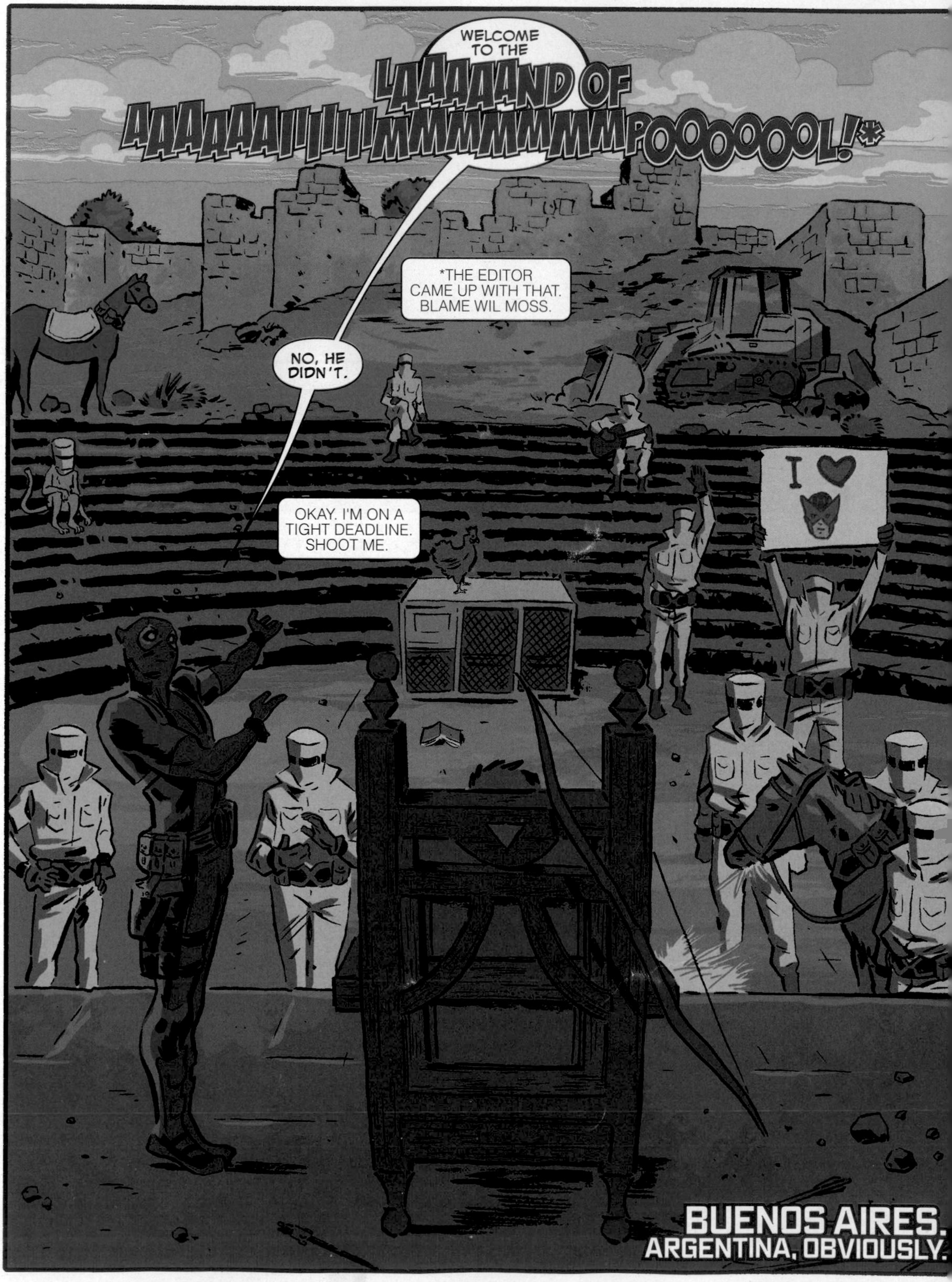

WELCOME TO THE LAAAAAND OF AAAAAAIIIIIIIIMMMMMMMMMPOOOOOOOL!*
*THE EDITOR CAME UP WITH THAT. BLAME WIL MOSS.
NO, HE DIDN'T.
OKAY. I'M ON A TIGHT DEADLINE. SHOOT ME.
I ♥
BUENOS AIRES. ARGENTINA, OBVIOUSLY.

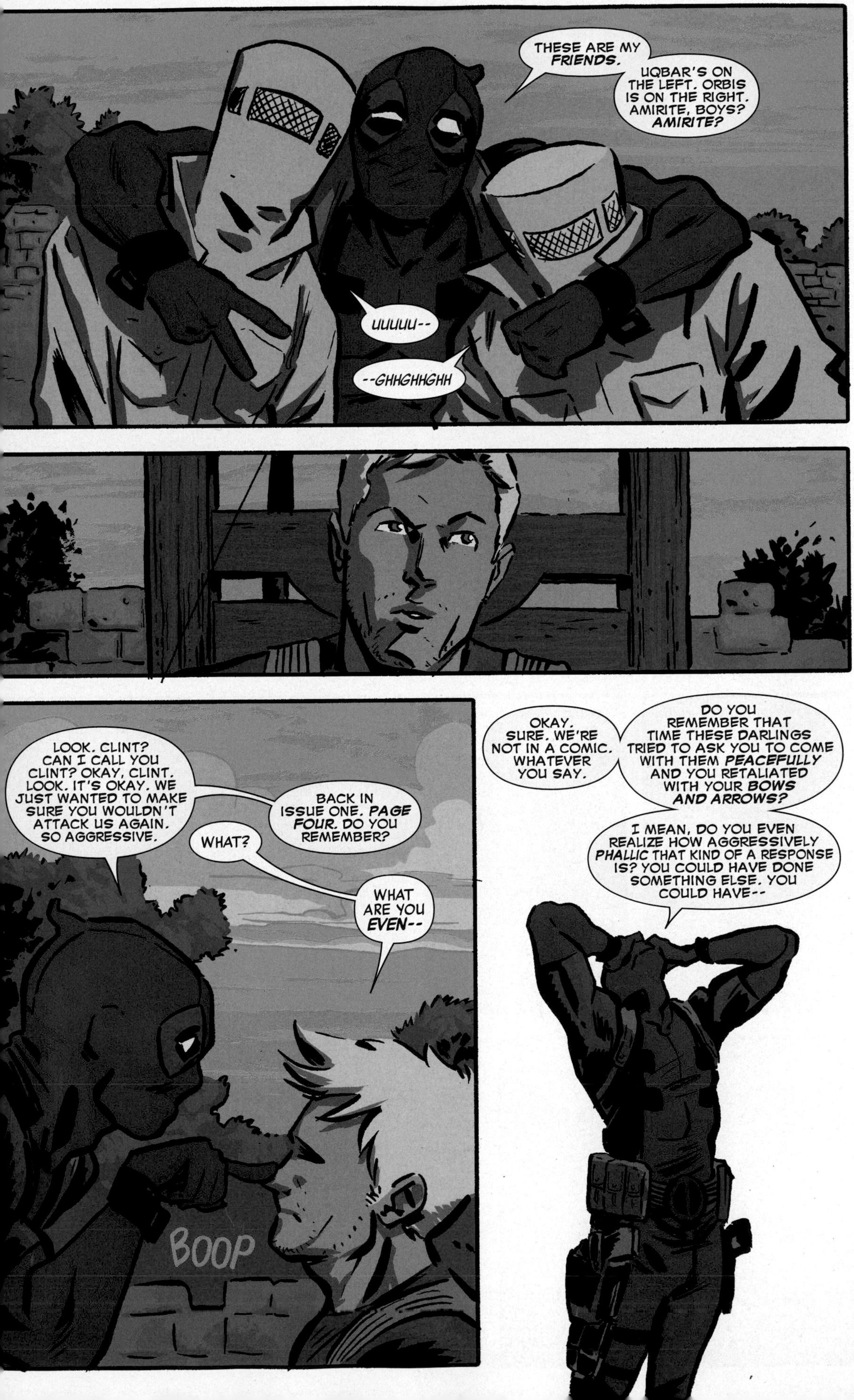
THESE ARE MY FRIENDS.
UQBAR'S ON THE LEFT. ORBIS IS ON THE RIGHT. AMIRITE, BOYS? AMIRITE?
UUUUU--
--GHHGHHGHH
LOOK. CLINT? CAN I CALL YOU CLINT? OKAY, CLINT. LOOK. IT'S OKAY. WE JUST WANTED TO MAKE SURE YOU WOULDN'T ATTACK US AGAIN. SO AGGRESSIVE.
BACK IN ISSUE ONE. PAGE FOUR. DO YOU REMEMBER?
WHAT?
WHAT ARE YOU EVEN--
BOOP
OKAY. SURE. WE'RE NOT IN A COMIC. WHATEVER YOU SAY.
DO YOU REMEMBER THAT TIME THESE DARLINGS TRIED TO ASK YOU TO COME WITH THEM PEACEFULLY AND YOU RETALIATED WITH YOUR BOWS AND ARROWS?
I MEAN, DO YOU EVEN REALIZE HOW AGGRESSIVELY PHALLIC THAT KIND OF A RESPONSE IS? YOU COULD HAVE DONE SOMETHING ELSE. YOU COULD HAVE--

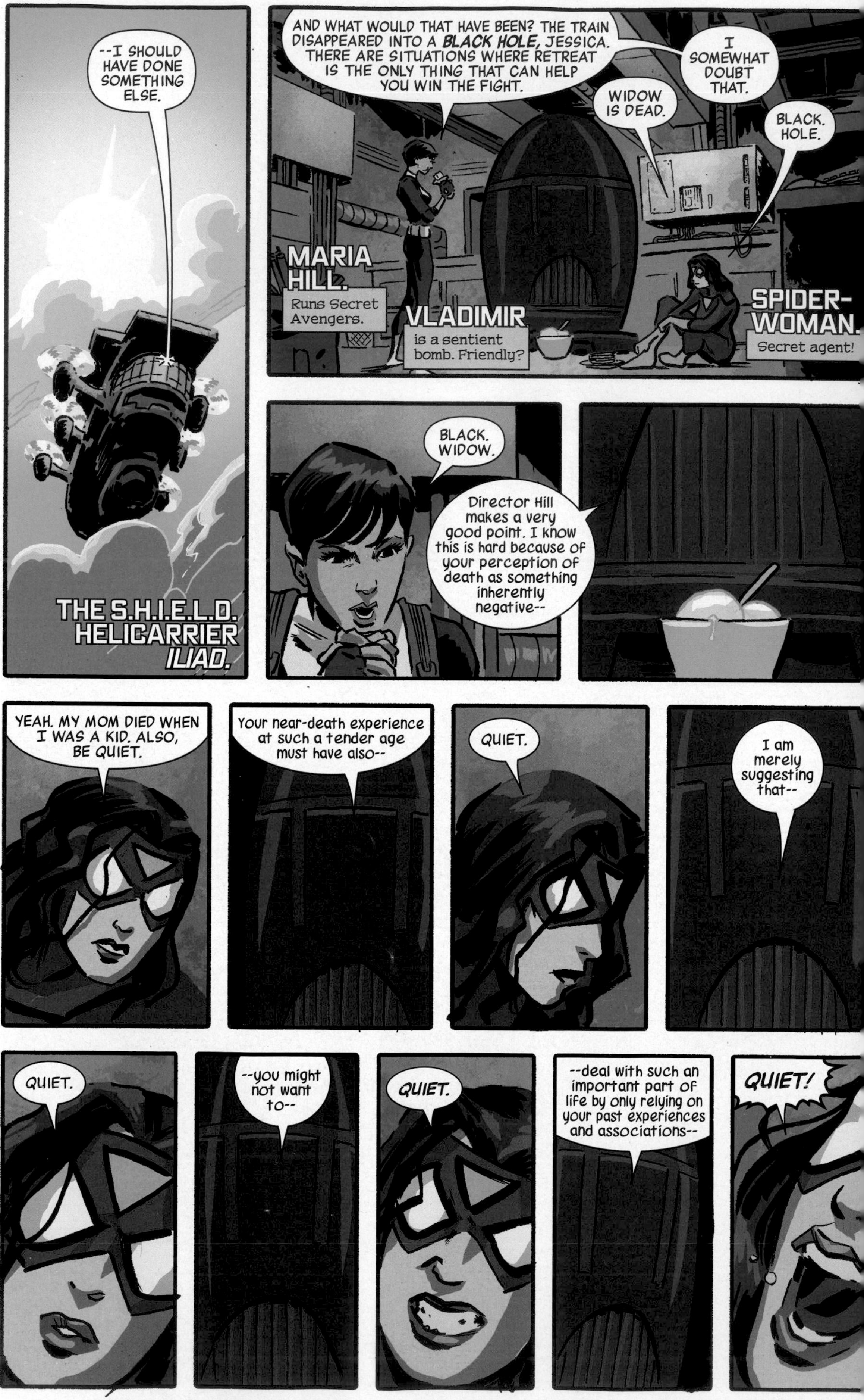
--I SHOULD HAVE DONE SOMETHING ELSE.
THE S.H.I.E.L.D. HELICARRIER ILIAD.
AND WHAT WOULD THAT HAVE BEEN? THE TRAIN DISAPPEARED INTO A BLACK HOLE, JESSICA. THERE ARE SITUATIONS WHERE RETREAT IS THE ONLY THING THAT CAN HELP YOU WIN THE FIGHT.
I SOMEWHAT DOUBT THAT.
WIDOW IS DEAD.
BLACK. HOLE.
MARIA HILL.
Runs Secret Avengers.
VLADIMIR
is a sentient bomb. Friendly?
SPIDER-WOMAN.
Secret agent!
BLACK. WIDOW.
Director Hill makes a very good point. I know this is hard because of your perception of death as something inherently negative--
YEAH. MY MOM DIED WHEN I WAS A KID. ALSO, BE QUIET.
Your near-death experience at such a tender age must have also--
QUIET.
I am merely suggesting that--
QUIET.
--you might not want to--
QUIET.
--deal with such an important part of life by only relying on your past experiences and associations--
QUIET!

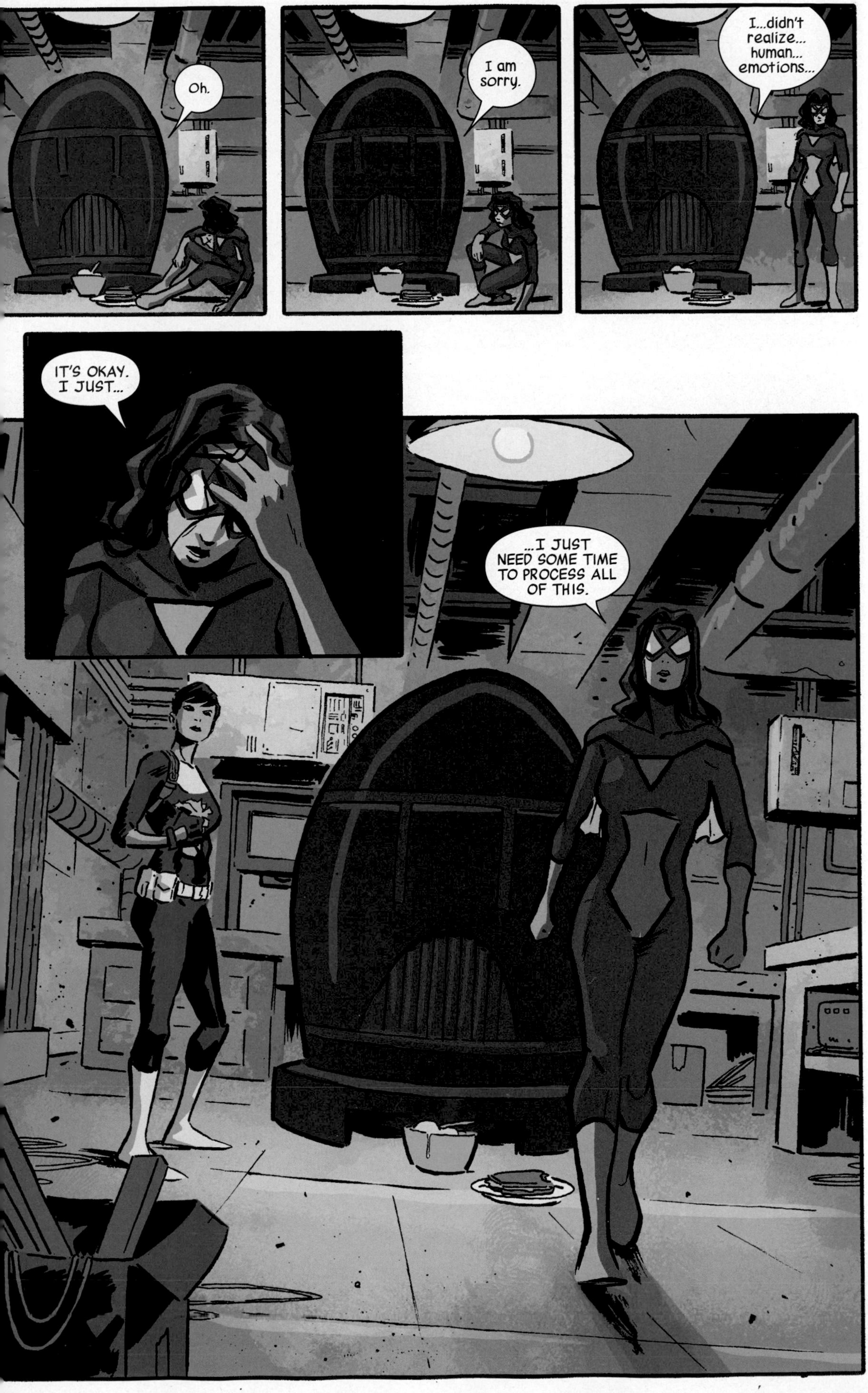
Oh.
I am sorry.
I...didn't realize... human... emotions...
IT'S OKAY. I JUST...
...I JUST NEED SOME TIME TO PROCESS ALL OF THIS.

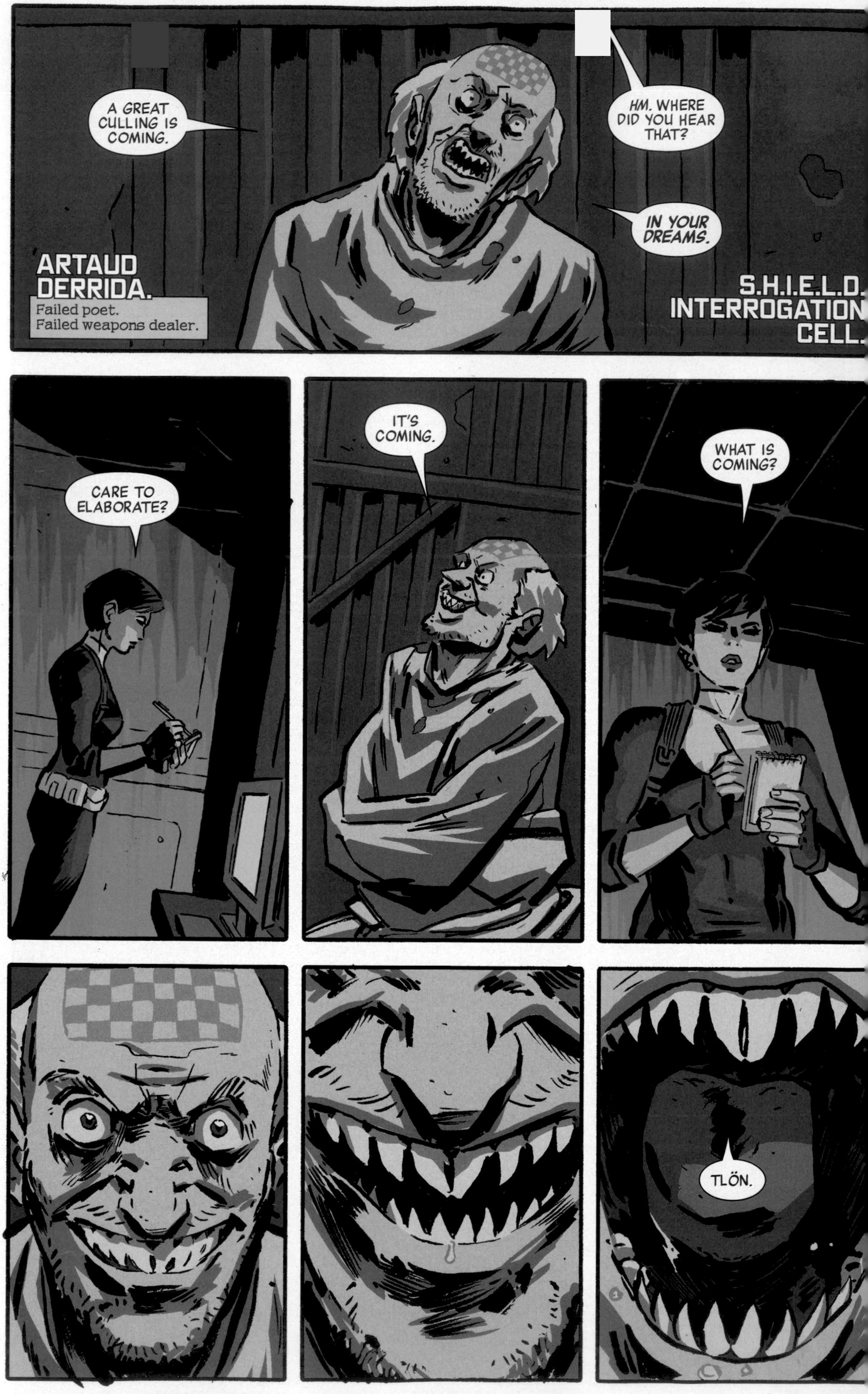
S.H.I.E.L.D. INTERROGATION CELL.
ARTAUD DERRIDA.
Failed poet.
Failed weapons dealer.
A GREAT CULLING IS COMING.
HM. WHERE DID YOU HEAR THAT?
IN YOUR DREAMS.
CARE TO ELABORATE?
IT'S COMING.
WHAT IS COMING?
TLÖN.

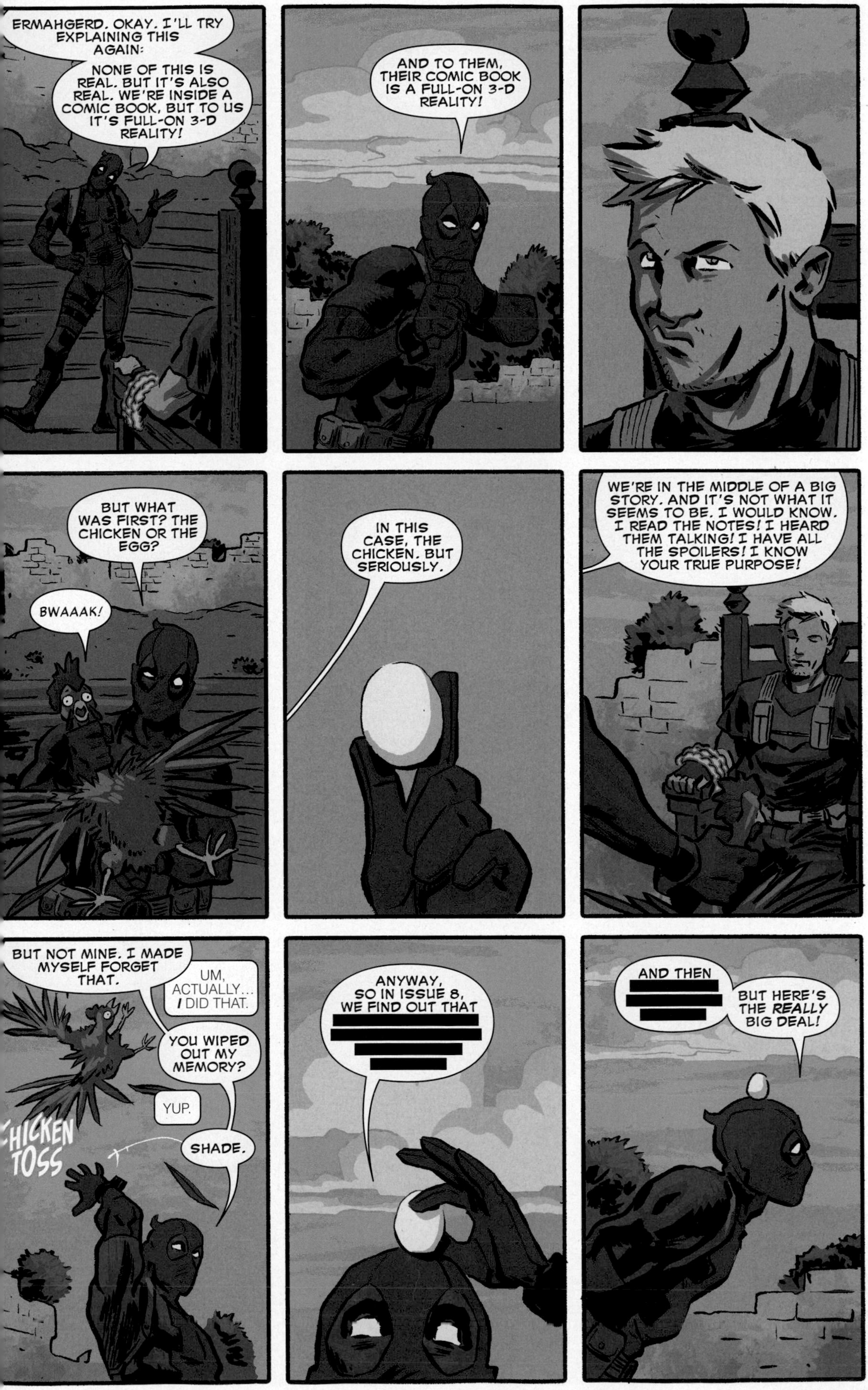
ERMAHGERD. OKAY. I'LL TRY EXPLAINING THIS AGAIN:
NONE OF THIS IS REAL. BUT IT'S ALSO REAL. WE'RE INSIDE A COMIC BOOK, BUT TO US IT'S FULL-ON 3-D REALITY!
AND TO THEM, THEIR COMIC BOOK IS A FULL-ON 3-D REALITY!
BUT WHAT WAS FIRST? THE CHICKEN OR THE EGG?
BWAAAK!
IN THIS CASE, THE CHICKEN. BUT SERIOUSLY.
WE'RE IN THE MIDDLE OF A BIG STORY. AND IT'S NOT WHAT IT SEEMS TO BE. I WOULD KNOW. I READ THE NOTES! I HEARD THEM TALKING! I HAVE ALL THE SPOILERS! I KNOW YOUR TRUE PURPOSE!
BUT NOT MINE. I MADE MYSELF FORGET THAT.
UM, ACTUALLY... *I* DID THAT.
YOU WIPED OUT MY MEMORY?
YUP.
SHADE.
HICKEN TOSS
ANYWAY, SO IN ISSUE 8, WE FIND OUT THAT [redacted]
AND THEN [redacted]
BUT HERE'S THE *REALLY* BIG DEAL!

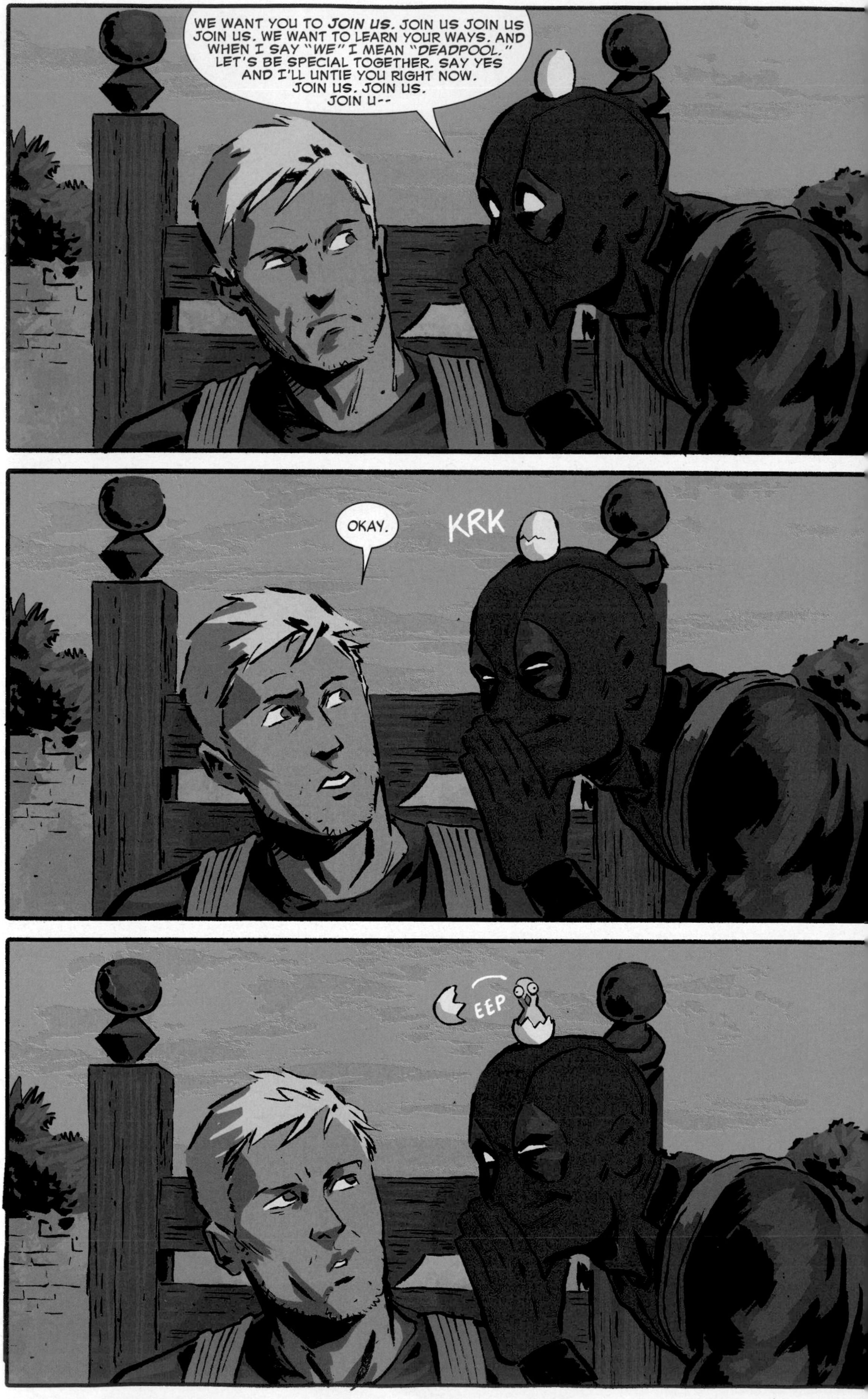
WE WANT YOU TO JOIN US. JOIN US JOIN US JOIN US. WE WANT TO LEARN YOUR WAYS. AND WHEN I SAY "WE" I MEAN "DEADPOOL." LET'S BE SPECIAL TOGETHER. SAY YES AND I'LL UNTIE YOU RIGHT NOW. JOIN US. JOIN US. JOIN U--
OKAY.
KRK
EEP

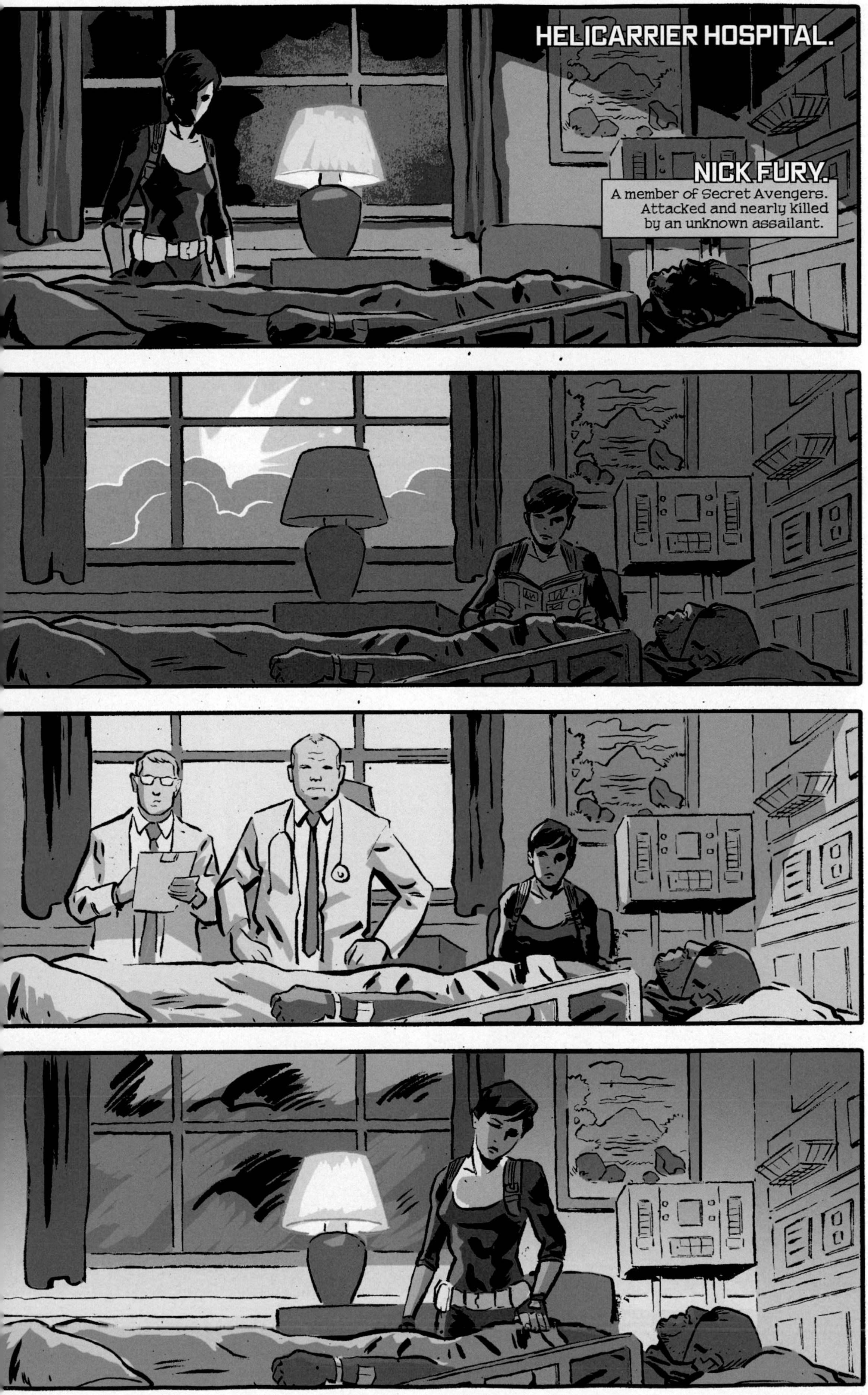
HELICARRIER HOSPITAL.
NICK FURY.
A member of Secret Avengers. Attacked and nearly killed by an unknown assailant.

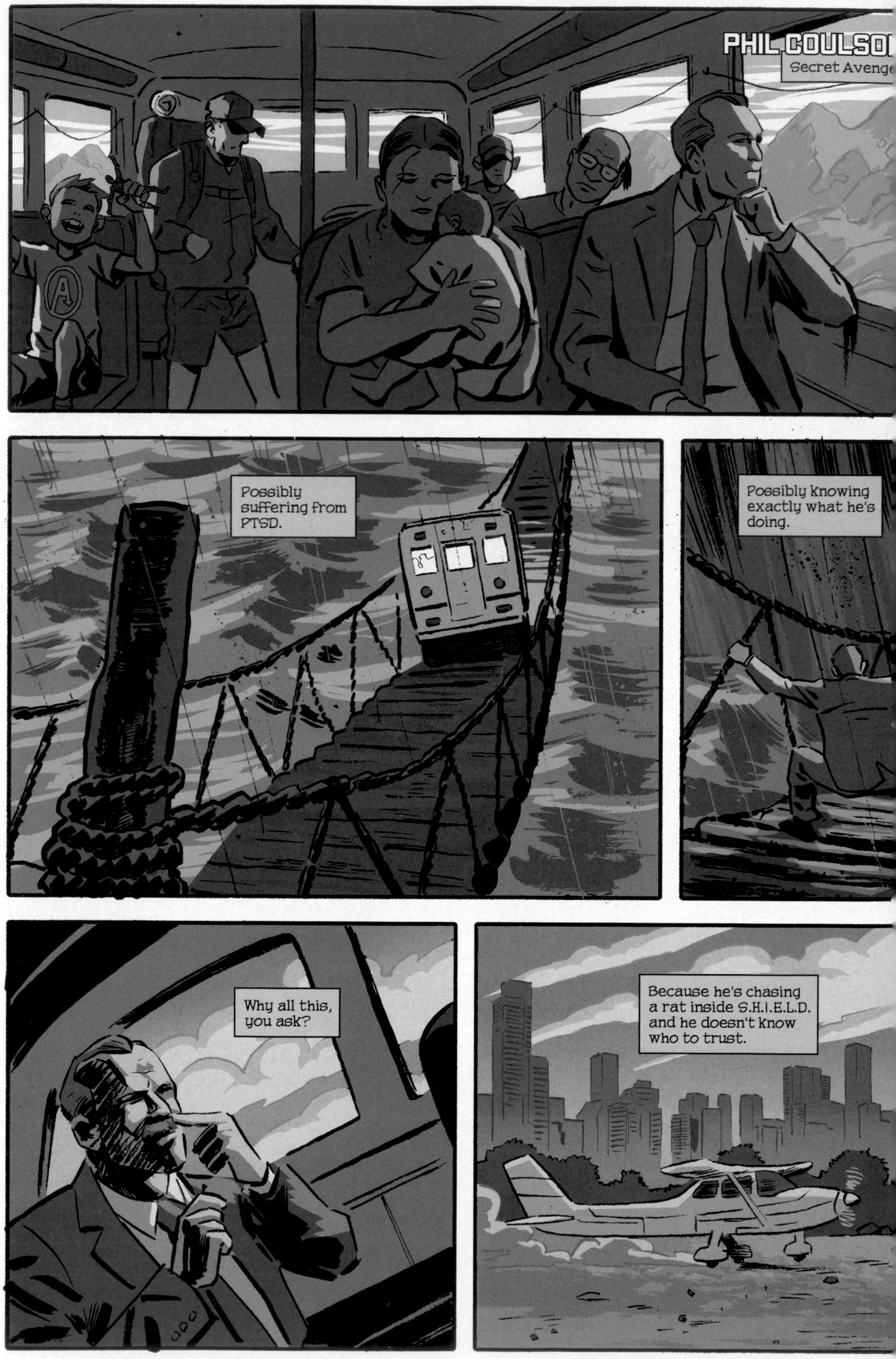
PHIL COULSO
Secret Aveng
Possibly suffering from PTSD.
Possibly knowing exactly what he's doing.
Why all this, you ask?
Because he's chasing a rat inside S.H.I.E.L.D. and he doesn't know who to trust.

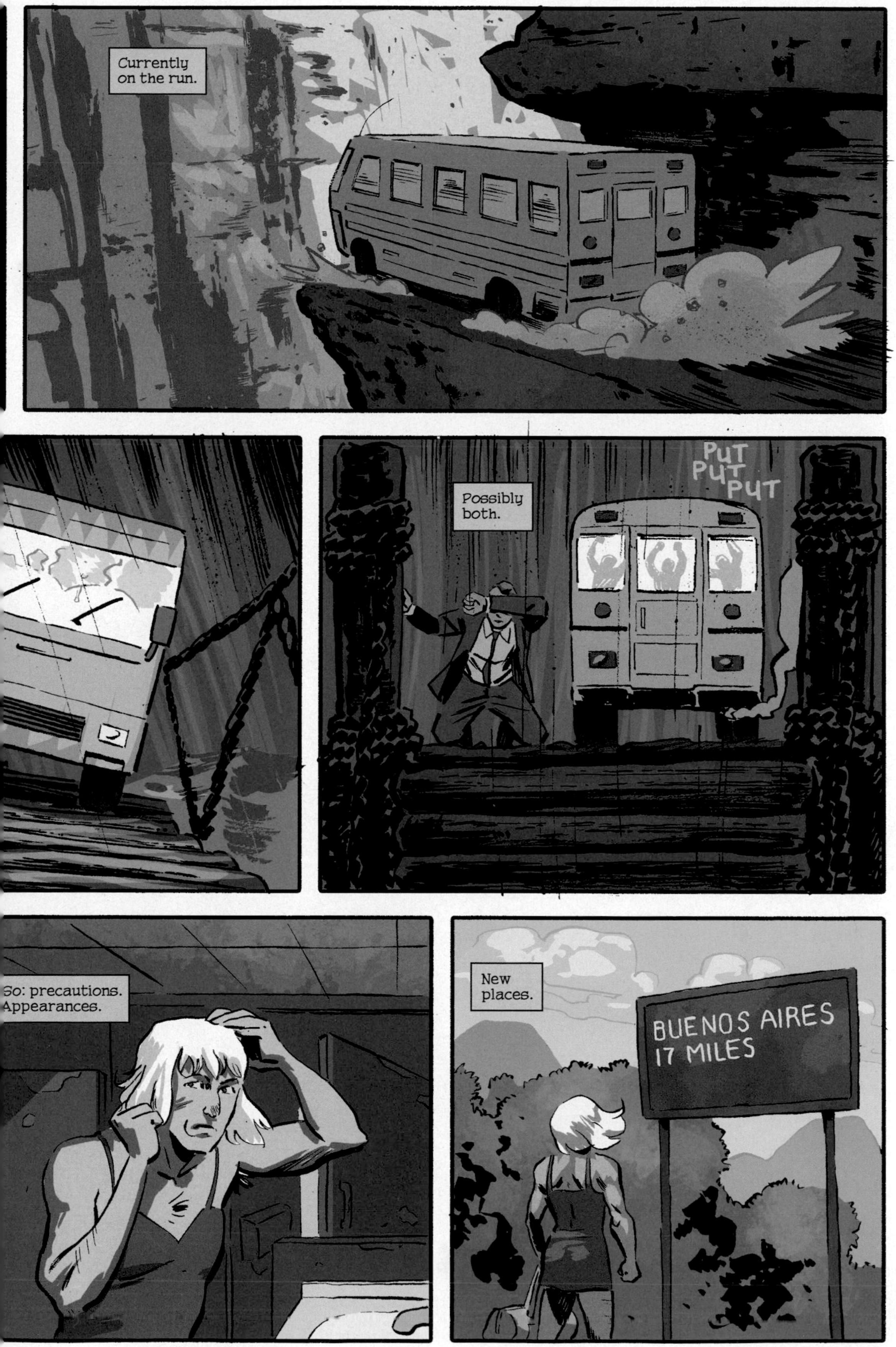
Currently on the run.
Possibly both.
PUT PUT PUT
So: precautions. Appearances.
New places.
BUENOS AIRES 17 MILES

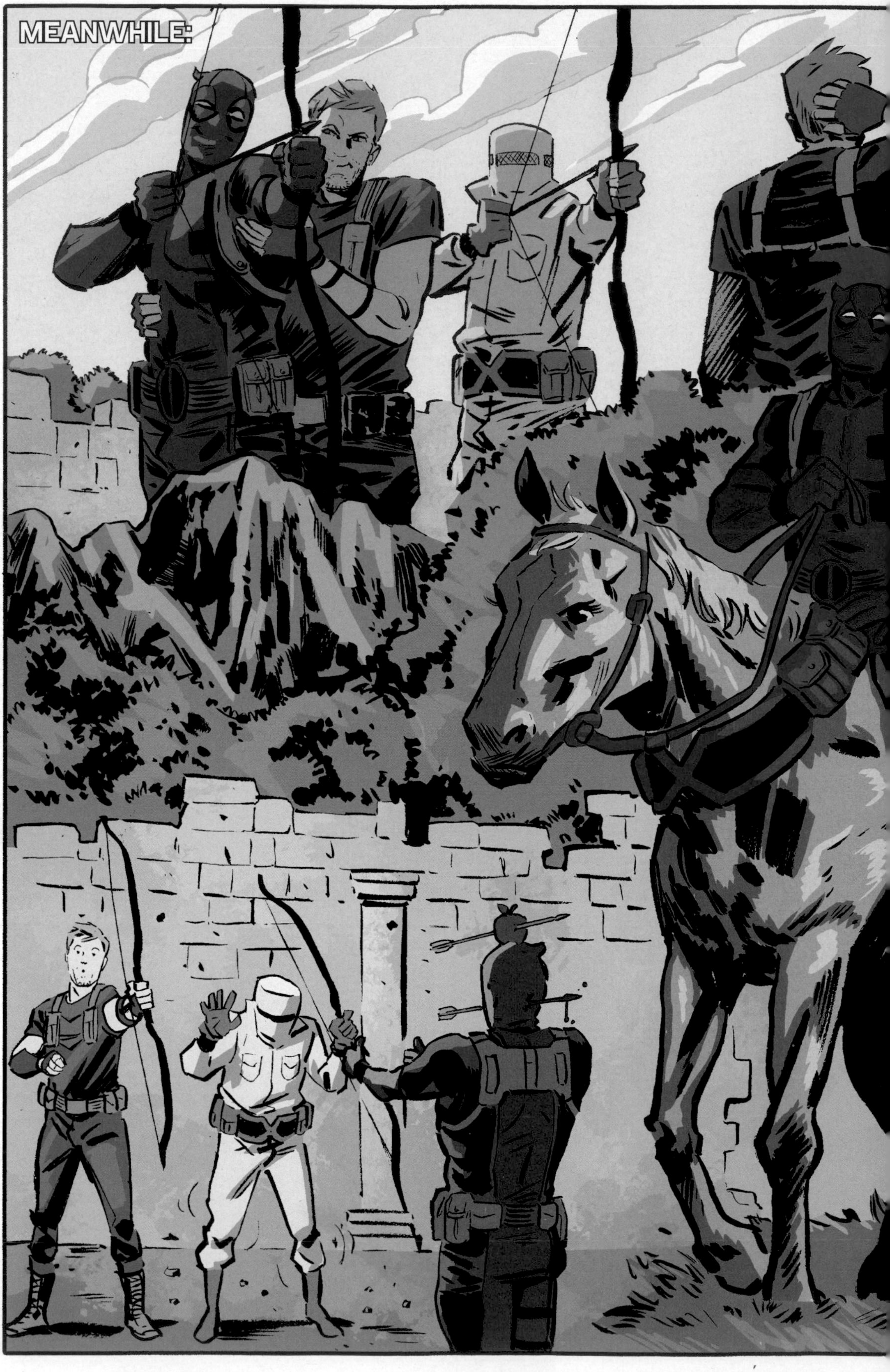
MEANWHILE:

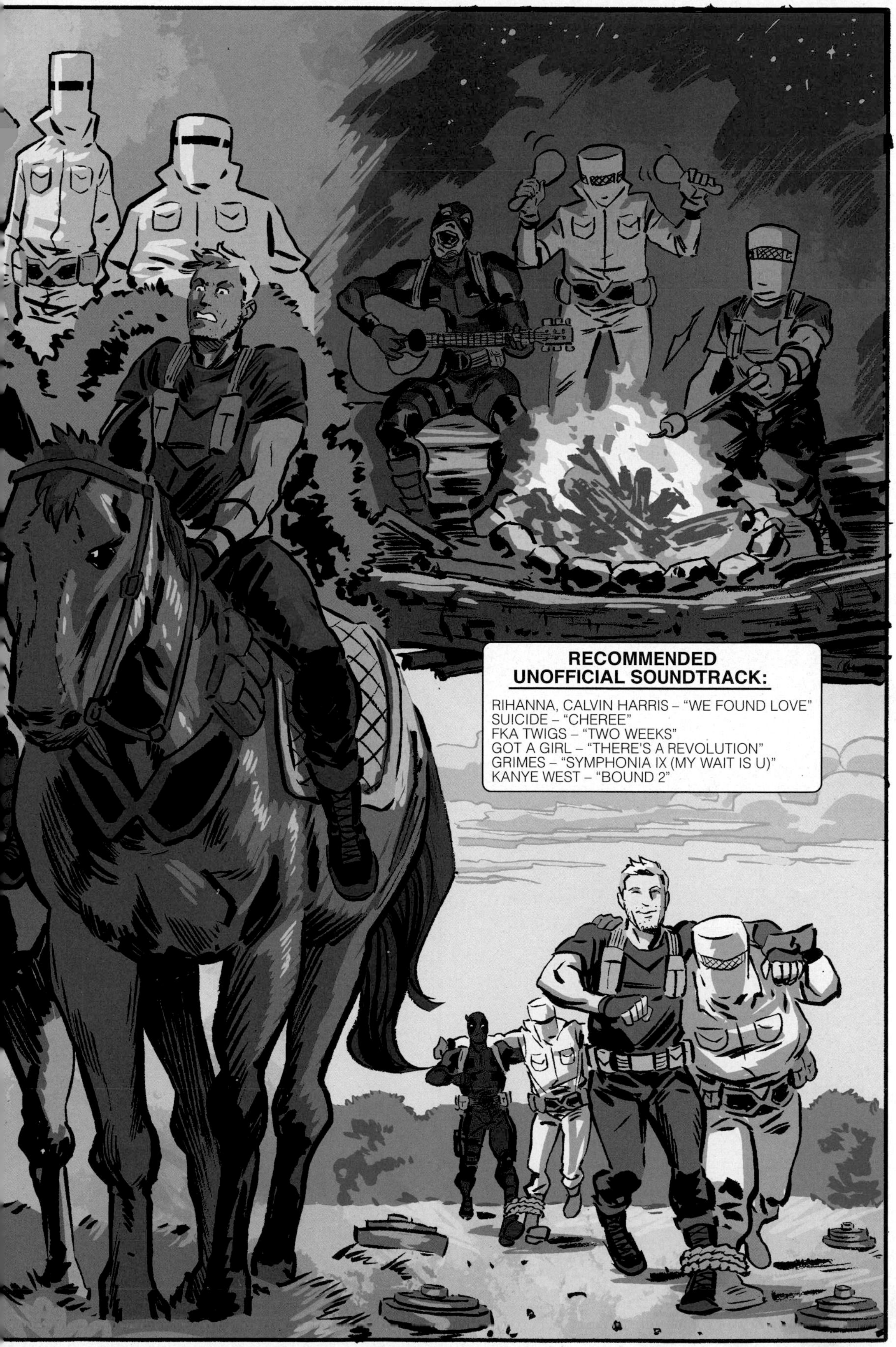
RECOMMENDED UNOFFICIAL SOUNDTRACK:
RIHANNA, CALVIN HARRIS – "WE FOUND LOVE"
SUICIDE – "CHEREE"
FKA TWIGS – "TWO WEEKS"
GOT A GIRL – "THERE'S A REVOLUTION"
GRIMES – "SYMPHONIA IX (MY WAIT IS U)"
KANYE WEST – "BOUND 2"

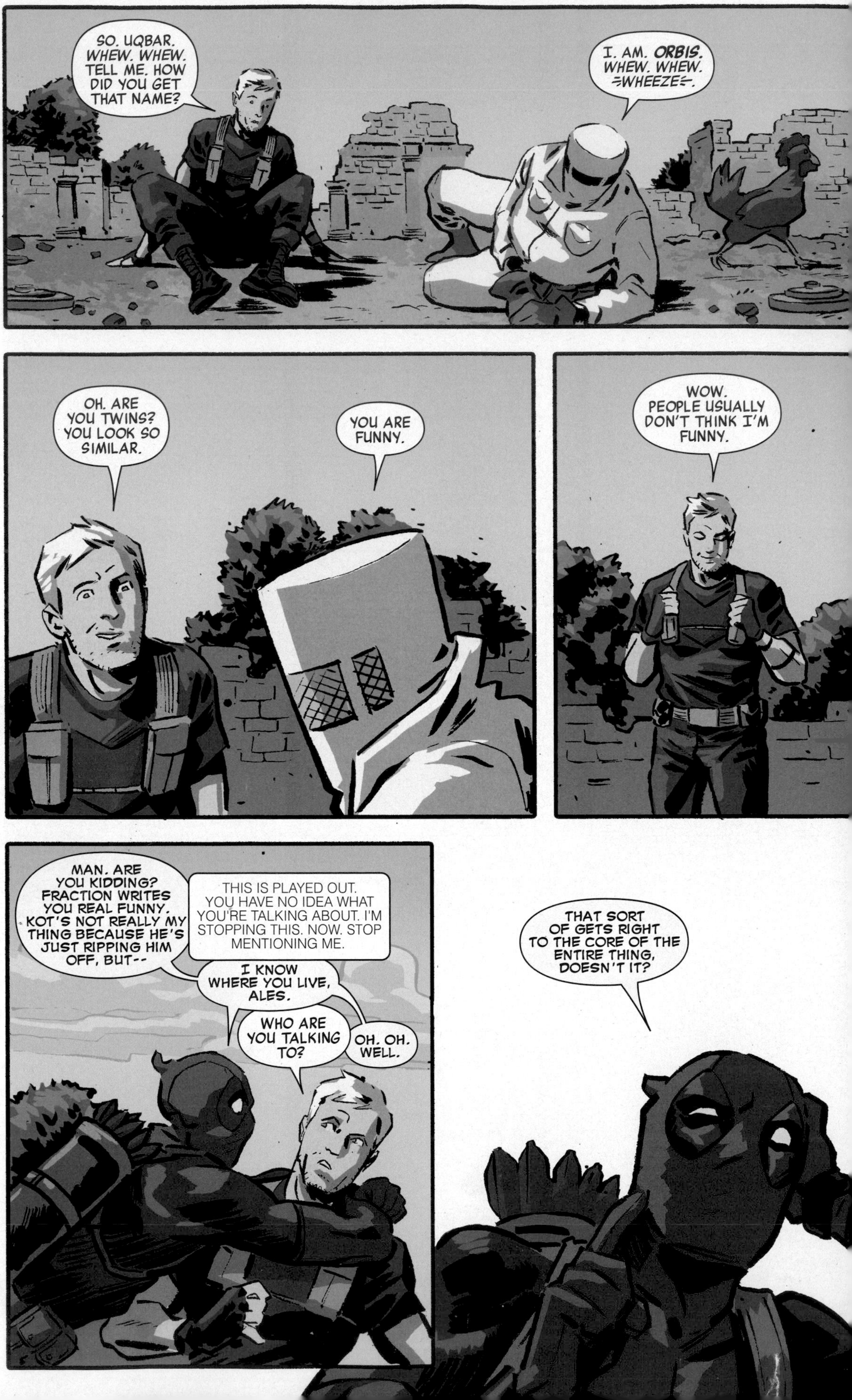

SO. UQBAR. WHEW. WHEW. TELL ME. HOW DID YOU GET THAT NAME?
I. AM. ORBIS. WHEW. WHEW. WHEEZE.
OH. ARE YOU TWINS? YOU LOOK SO SIMILAR.
YOU ARE FUNNY.
WOW. PEOPLE USUALLY DON'T THINK I'M FUNNY.
MAN. ARE YOU KIDDING? FRACTION WRITES YOU REAL FUNNY. KOT'S NOT REALLY MY THING BECAUSE HE'S JUST RIPPING HIM OFF, BUT--
THIS IS PLAYED OUT. YOU HAVE NO IDEA WHAT YOU'RE TALKING ABOUT. I'M STOPPING THIS. NOW. STOP MENTIONING ME.
I KNOW WHERE YOU LIVE, ALES.
WHO ARE YOU TALKING TO?
OH. OH. WELL.
THAT SORT OF GETS RIGHT TO THE CORE OF THE ENTIRE THING, DOESN'T IT?

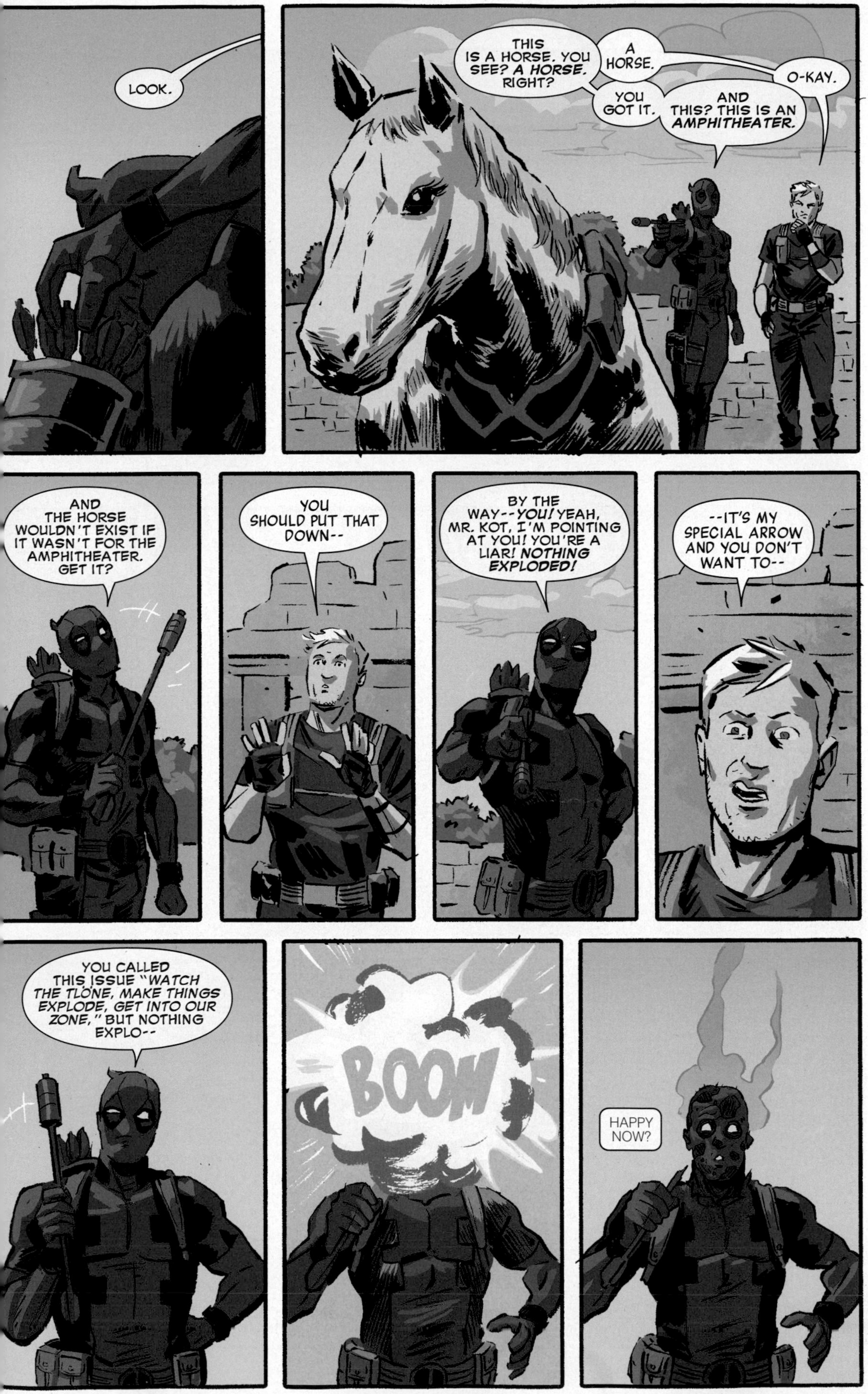
LOOK.
THIS IS A HORSE. YOU SEE? A HORSE. RIGHT?
A HORSE.
O-KAY.
YOU GOT IT.
AND THIS? THIS IS AN AMPHITHEATER.
AND THE HORSE WOULDN'T EXIST IF IT WASN'T FOR THE AMPHITHEATER. GET IT?
YOU SHOULD PUT THAT DOWN--
BY THE WAY--YOU! YEAH, MR. KOT, I'M POINTING AT YOU! YOU'RE A LIAR! NOTHING EXPLODED!
--IT'S MY SPECIAL ARROW AND YOU DON'T WANT TO--
YOU CALLED THIS ISSUE "WATCH THE TLONE, MAKE THINGS EXPLODE, GET INTO OUR ZONE," BUT NOTHING EXPLO--
BOOM
HAPPY NOW?

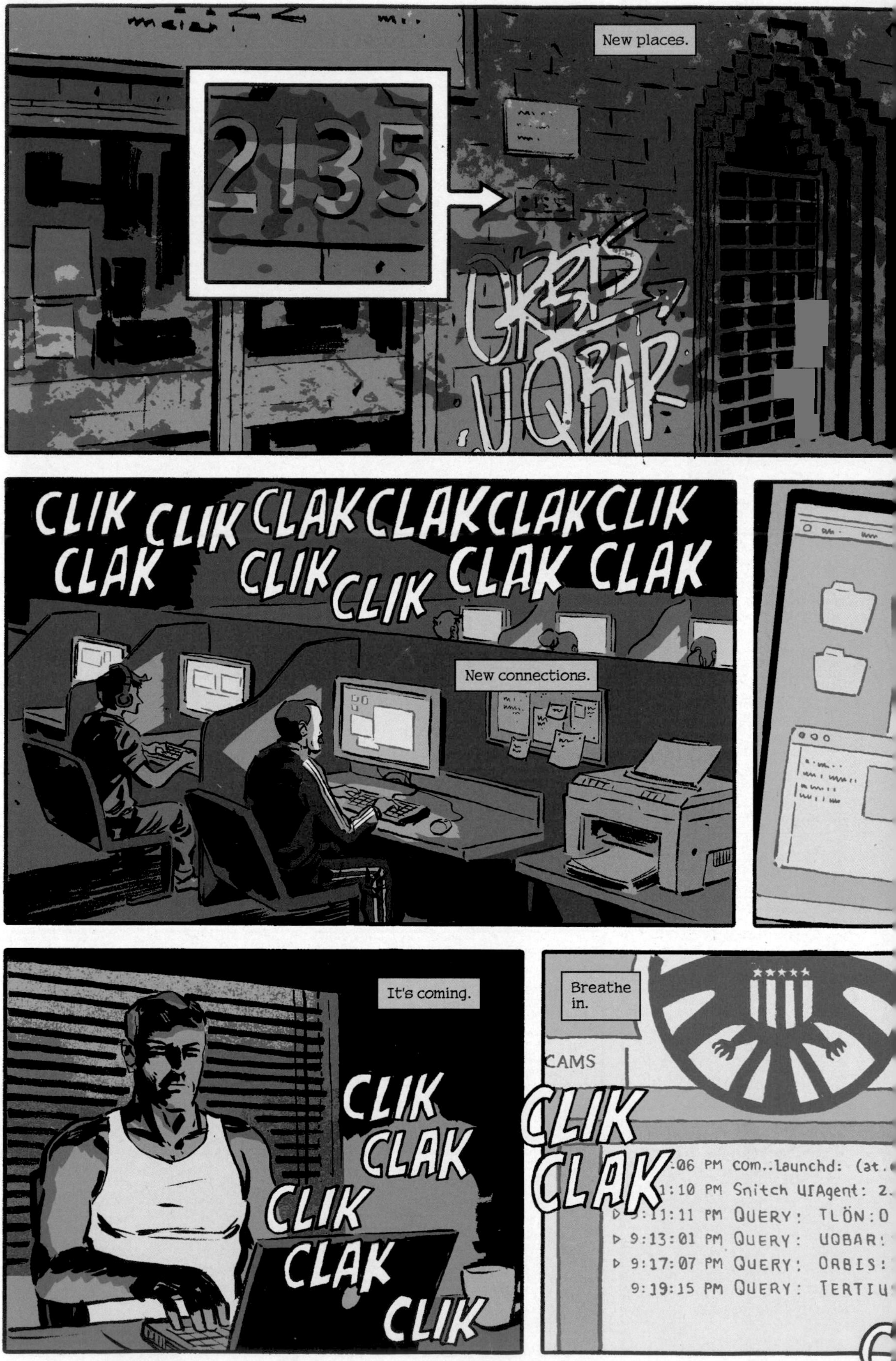

New places.
2135
UQBAR
CLIK CLIK CLAK CLAK CLAK CLIK
CLAK
CLIK CLIK CLAK CLAK
New connections.
It's coming.
CLIK
CLAK
CLIK
CLAK
CLIK
Breathe in.
CAMS
CLIK
CLAK
:06 PM com..launchd: (at.
1:10 PM Snitch UIAgent: 2.
9:13:01 PM QUERY: UQBAR:
9:17:07 PM QUERY: ORBIS:
9:19:15 PM QUERY: TERTIU

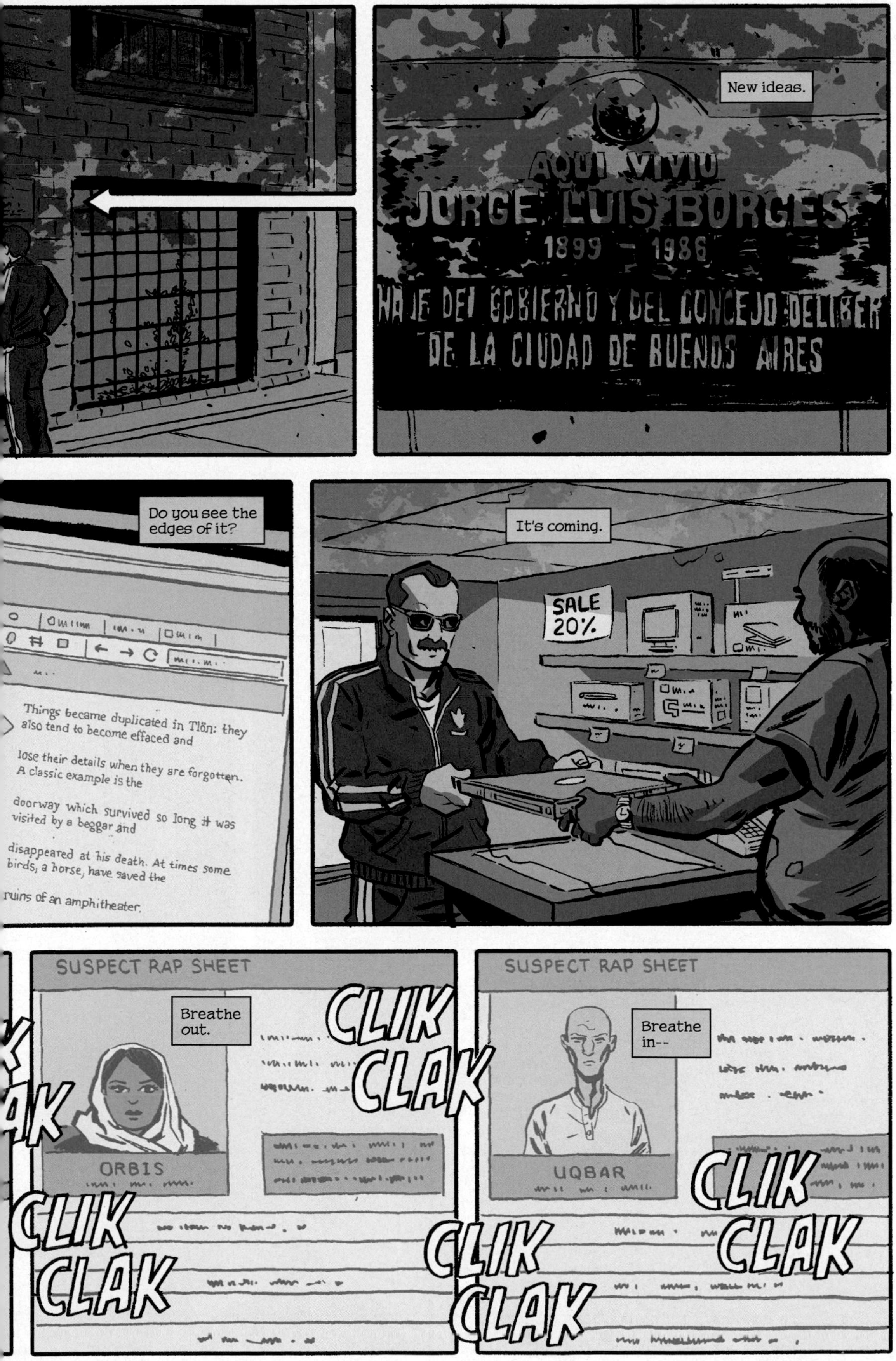
New ideas.
AQUI VIVIO
JORGE LUIS BORGES
1899 - 1986
HAJE DEL GOBIERNO Y DEL CONCEJO DELIBER
DE LA CIUDAD DE BUENOS AIRES
Do you see the edges of it?
Things became duplicated in Tlön: they also tend to become effaced and
lose their details when they are forgotten. A classic example is the
doorway which survived so long it was visited by a beggar and
disappeared at his death. At times some birds, a horse, have saved the
ruins of an amphitheater.
It's coming.
SALE 20%
SUSPECT RAP SHEET
Breathe out.
ORBIS
CLIK CLAK
CLIK CLAK
SUSPECT RAP SHEET
Breathe in--
UQBAR
CLIK CLAK
CLIK CLAK

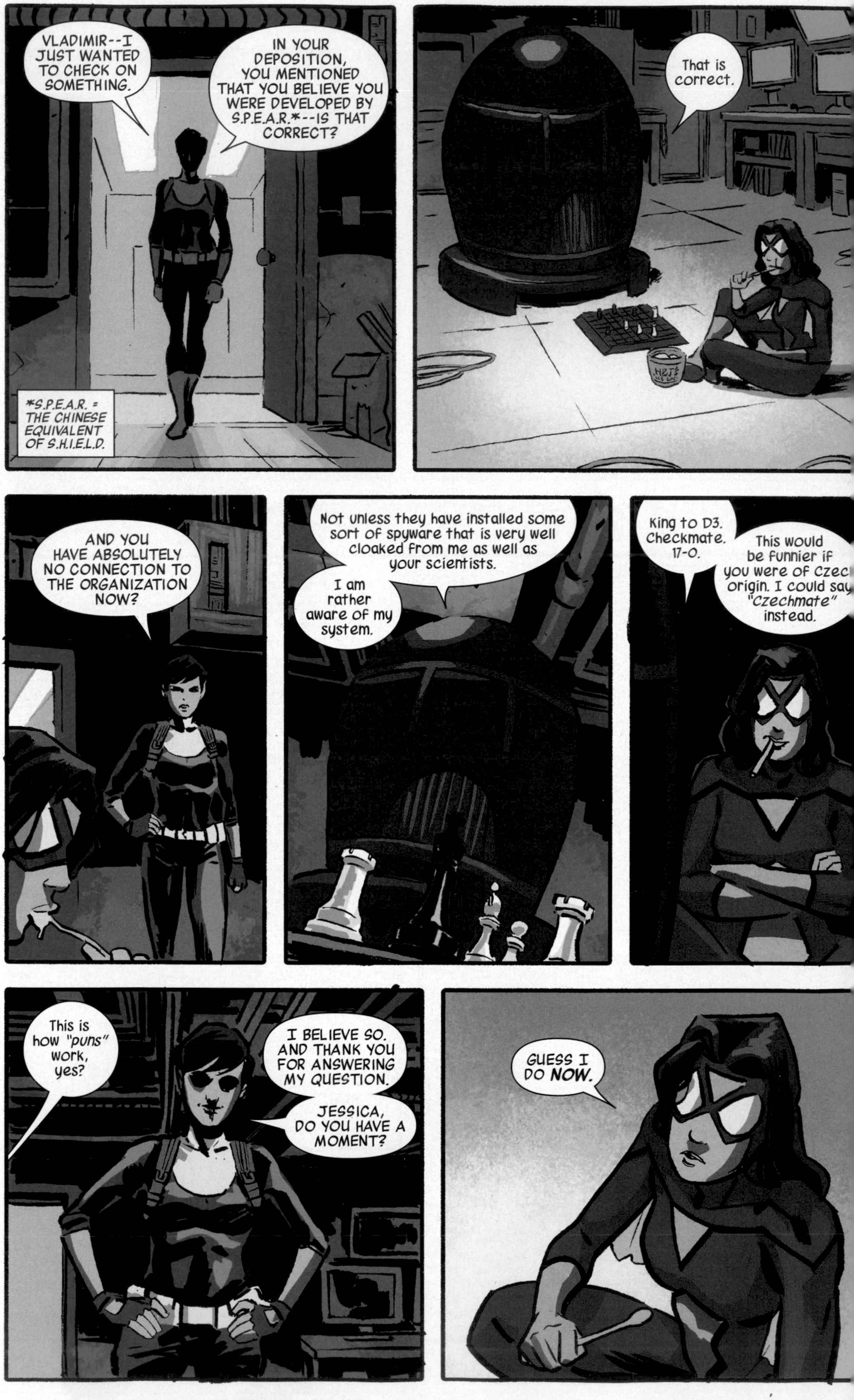
VLADIMIR--I JUST WANTED TO CHECK ON SOMETHING.
IN YOUR DEPOSITION, YOU MENTIONED THAT YOU BELIEVE YOU WERE DEVELOPED BY S.P.E.A.R.*--IS THAT CORRECT?
*S.P.E.A.R. = THE CHINESE EQUIVALENT OF S.H.I.E.L.D.
That is correct.
AND YOU HAVE ABSOLUTELY NO CONNECTION TO THE ORGANIZATION NOW?
Not unless they have installed some sort of spyware that is very well cloaked from me as well as your scientists.
I am rather aware of my system.
King to D3. Checkmate. 17-0.
This would be funnier if you were of Czec origin. I could say "Czechmate" instead.
This is how "puns" work, yes?
I BELIEVE SO. AND THANK YOU FOR ANSWERING MY QUESTION.
JESSICA, DO YOU HAVE A MOMENT?
GUESS I DO NOW.

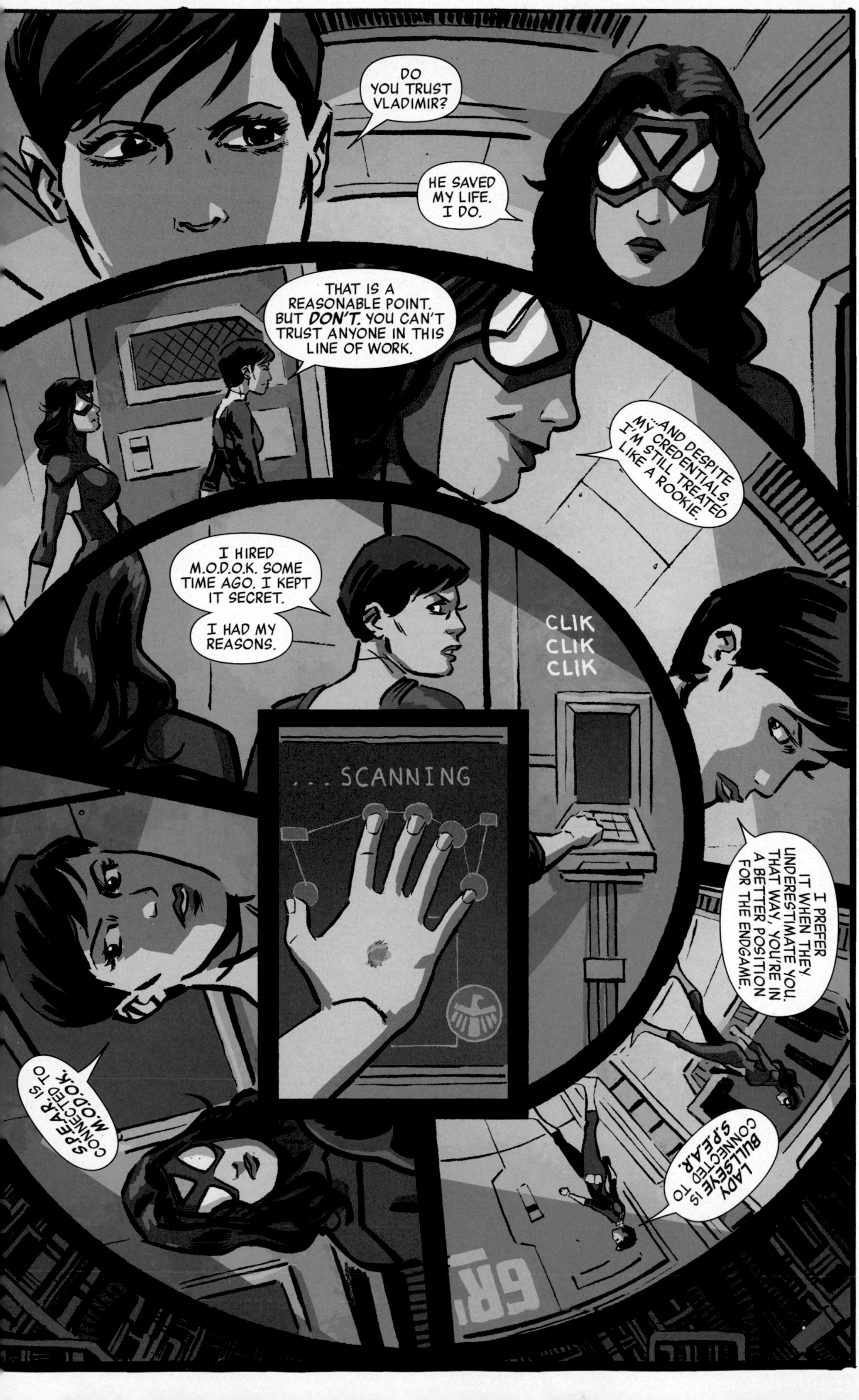
DO YOU TRUST VLADIMIR?
HE SAVED MY LIFE. I DO.
THAT IS A REASONABLE POINT. BUT **DON'T.** YOU CAN'T TRUST ANYONE IN THIS LINE OF WORK.
...AND DESPITE MY CREDENTIALS, I'M STILL TREATED LIKE A ROOKIE.
I HIRED M.O.D.O.K. SOME TIME AGO. I KEPT IT SECRET.
I HAD MY REASONS.
CLIK CLIK CLIK
...SCANNING
I PREFER IT WHEN THEY UNDERESTIMATE YOU. THAT WAY, YOU'RE IN A BETTER POSITION FOR THE ENDGAME.
LADY BULLSEYE IS CONNECTED TO **S.P.E.A.R.**
S.P.E.A.R. IS CONNECTED TO **M.O.D.O.K.**

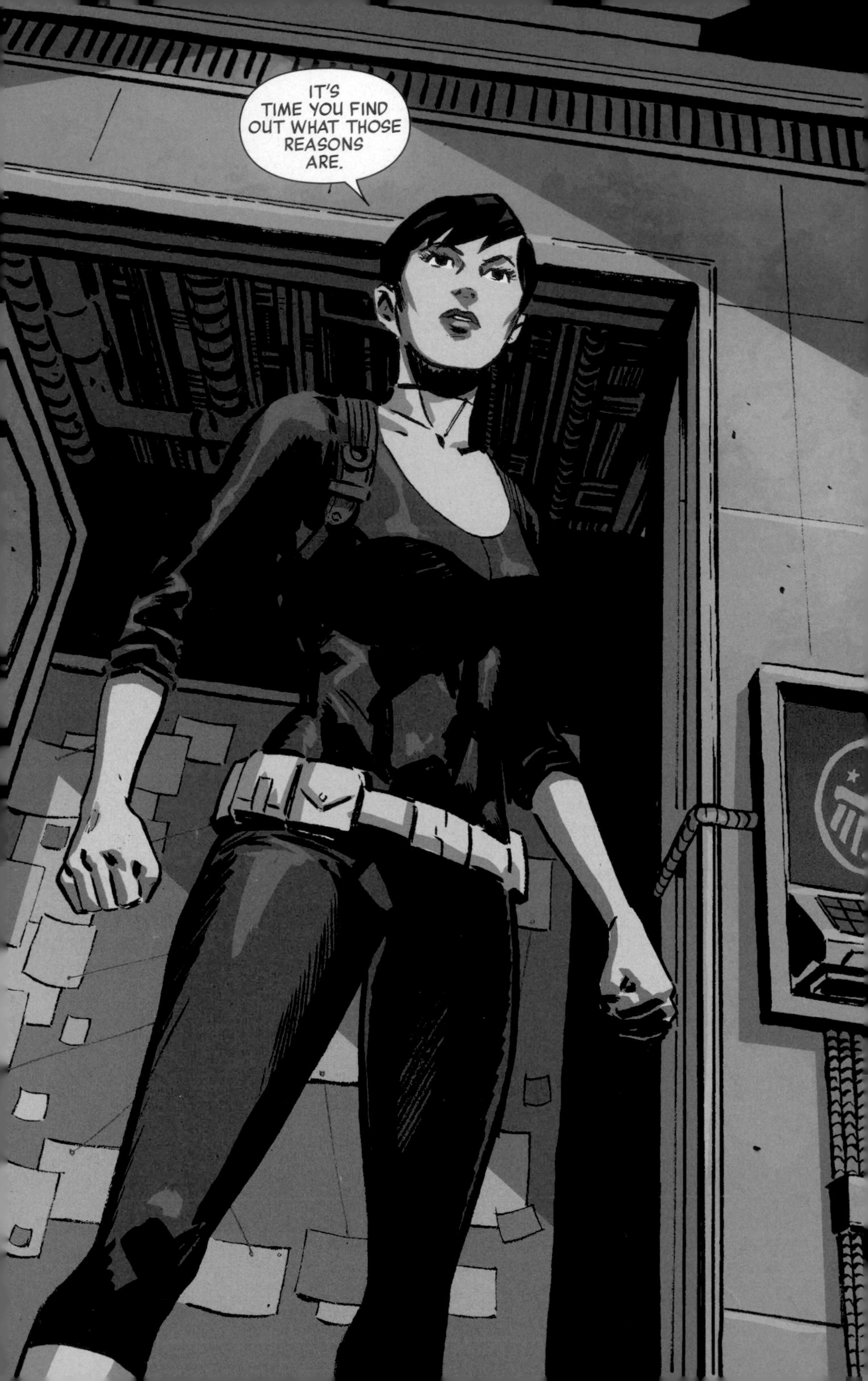
IT'S TIME YOU FIND OUT WHAT THOSE REASONS ARE.

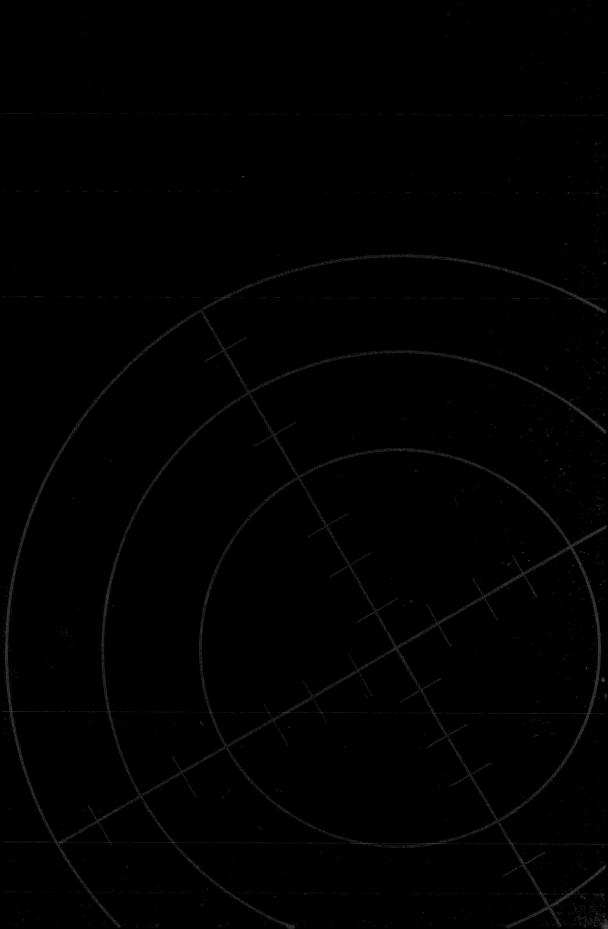

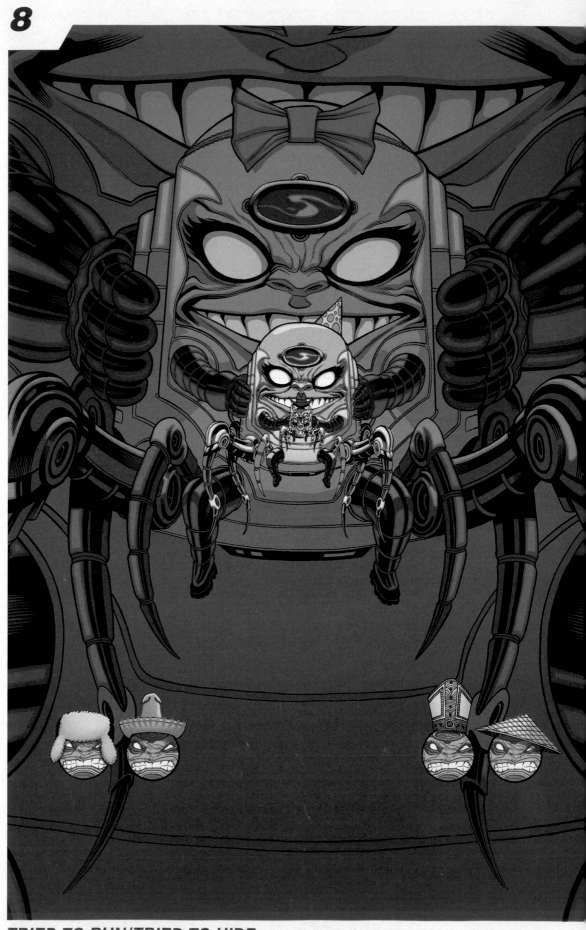

TRIED TO RUN/TRIED TO HIDE

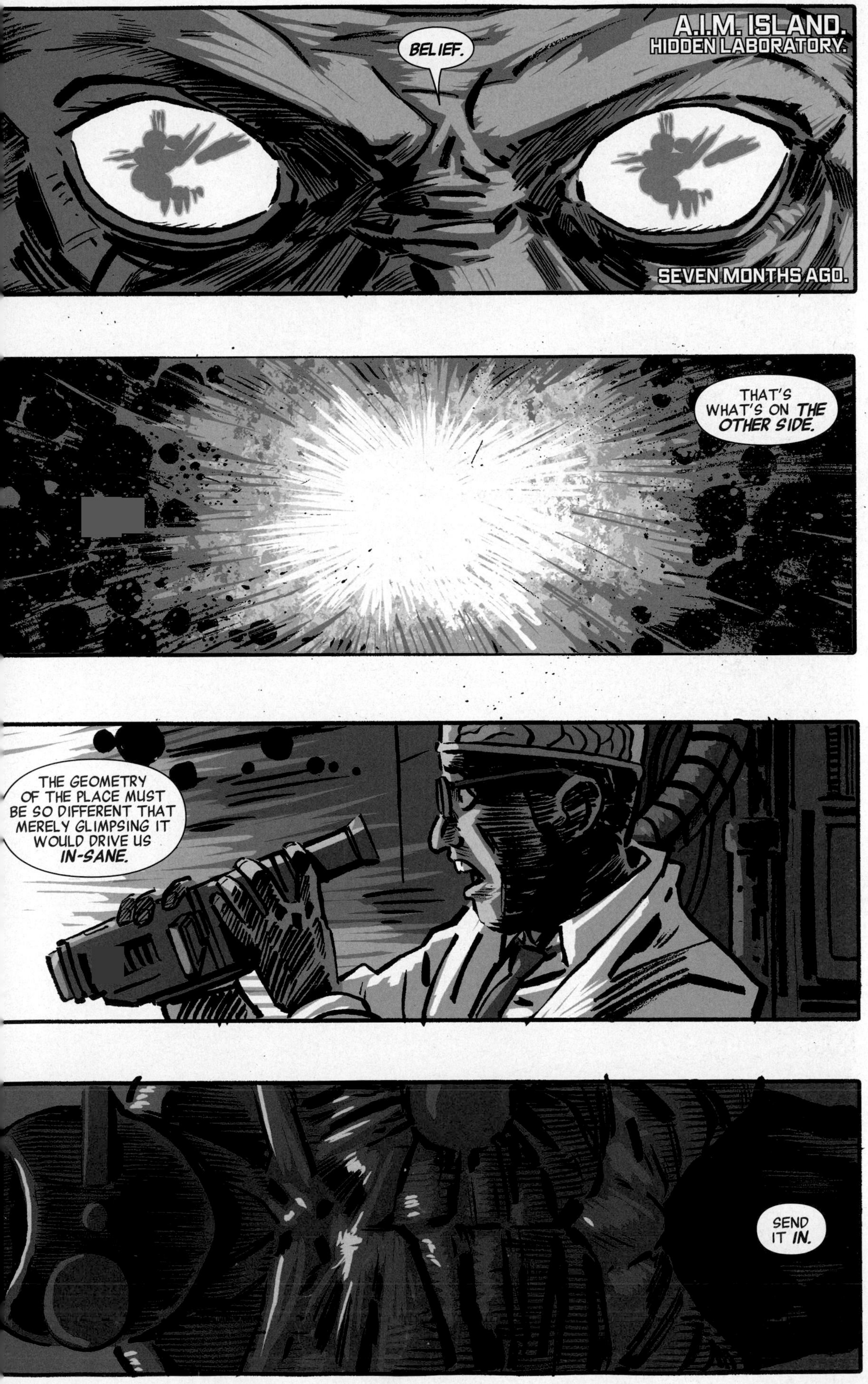
A.I.M. ISLAND.
HIDDEN LABORATORY.
BELIEF.
SEVEN MONTHS AGO.
THAT'S WHAT'S ON THE OTHER SIDE.
THE GEOMETRY OF THE PLACE MUST BE SO DIFFERENT THAT MERELY GLIMPSING IT WOULD DRIVE US IN-SANE.
SEND IT IN.

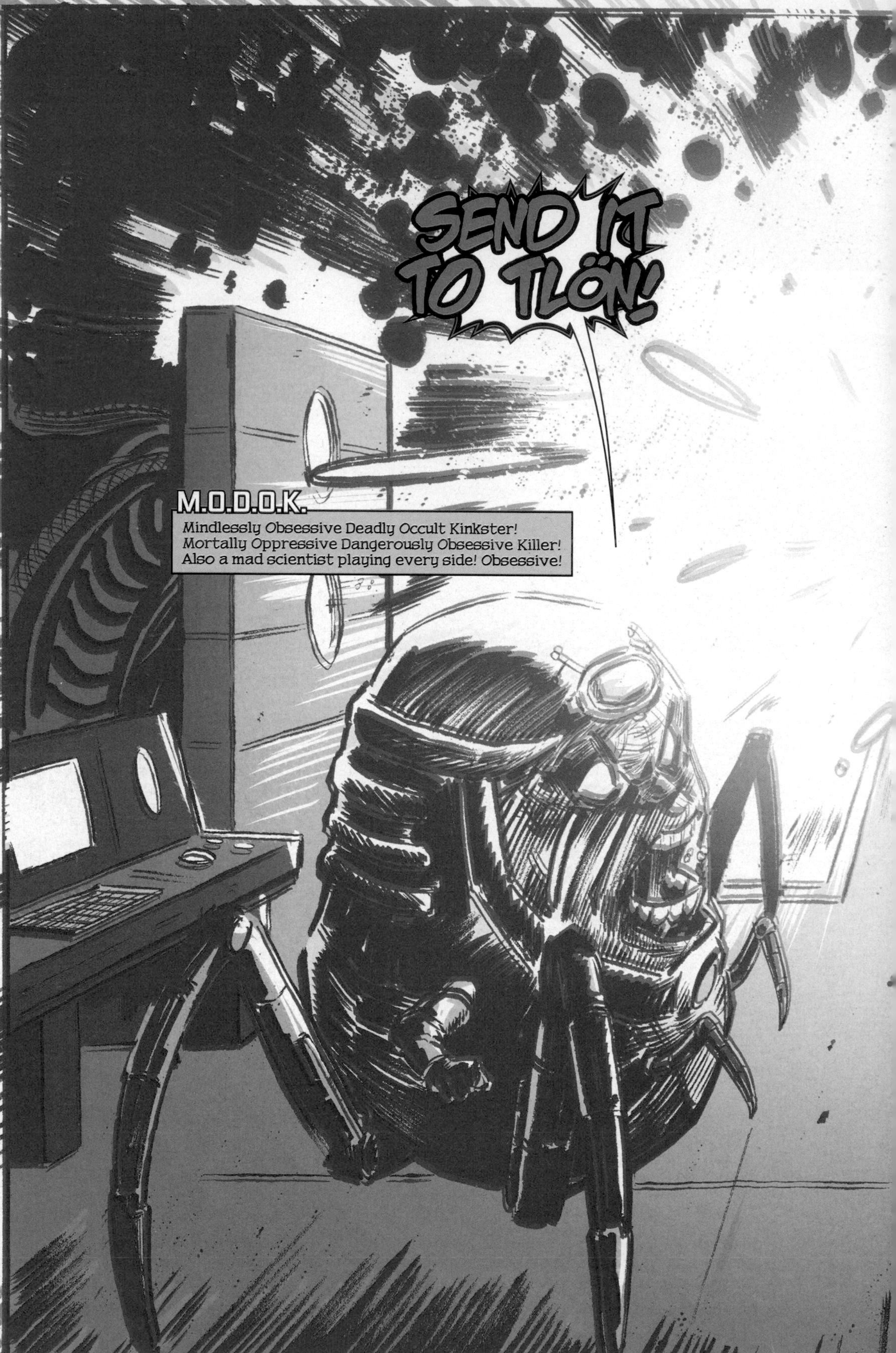
SEND IT TO TLÖN!
M.O.D.O.K.
Mindlessly Obsessive Deadly Occult Kinkster!
Mortally Oppressive Dangerously Obsessive Killer!
Also a mad scientist playing every side! Obsessive!

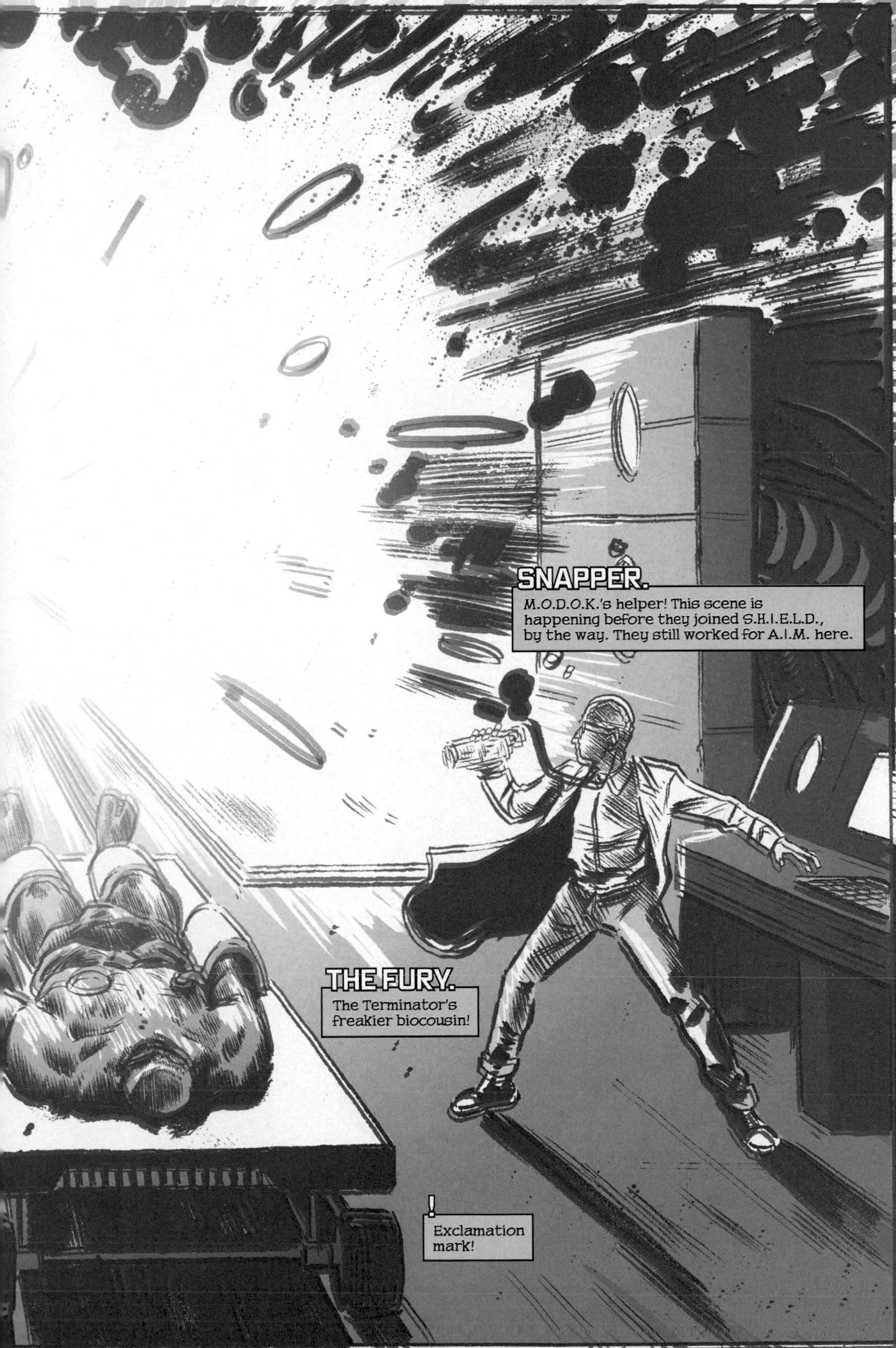
SNAPPER.
M.O.D.O.K.'s helper! This scene is happening before they joined S.H.I.E.L.D., by the way. They still worked for A.I.M. here.
THE FURY.
The Terminator's freakier biocousin!
!
Exclamation mark!

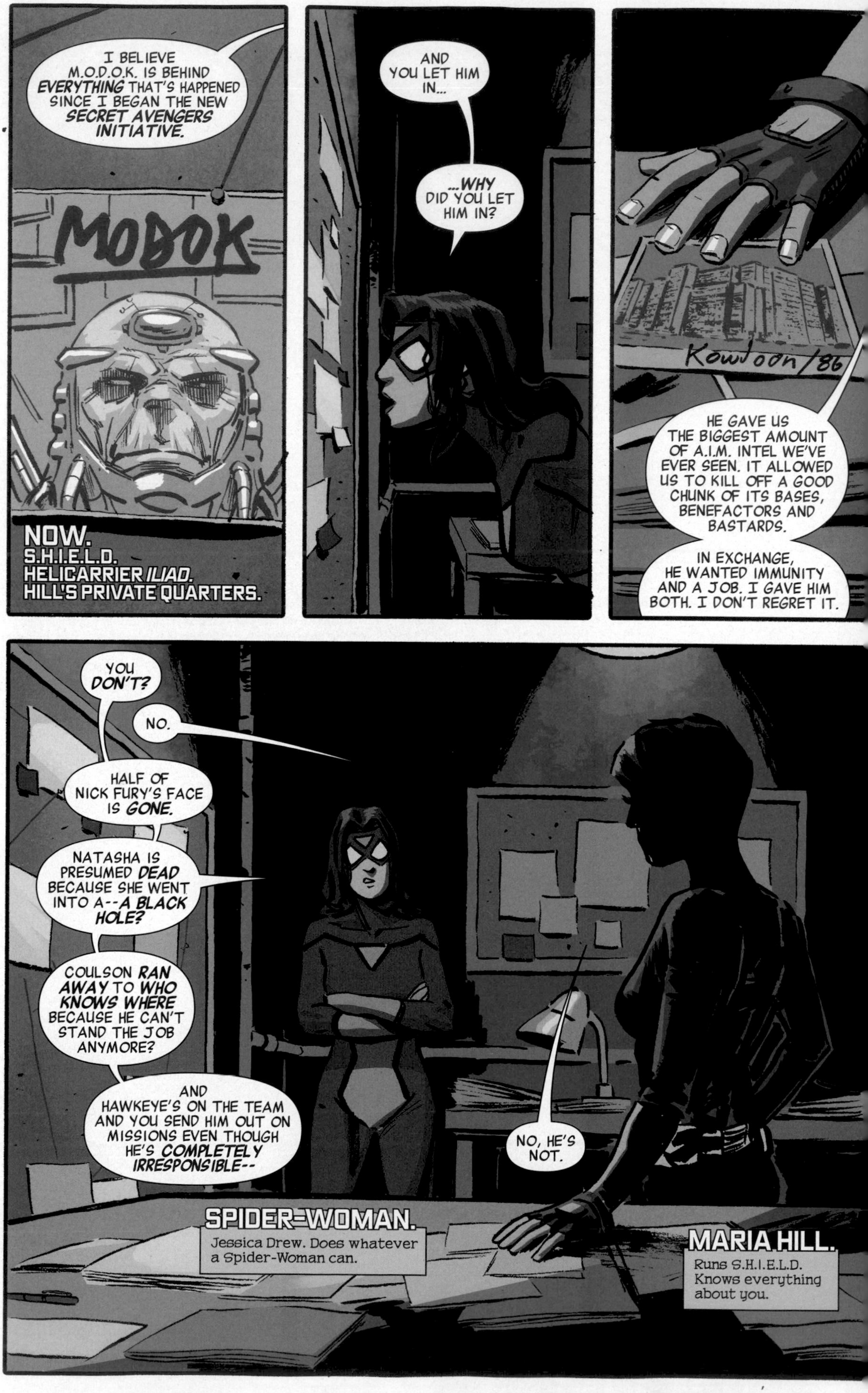
I BELIEVE M.O.D.O.K. IS BEHIND EVERYTHING THAT'S HAPPENED SINCE I BEGAN THE NEW SECRET AVENGERS INITIATIVE.
MODOK
NOW. S.H.I.E.L.D. HELICARRIER ILIAD. HILL'S PRIVATE QUARTERS.
AND YOU LET HIM IN...
...WHY DID YOU LET HIM IN?
Kowloon/86
HE GAVE US THE BIGGEST AMOUNT OF A.I.M. INTEL WE'VE EVER SEEN. IT ALLOWED US TO KILL OFF A GOOD CHUNK OF ITS BASES, BENEFACTORS AND BASTARDS.
IN EXCHANGE, HE WANTED IMMUNITY AND A JOB. I GAVE HIM BOTH. I DON'T REGRET IT.
YOU DON'T?
NO.
HALF OF NICK FURY'S FACE IS GONE.
NATASHA IS PRESUMED DEAD BECAUSE SHE WENT INTO A--A BLACK HOLE?
COULSON RAN AWAY TO WHO KNOWS WHERE BECAUSE HE CAN'T STAND THE JOB ANYMORE?
AND HAWKEYE'S ON THE TEAM AND YOU SEND HIM OUT ON MISSIONS EVEN THOUGH HE'S COMPLETELY IRRESPONSIBLE--
NO, HE'S NOT.
SPIDER-WOMAN.
Jessica Drew. Does whatever a Spider-Woman can.
MARIA HILL.
Runs S.H.I.E.L.D. Knows everything about you.

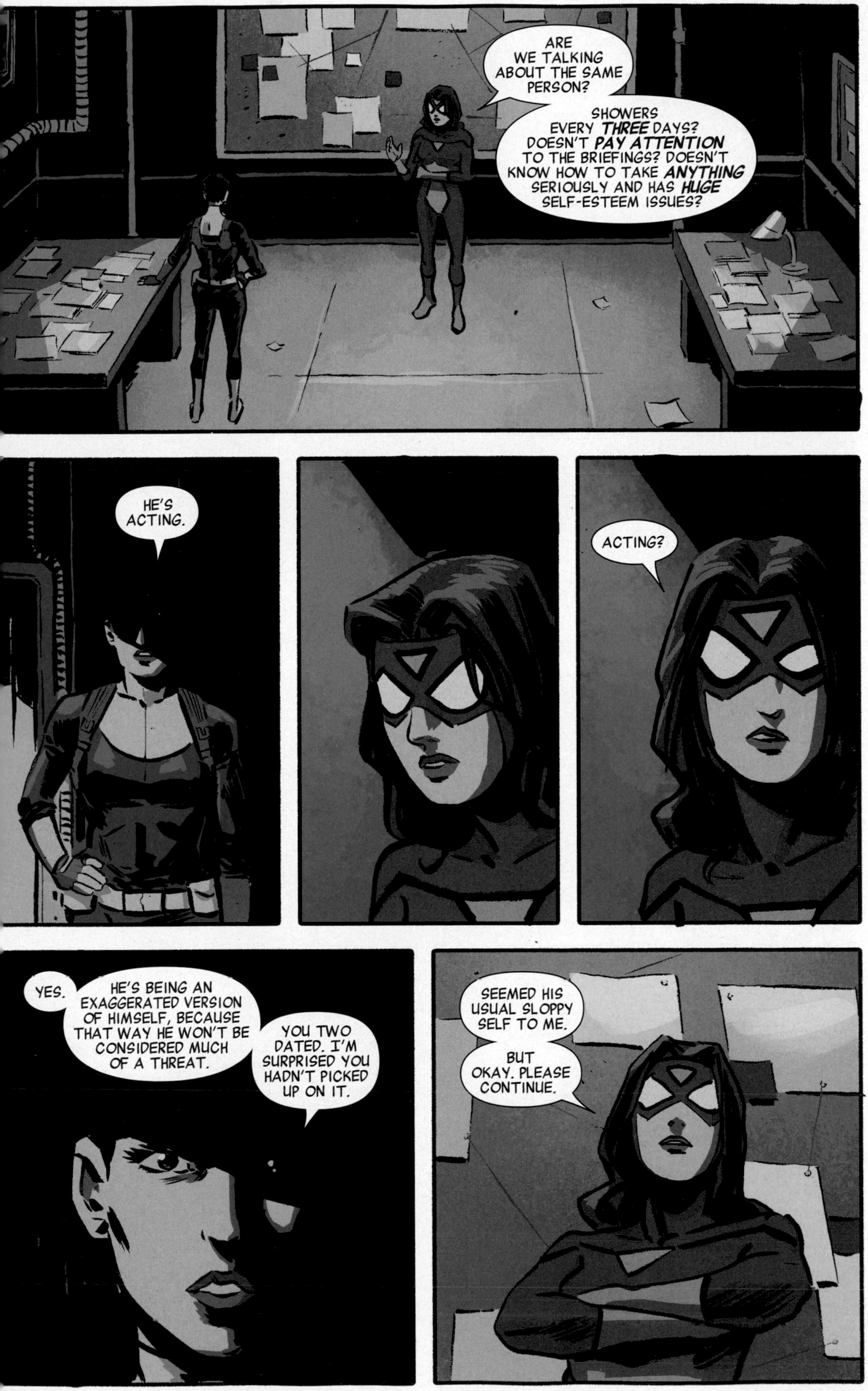
ARE WE TALKING ABOUT THE SAME PERSON?
SHOWERS EVERY THREE DAYS? DOESN'T PAY ATTENTION TO THE BRIEFINGS? DOESN'T KNOW HOW TO TAKE ANYTHING SERIOUSLY AND HAS HUGE SELF-ESTEEM ISSUES?
HE'S ACTING.
ACTING?
YES.
HE'S BEING AN EXAGGERATED VERSION OF HIMSELF, BECAUSE THAT WAY HE WON'T BE CONSIDERED MUCH OF A THREAT.
YOU TWO DATED. I'M SURPRISED YOU HADN'T PICKED UP ON IT.
SEEMED HIS USUAL SLOPPY SELF TO ME.
BUT OKAY. PLEASE CONTINUE.

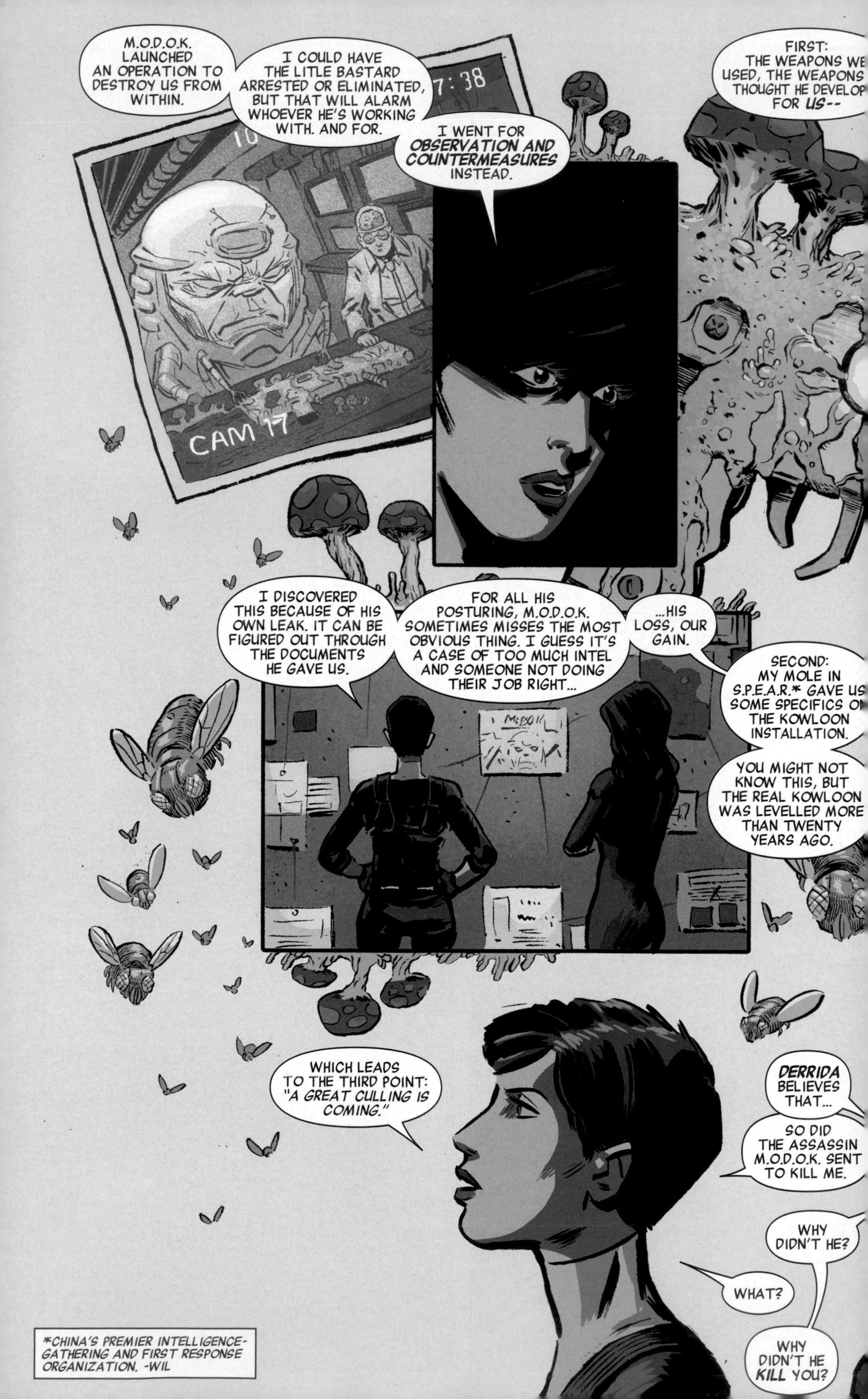
M.O.D.O.K. LAUNCHED AN OPERATION TO DESTROY US FROM WITHIN.
I COULD HAVE THE LITLE BASTARD ARRESTED OR ELIMINATED, BUT THAT WILL ALARM WHOEVER HE'S WORKING WITH. AND FOR.
7:38
I WENT FOR *OBSERVATION AND COUNTERMEASURES* INSTEAD.
CAM 17
FIRST: THE WEAPONS WE USED, THE WEAPONS THOUGHT HE DEVELOP FOR *US*--
I DISCOVERED THIS BECAUSE OF HIS OWN LEAK. IT CAN BE FIGURED OUT THROUGH THE DOCUMENTS HE GAVE US.
FOR ALL HIS POSTURING, M.O.D.O.K. SOMETIMES MISSES THE MOST OBVIOUS THING. I GUESS IT'S A CASE OF TOO MUCH INTEL AND SOMEONE NOT DOING THEIR JOB RIGHT...
...HIS LOSS, OUR GAIN.
SECOND: MY MOLE IN S.P.E.A.R.* GAVE US SOME SPECIFICS O THE KOWLOON INSTALLATION.
YOU MIGHT NOT KNOW THIS, BUT THE REAL KOWLOON WAS LEVELLED MORE THAN TWENTY YEARS AGO.
WHICH LEADS TO THE THIRD POINT: "*A GREAT CULLING IS COMING.*"
DERRIDA BELIEVES THAT...
SO DID THE ASSASSIN M.O.D.O.K. SENT TO KILL ME.
WHY DIDN'T HE?
WHAT?
WHY DIDN'T HE *KILL* YOU?
*CHINA'S PREMIER INTELLIGENCE-GATHERING AND FIRST RESPONSE ORGANIZATION. -WIL

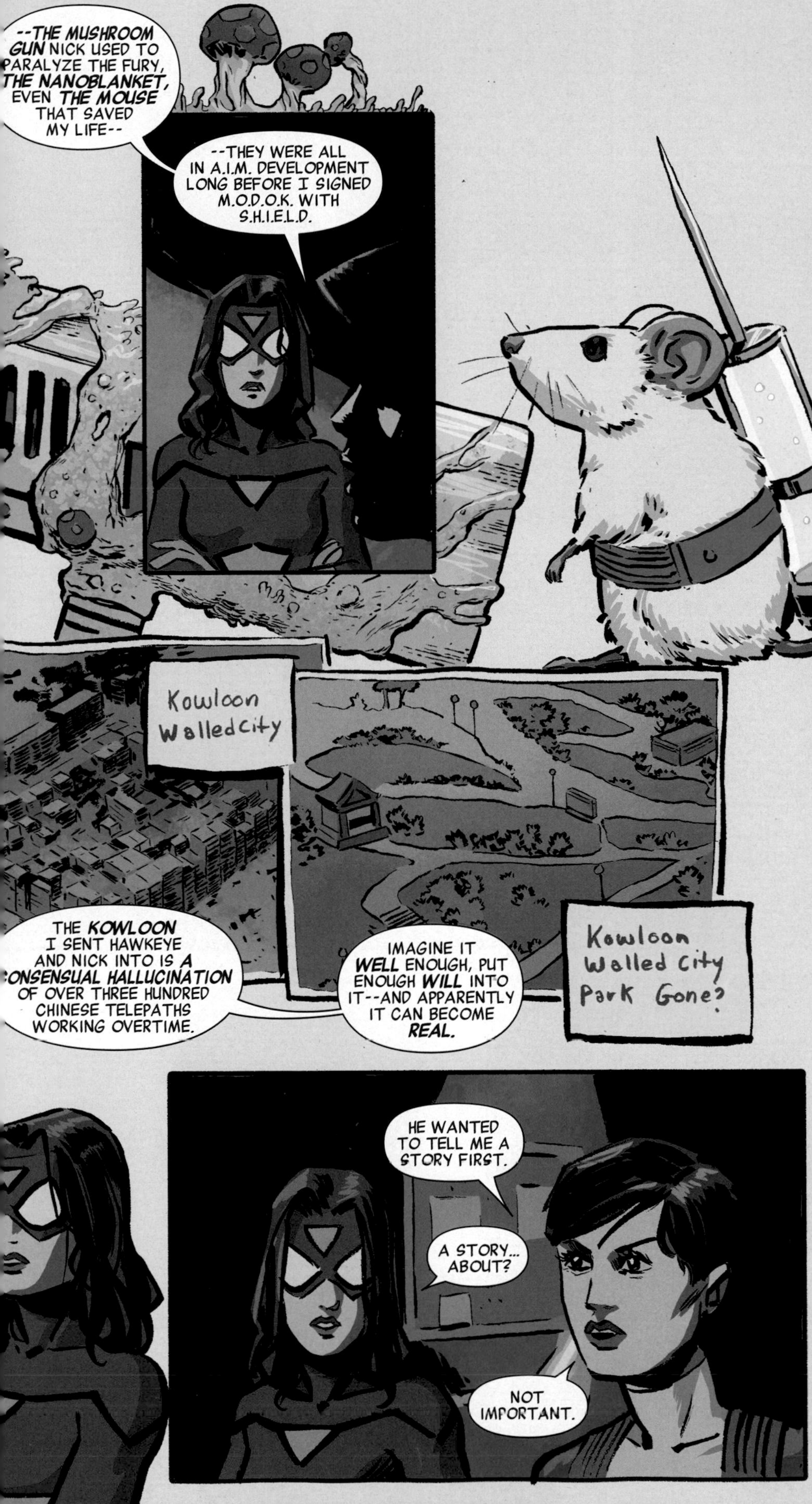
--THE MUSHROOM GUN NICK USED TO PARALYZE THE FURY, THE NANOBLANKET, EVEN THE MOUSE THAT SAVED MY LIFE--
--THEY WERE ALL IN A.I.M. DEVELOPMENT LONG BEFORE I SIGNED M.O.D.O.K. WITH S.H.I.E.L.D.
Kowloon Walledcity
THE KOWLOON I SENT HAWKEYE AND NICK INTO IS A CONSENSUAL HALLUCINATION OF OVER THREE HUNDRED CHINESE TELEPATHS WORKING OVERTIME.
IMAGINE IT WELL ENOUGH, PUT ENOUGH WILL INTO IT--AND APPARENTLY IT CAN BECOME REAL.
Kowloon Walled City Park Gone?
HE WANTED TO TELL ME A STORY FIRST.
A STORY... ABOUT?
NOT IMPORTANT.

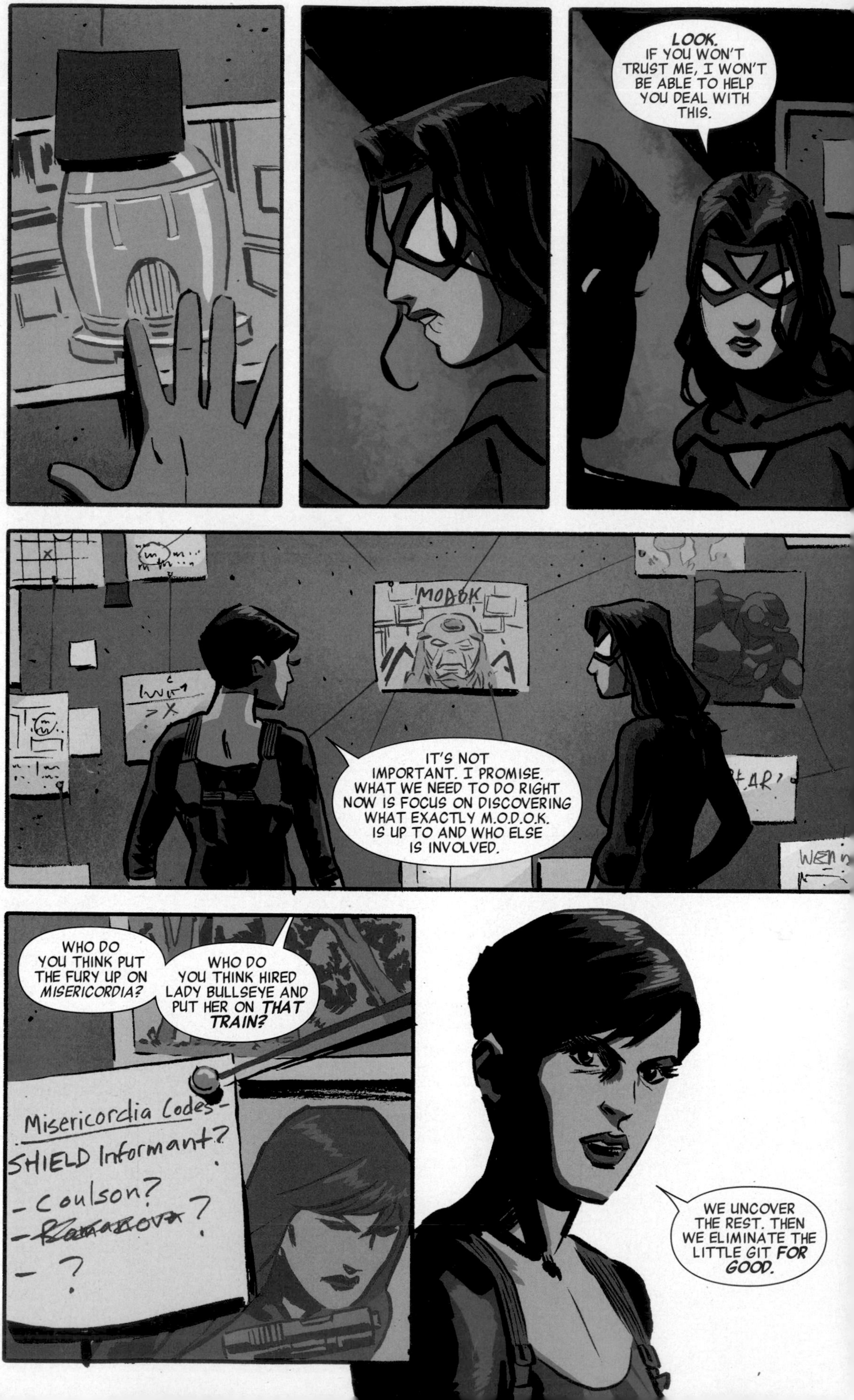
LOOK. IF YOU WON'T TRUST ME, I WON'T BE ABLE TO HELP YOU DEAL WITH THIS.
MODOK
IT'S NOT IMPORTANT. I PROMISE. WHAT WE NEED TO DO RIGHT NOW IS FOCUS ON DISCOVERING WHAT EXACTLY M.O.D.O.K. IS UP TO AND WHO ELSE IS INVOLVED.
WHO DO YOU THINK PUT THE FURY UP ON MISERICORDIA?
WHO DO YOU THINK HIRED LADY BULLSEYE AND PUT HER ON THAT TRAIN?
Misericordia Codes
SHIELD Informant?
- Coulson?
WE UNCOVER THE REST. THEN WE ELIMINATE THE LITTLE GIT FOR GOOD.

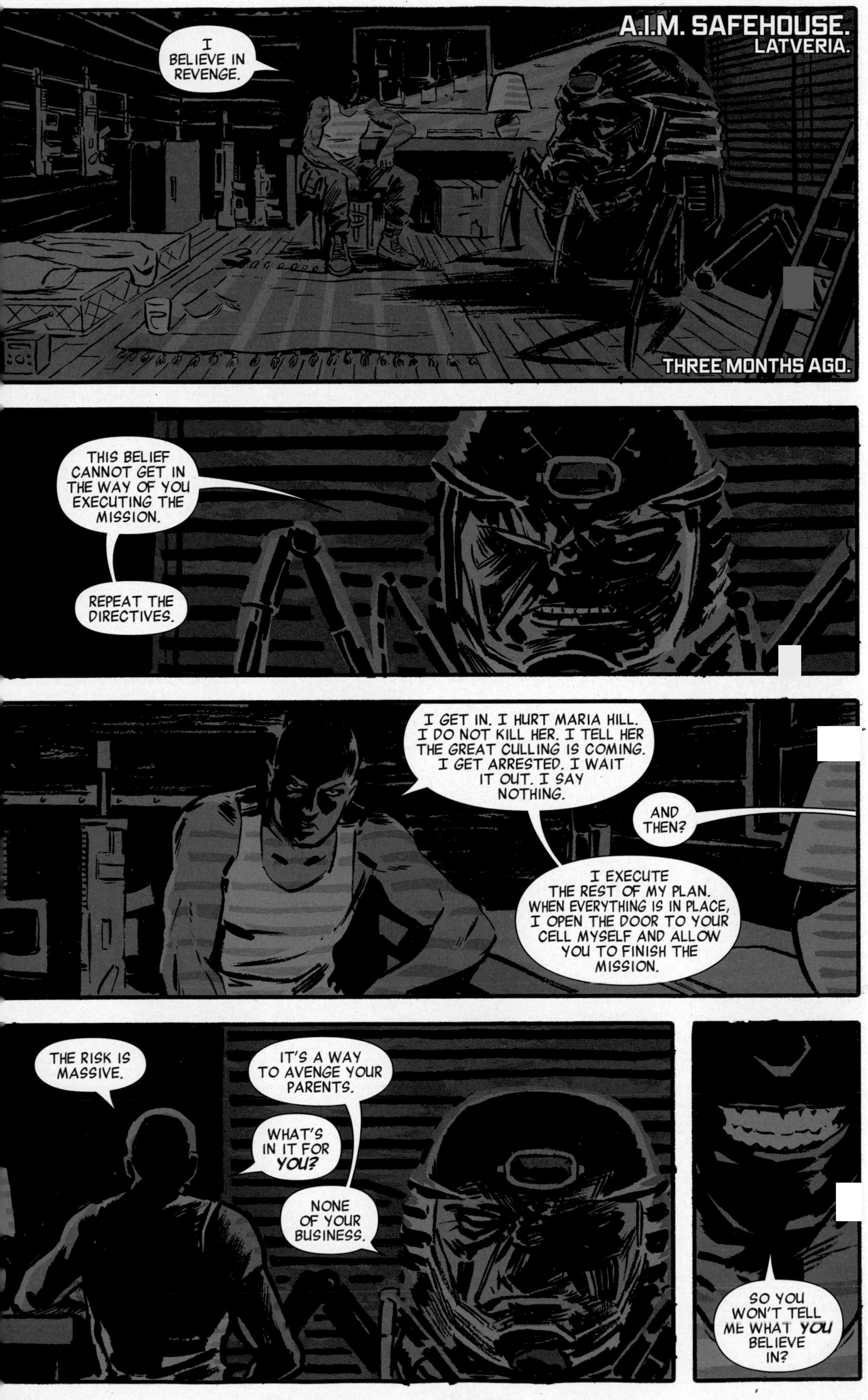
A.I.M. SAFEHOUSE. LATVERIA.
I BELIEVE IN REVENGE.
THREE MONTHS AGO.
THIS BELIEF CANNOT GET IN THE WAY OF YOU EXECUTING THE MISSION.
REPEAT THE DIRECTIVES.
I GET IN. I HURT MARIA HILL. I DO NOT KILL HER. I TELL HER THE GREAT CULLING IS COMING. I GET ARRESTED. I WAIT IT OUT. I SAY NOTHING.
AND THEN?
I EXECUTE THE REST OF MY PLAN. WHEN EVERYTHING IS IN PLACE, I OPEN THE DOOR TO YOUR CELL MYSELF AND ALLOW YOU TO FINISH THE MISSION.
THE RISK IS MASSIVE.
IT'S A WAY TO AVENGE YOUR PARENTS.
WHAT'S IN IT FOR YOU?
NONE OF YOUR BUSINESS.
SO YOU WON'T TELL ME WHAT YOU BELIEVE IN?

WHAT HAPPENED TO IT?

NOW.
IUAD. S.H.I.E.L.D.
HOLDING FACILITY.

IT CAME FROM SOMEWHERE FAR AWAY.

COULD YOU BE MORE SPECIFIC?

I DON'T HAVE THE KNOWLEDGE NECESSARY TO SPECIFY WHERE IT WENT. I DON'T KNOW WHAT IT ENCOUNTERED OR HOW TO DESCRIBE THE ATMOSPHERIC PRESSURES IT MIGHT HAVE UNDERGONE...

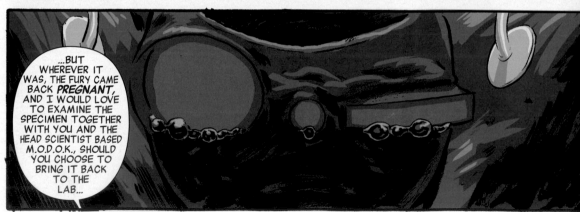

...BUT WHEREVER IT WAS, THE FURY CAME BACK *PREGNANT*, AND I WOULD LOVE TO EXAMINE THE SPECIMEN TOGETHER WITH YOU AND THE HEAD SCIENTIST BASED M.O.D.O.K., SHOULD YOU CHOOSE TO BRING IT BACK TO THE LAB...

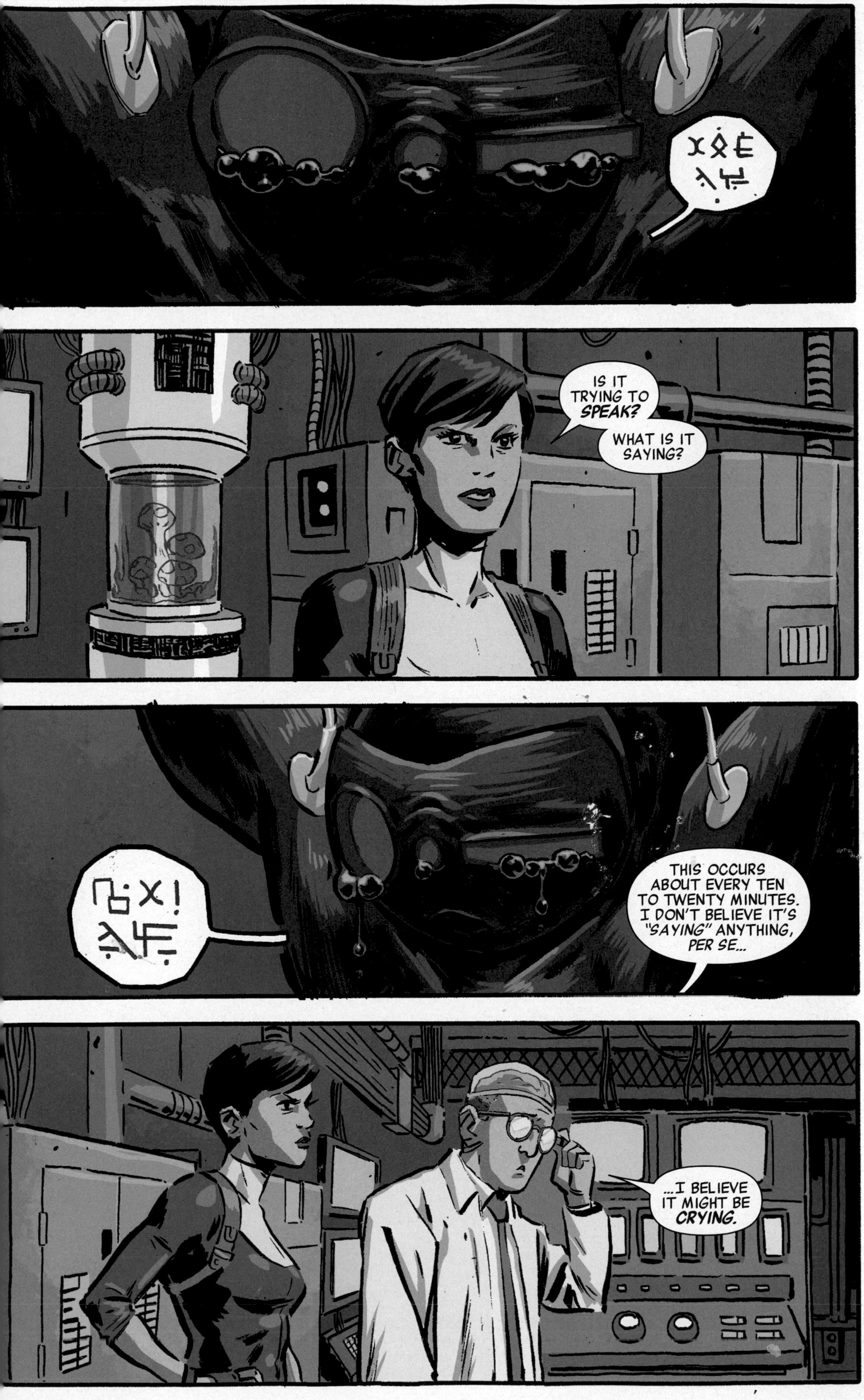
IS IT TRYING TO SPEAK?
WHAT IS IT SAYING?
THIS OCCURS ABOUT EVERY TEN TO TWENTY MINUTES. I DON'T BELIEVE IT'S "SAYING" ANYTHING, PER SE...
...I BELIEVE IT MIGHT BE CRYING.

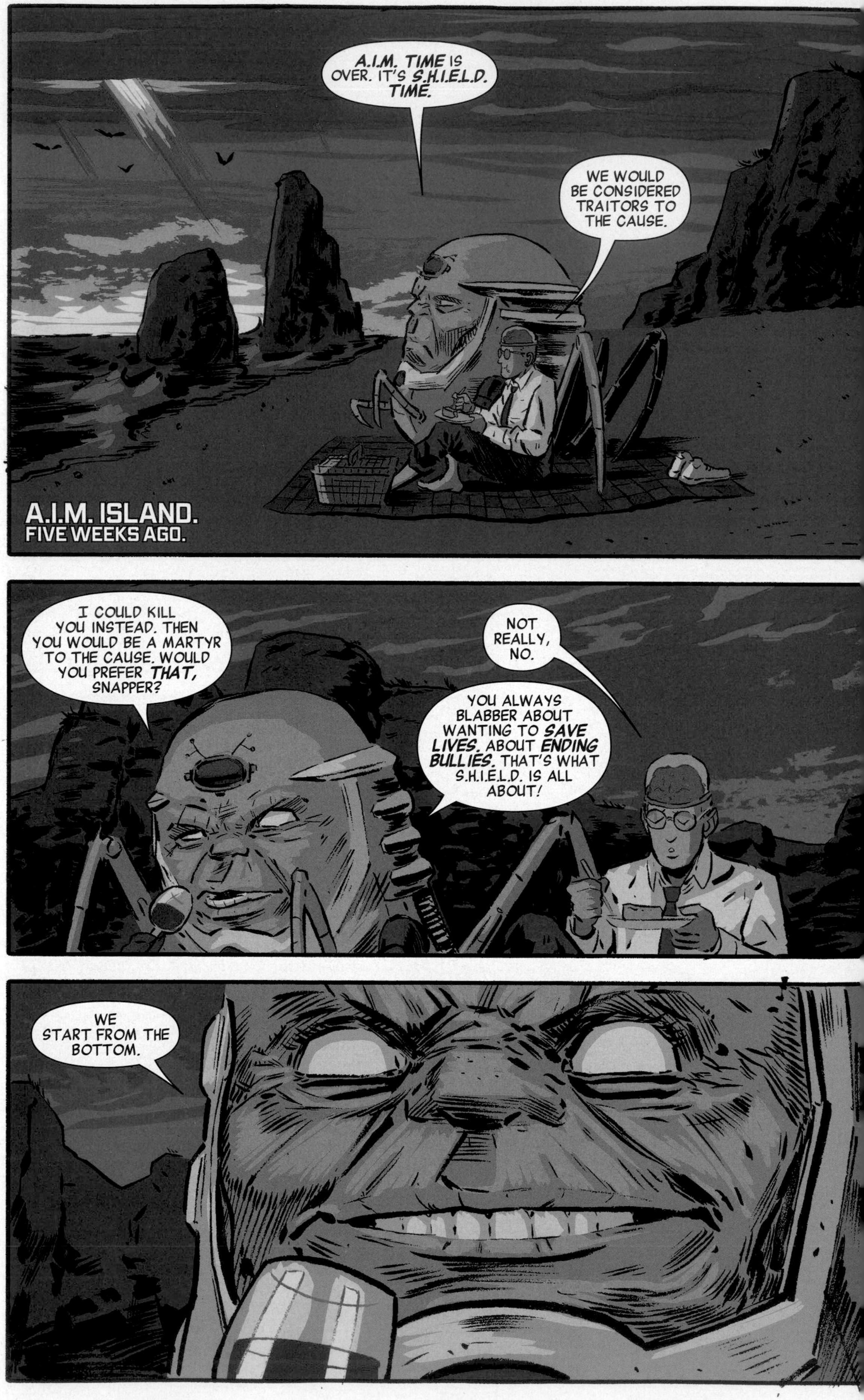
A.I.M. TIME IS OVER. IT'S S.H.I.E.L.D. TIME.
WE WOULD BE CONSIDERED TRAITORS TO THE CAUSE.
A.I.M. ISLAND. FIVE WEEKS AGO.
I COULD KILL YOU INSTEAD. THEN YOU WOULD BE A MARTYR TO THE CAUSE. WOULD YOU PREFER THAT, SNAPPER?
NOT REALLY, NO.
YOU ALWAYS BLABBER ABOUT WANTING TO SAVE LIVES. ABOUT ENDING BULLIES. THAT'S WHAT S.H.I.E.L.D. IS ALL ABOUT!
WE START FROM THE BOTTOM.

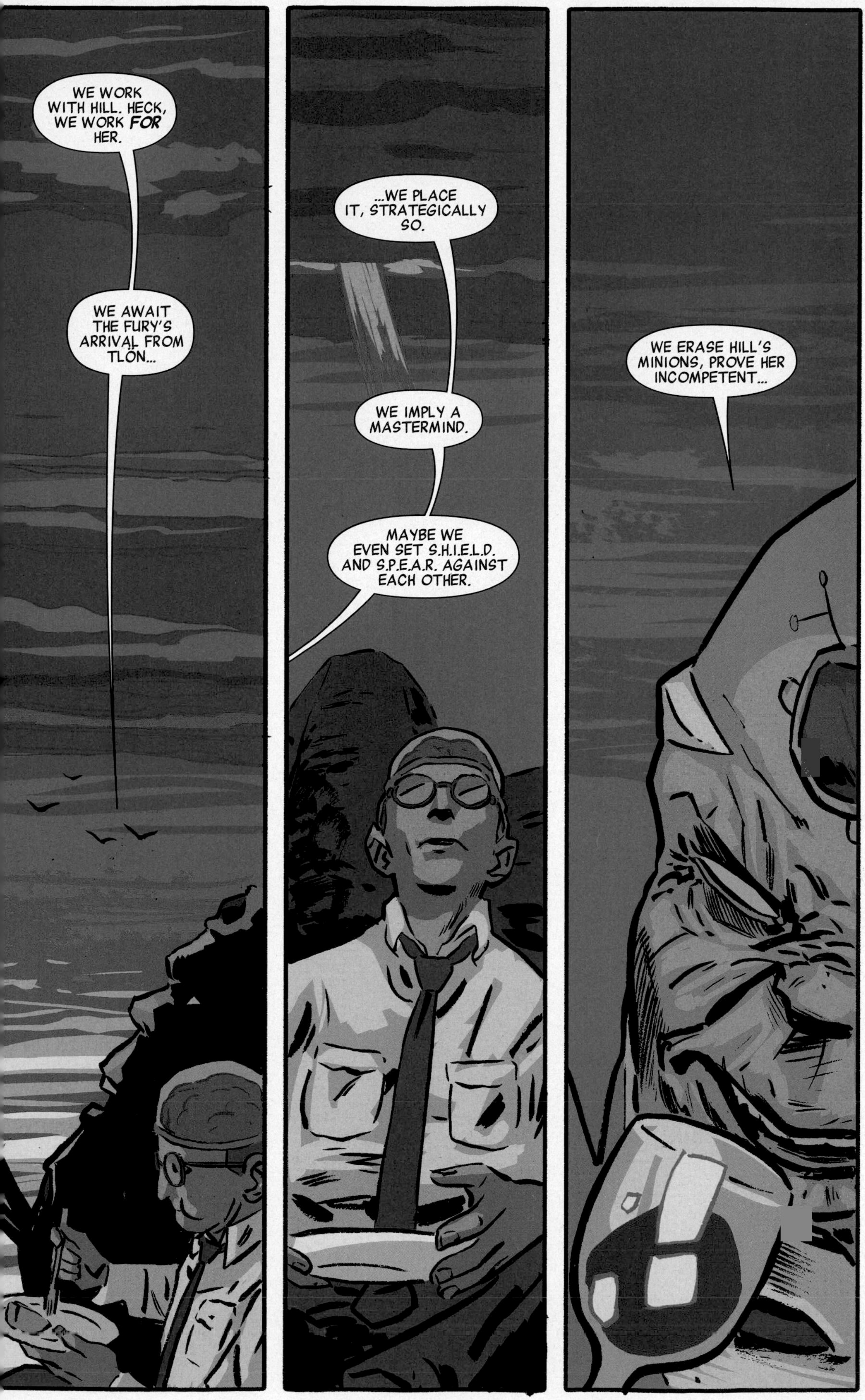
WE WORK WITH HILL. HECK, WE WORK **FOR** HER.
WE AWAIT THE FURY'S ARRIVAL FROM TLÖN...
...WE PLACE IT, STRATEGICALLY SO.
WE IMPLY A MASTERMIND.
MAYBE WE EVEN SET S.H.I.E.L.D. AND S.P.E.A.R. AGAINST EACH OTHER.
WE ERASE HILL'S MINIONS, PROVE HER INCOMPETENT...

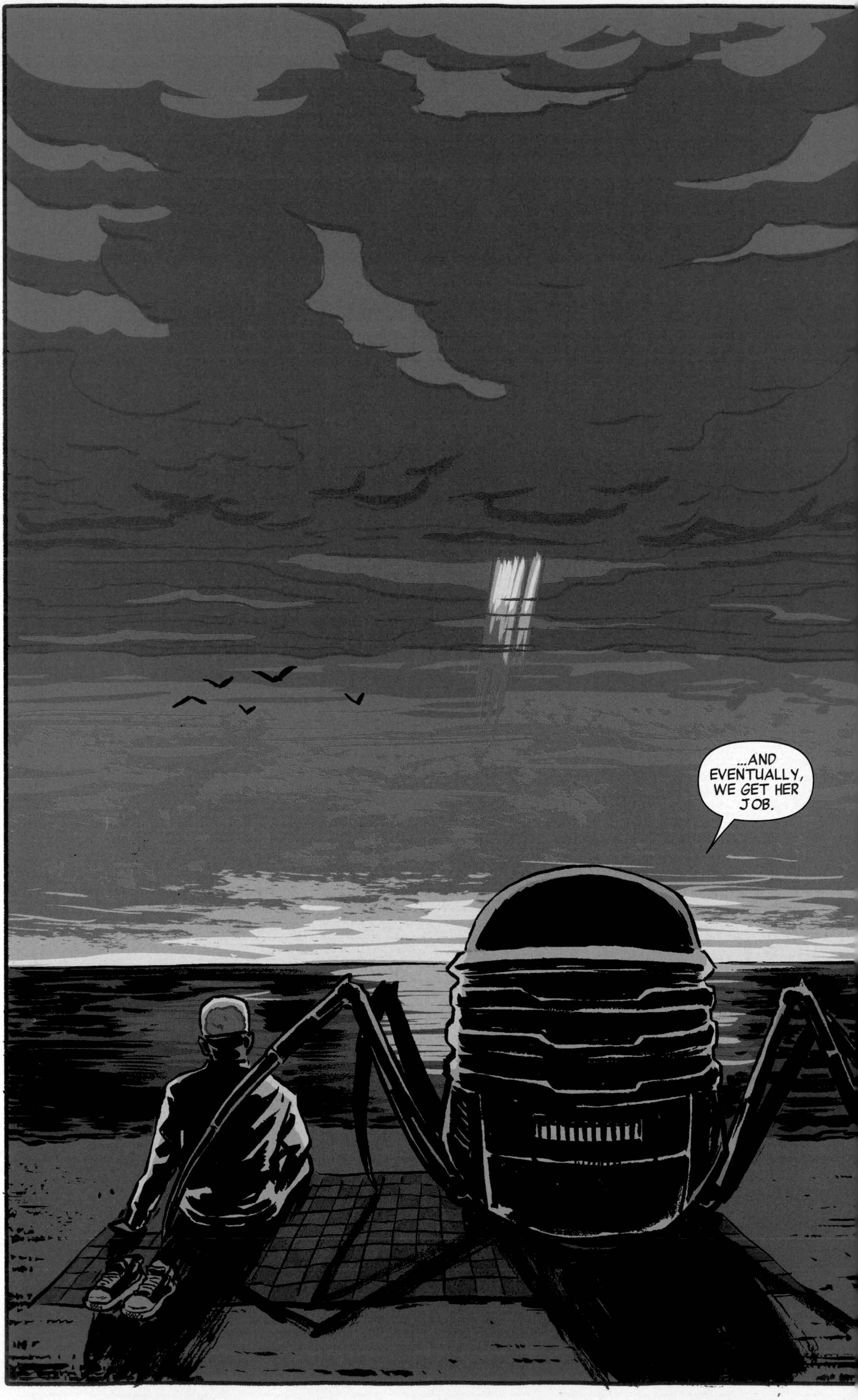
...AND EVENTUALLY, WE GET HER JOB.

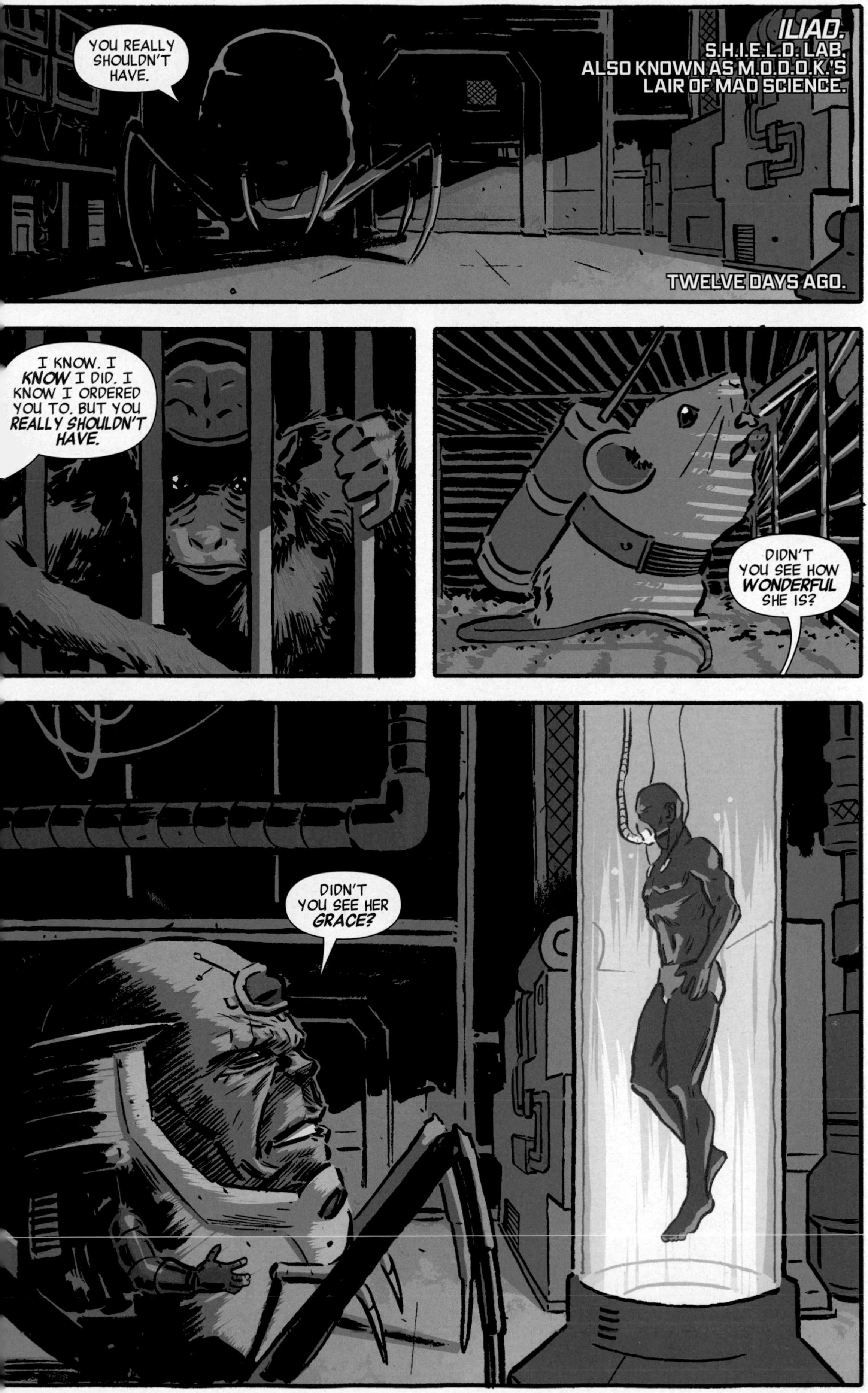
ILIAD.
S.H.I.E.L.D. LAB.
ALSO KNOWN AS M.O.D.O.K.'S LAIR OF MAD SCIENCE.
YOU REALLY SHOULDN'T HAVE.
TWELVE DAYS AGO.
I KNOW. I KNOW I DID. I KNOW I ORDERED YOU TO. BUT YOU REALLY SHOULDN'T HAVE.
DIDN'T YOU SEE HOW WONDERFUL SHE IS?
DIDN'T YOU SEE HER GRACE?

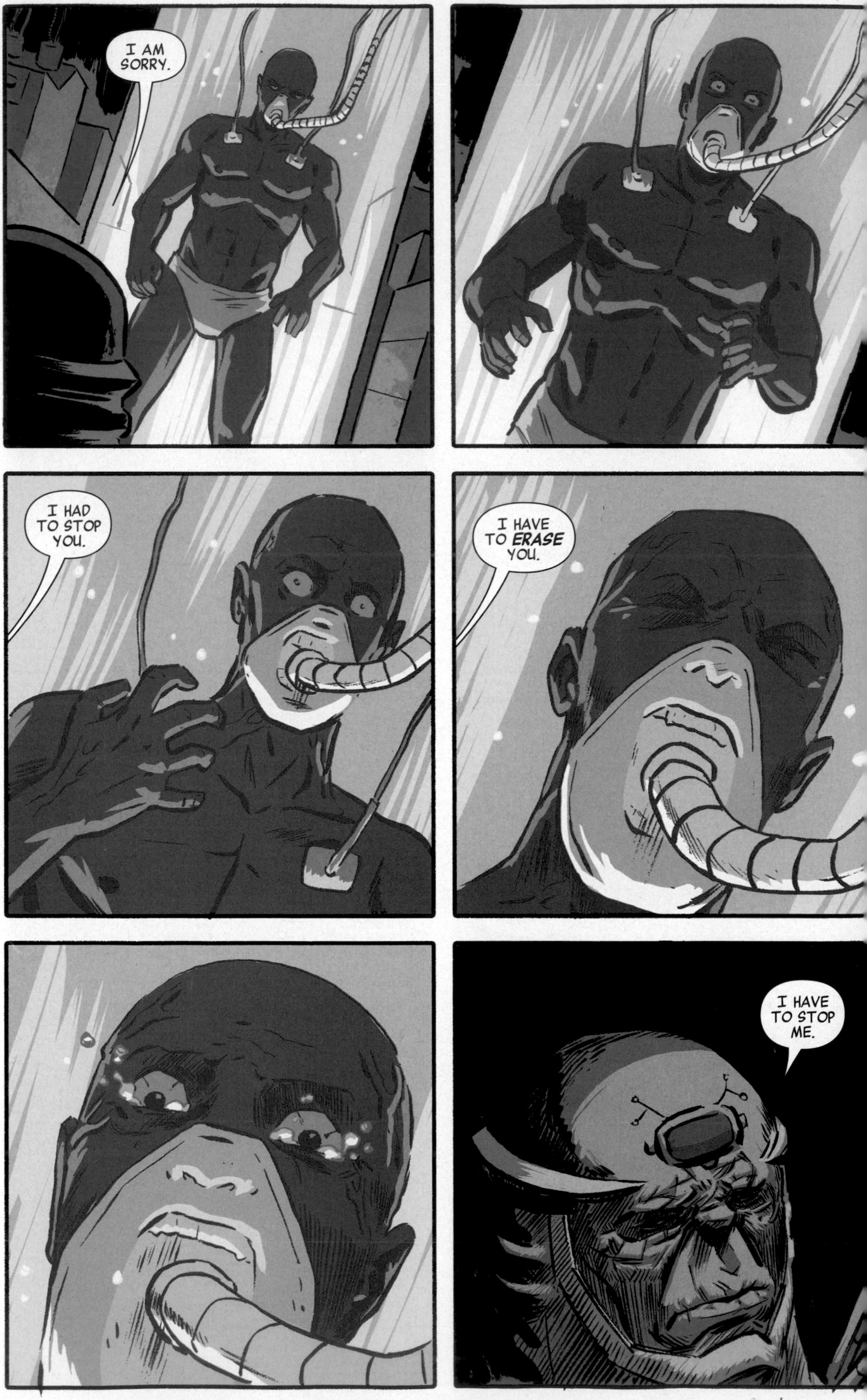
I AM SORRY.
I HAD TO STOP YOU.
I HAVE TO **ERASE** YOU.
I HAVE TO STOP ME.

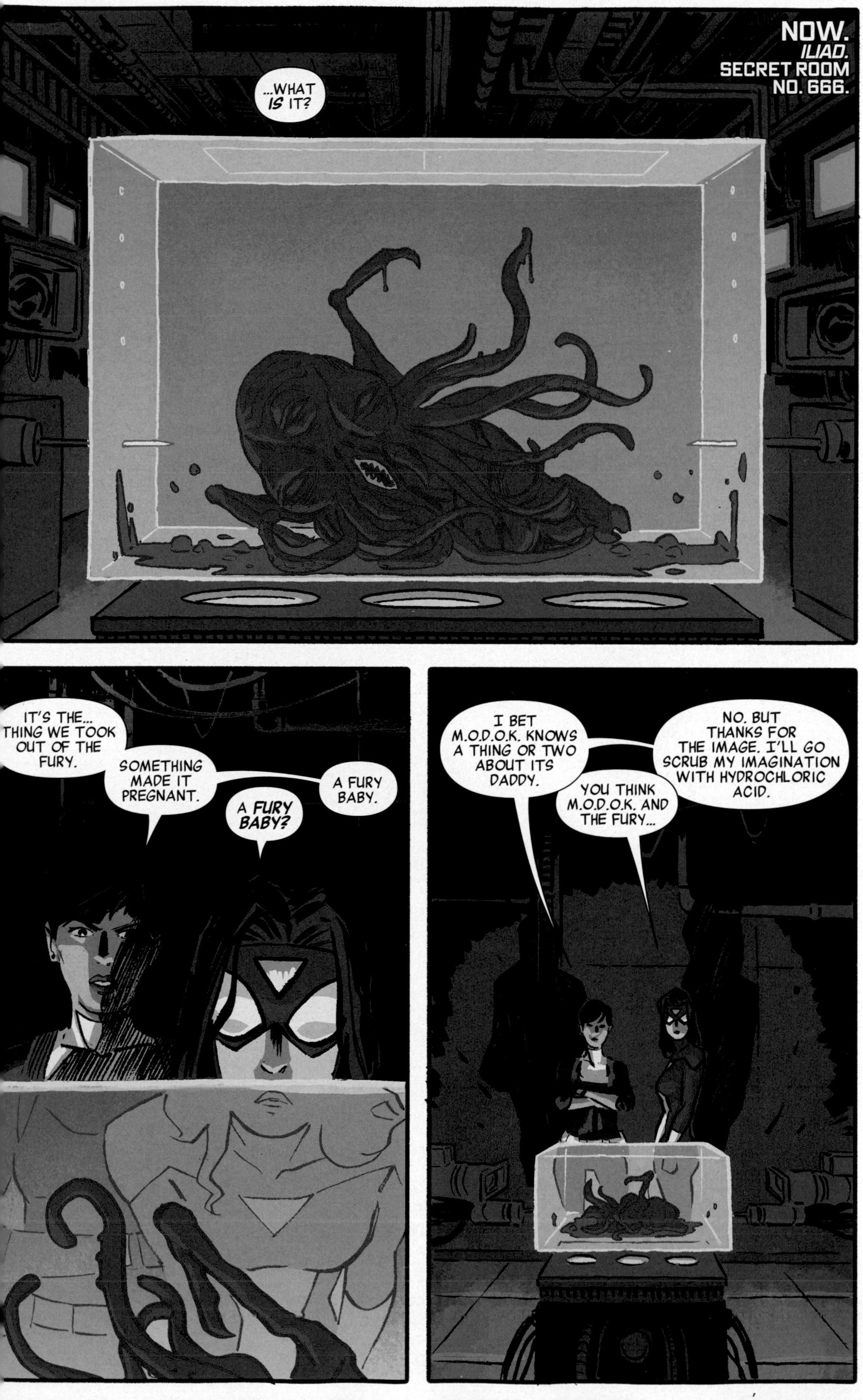
NOW.
ILIAD.
SECRET ROOM
NO. 666.
...WHAT IS IT?
IT'S THE... THING WE TOOK OUT OF THE FURY.
SOMETHING MADE IT PREGNANT.
A FURY BABY?
A FURY BABY.
I BET M.O.D.O.K. KNOWS A THING OR TWO ABOUT ITS DADDY.
YOU THINK M.O.D.O.K. AND THE FURY...
NO. BUT THANKS FOR THE IMAGE. I'LL GO SCRUB MY IMAGINATION WITH HYDROCHLORIC ACID.

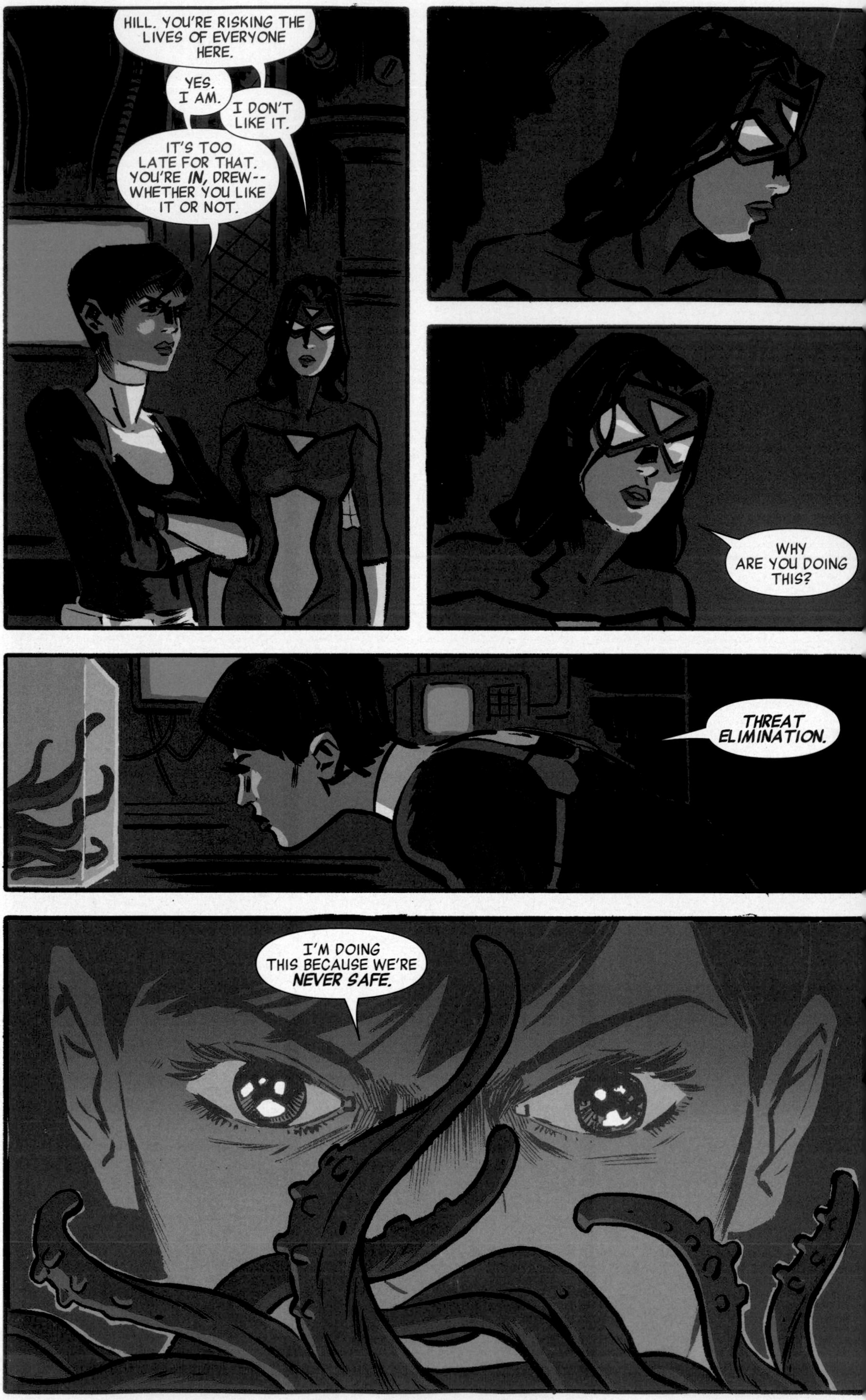
HILL. YOU'RE RISKING THE LIVES OF EVERYONE HERE.
YES. I AM.
I DON'T LIKE IT.
IT'S TOO LATE FOR THAT. YOU'RE *IN,* DREW-- WHETHER YOU LIKE IT OR NOT.
WHY ARE YOU DOING THIS?
THREAT ELIMINATION.
I'M DOING THIS BECAUSE WE'RE *NEVER SAFE.*

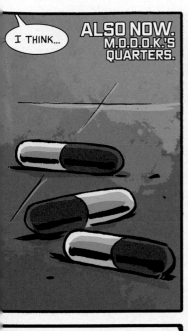

I THINK...

ALSO NOW. M.O.D.O.K.'S QUARTERS.

...I THINK I AM SABOTAGING MY OWN PLAN. I THOUGHT DOING THIS WOULD BE A **GOOD** THING...

...I THOUGHT I--I COULD BE GOOD AT THIS, SO GOOD, **BETTER** THAN SHE IS, BUT **SHE'S SO**...

...**SOMETHING** CAME BACK WITH **IT**, DIDN'T IT? **SOMETHING** CAME BACK WITH IT FROM **TLÖN**.

THAT'S WHAT S.P.E.A.R. IS HIDING. THE WALLED CITY WAS **A BREEDING GROUND.** IT'S WHAT **I** WOULD DO. IT'S WHAT YOUR CONTACT **"FORGOT"** TO TELL US.

IMAGINE HOW MANY TELEPATHS THEY NEED TO RUN SUCH A PERFECT SIMULATION OF A--

SIR. I BELIEVE YOU NEED SLEEP. YOUR MEDICATION WON'T HELP HERE.

I THINK YOU'RE **RIGHT.** I THINK YOU'RE RIGHT, SNAPPER.

I THINK I JUST HAVE TO FINALLY ADMIT IT...

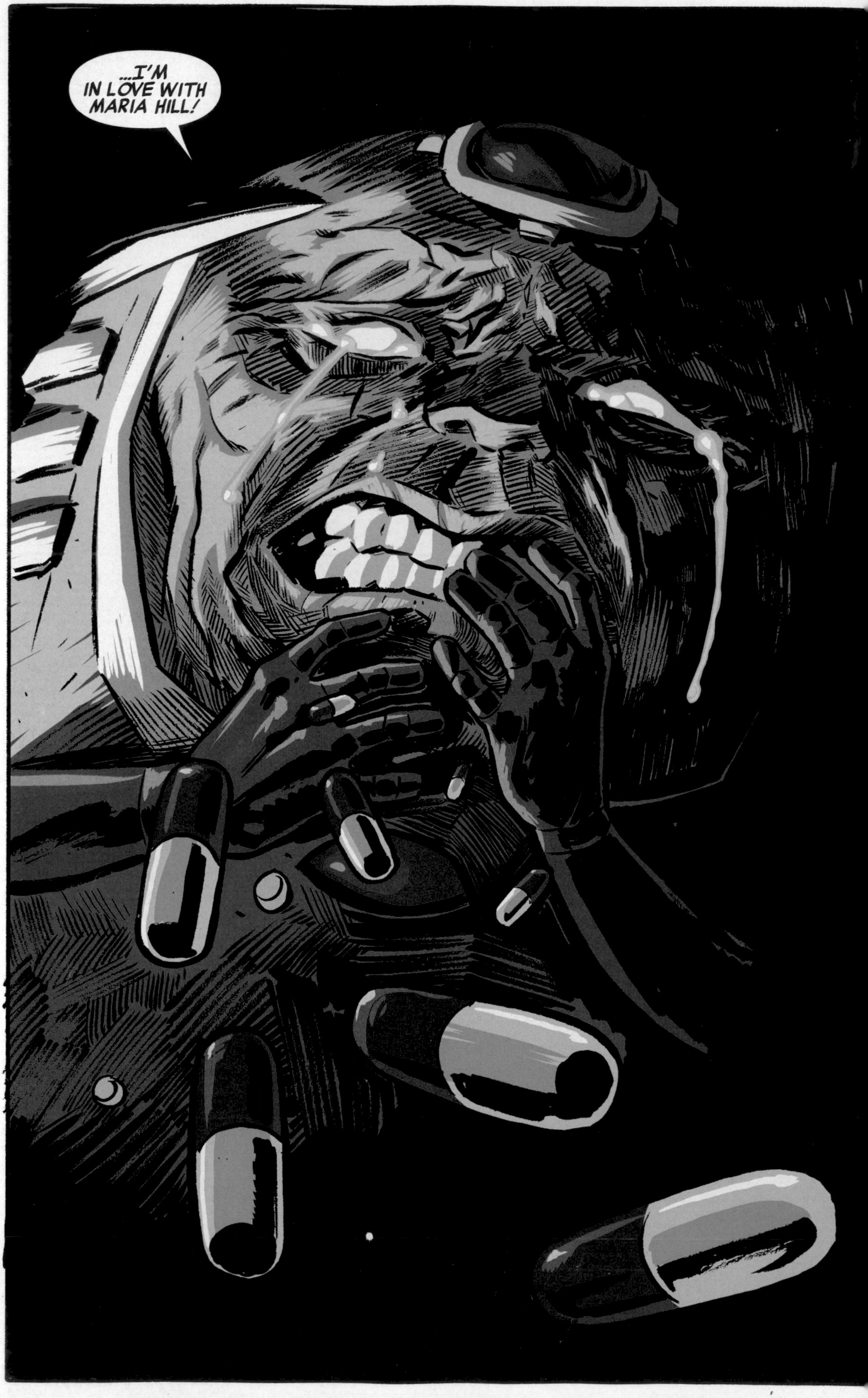
...I'M IN LOVE WITH MARIA HILL!

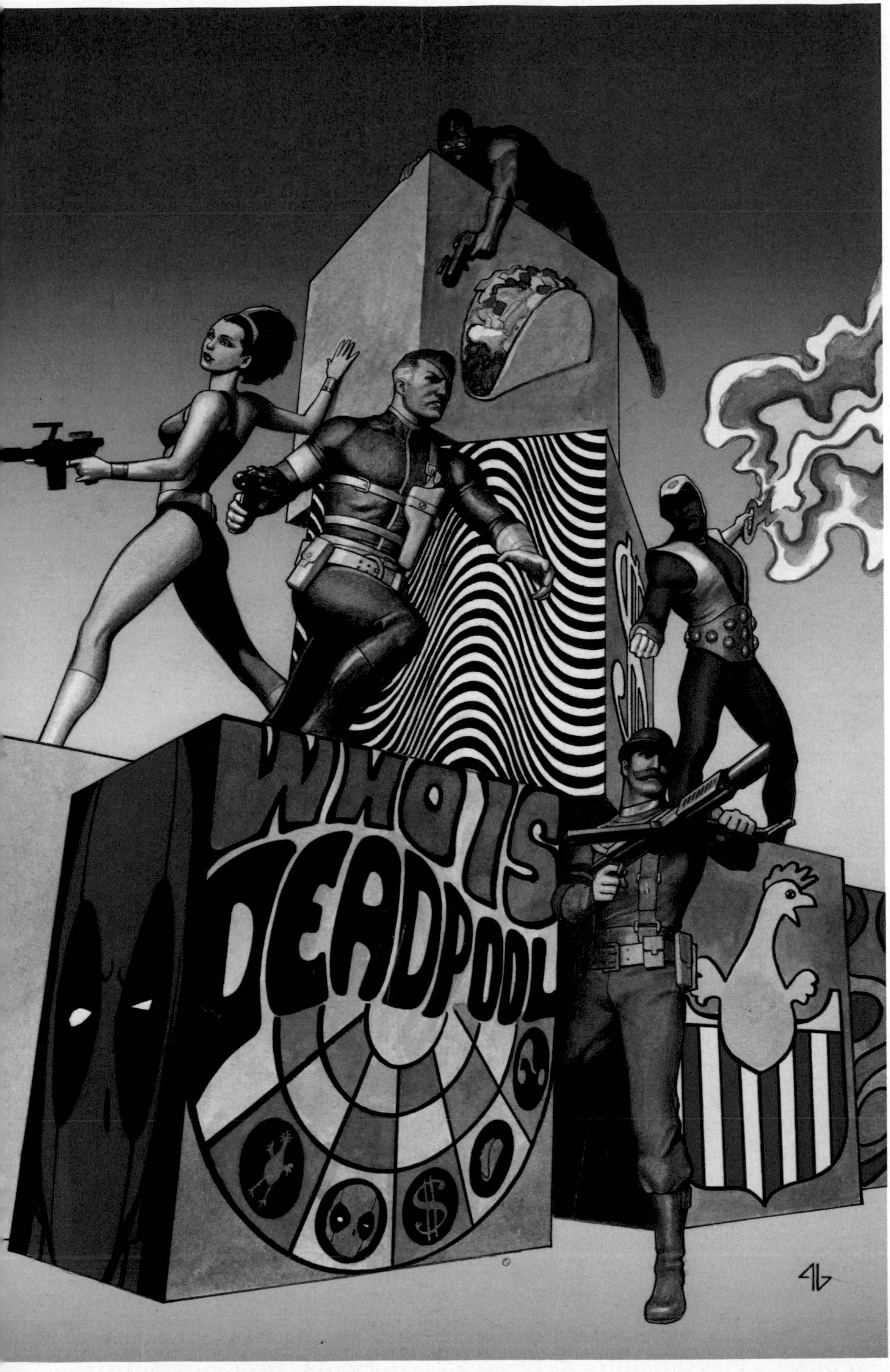
WHO IS DEADPOOL

#9 DEADPOOL 75TH ANNIVERSARY VARIANT BY ADI GRANOV

9

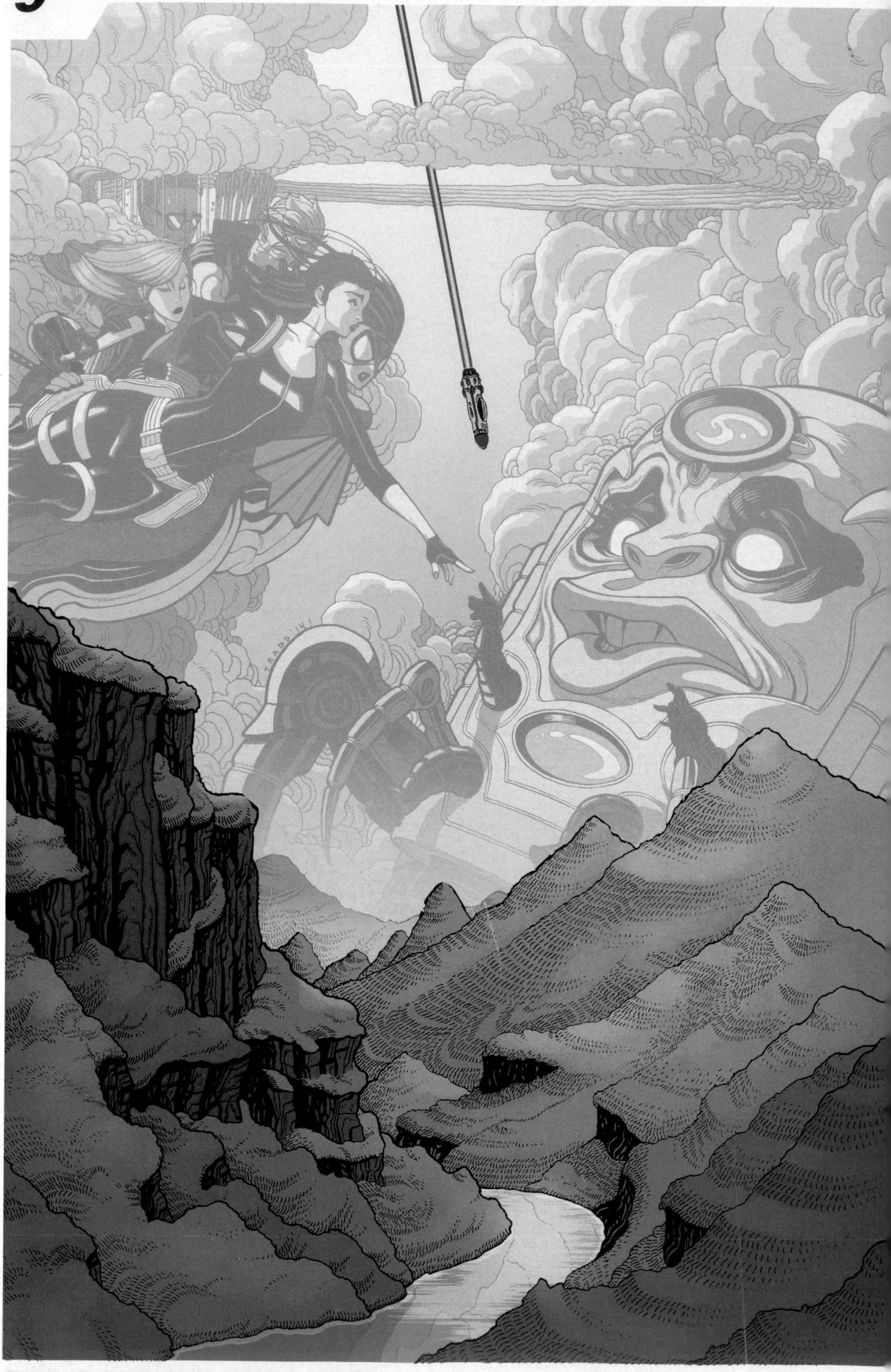

THIS IS THE WAY, STEP INSIDE

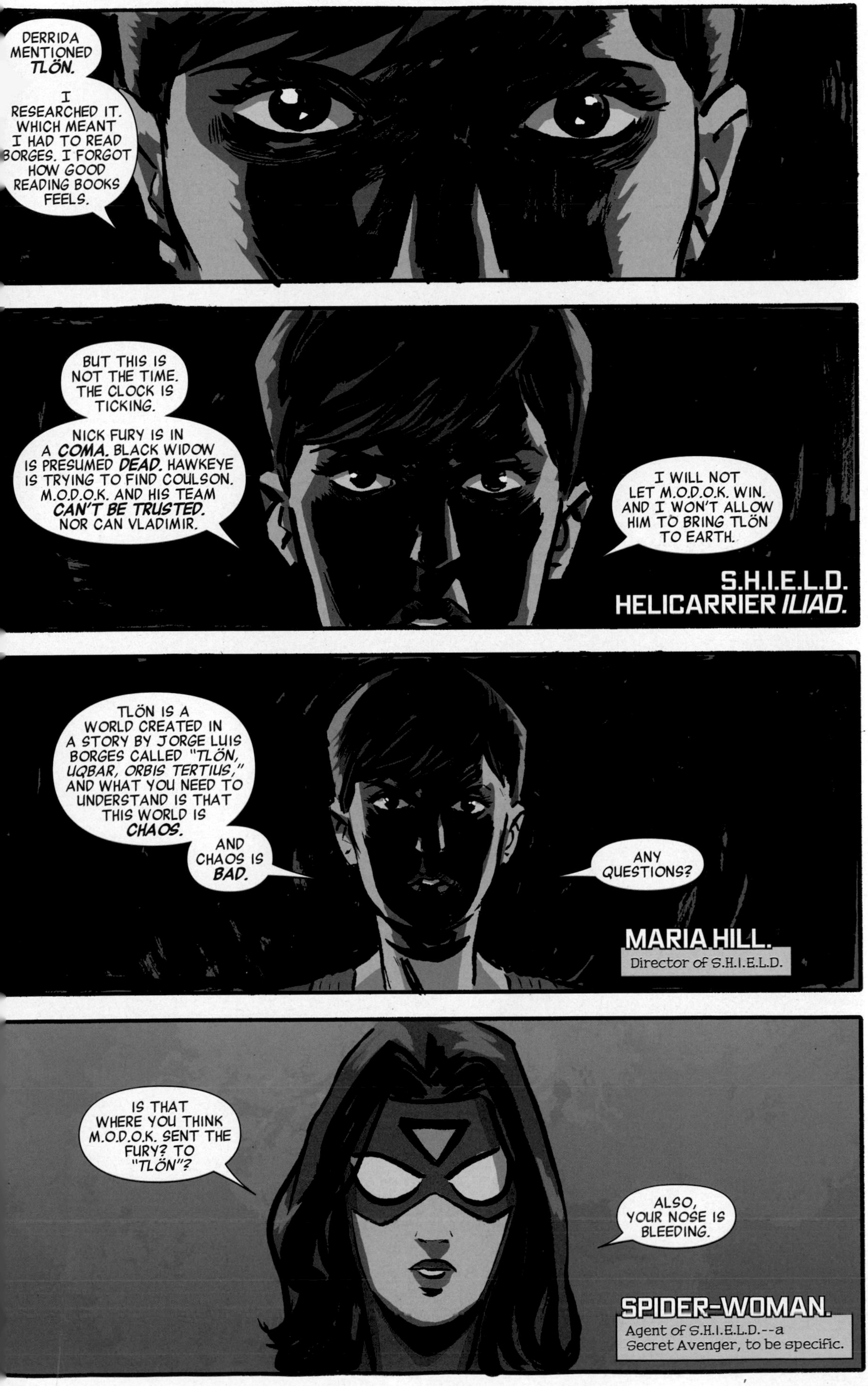
DERRIDA MENTIONED TLÖN.
I RESEARCHED IT. WHICH MEANT I HAD TO READ BORGES. I FORGOT HOW GOOD READING BOOKS FEELS.
BUT THIS IS NOT THE TIME. THE CLOCK IS TICKING.
NICK FURY IS IN A COMA. BLACK WIDOW IS PRESUMED DEAD. HAWKEYE IS TRYING TO FIND COULSON. M.O.D.O.K. AND HIS TEAM CAN'T BE TRUSTED. NOR CAN VLADIMIR.
I WILL NOT LET M.O.D.O.K. WIN. AND I WON'T ALLOW HIM TO BRING TLÖN TO EARTH.
S.H.I.E.L.D. HELICARRIER ILIAD.
TLÖN IS A WORLD CREATED IN A STORY BY JORGE LUIS BORGES CALLED "TLÖN, UQBAR, ORBIS TERTIUS," AND WHAT YOU NEED TO UNDERSTAND IS THAT THIS WORLD IS CHAOS.
AND CHAOS IS BAD.
ANY QUESTIONS?
MARIA HILL.
Director of S.H.I.E.L.D.
IS THAT WHERE YOU THINK M.O.D.O.K. SENT THE FURY? TO "TLÖN"?
ALSO, YOUR NOSE IS BLEEDING.
SPIDER-WOMAN.
Agent of S.H.I.E.L.D.--a Secret Avenger, to be specific.

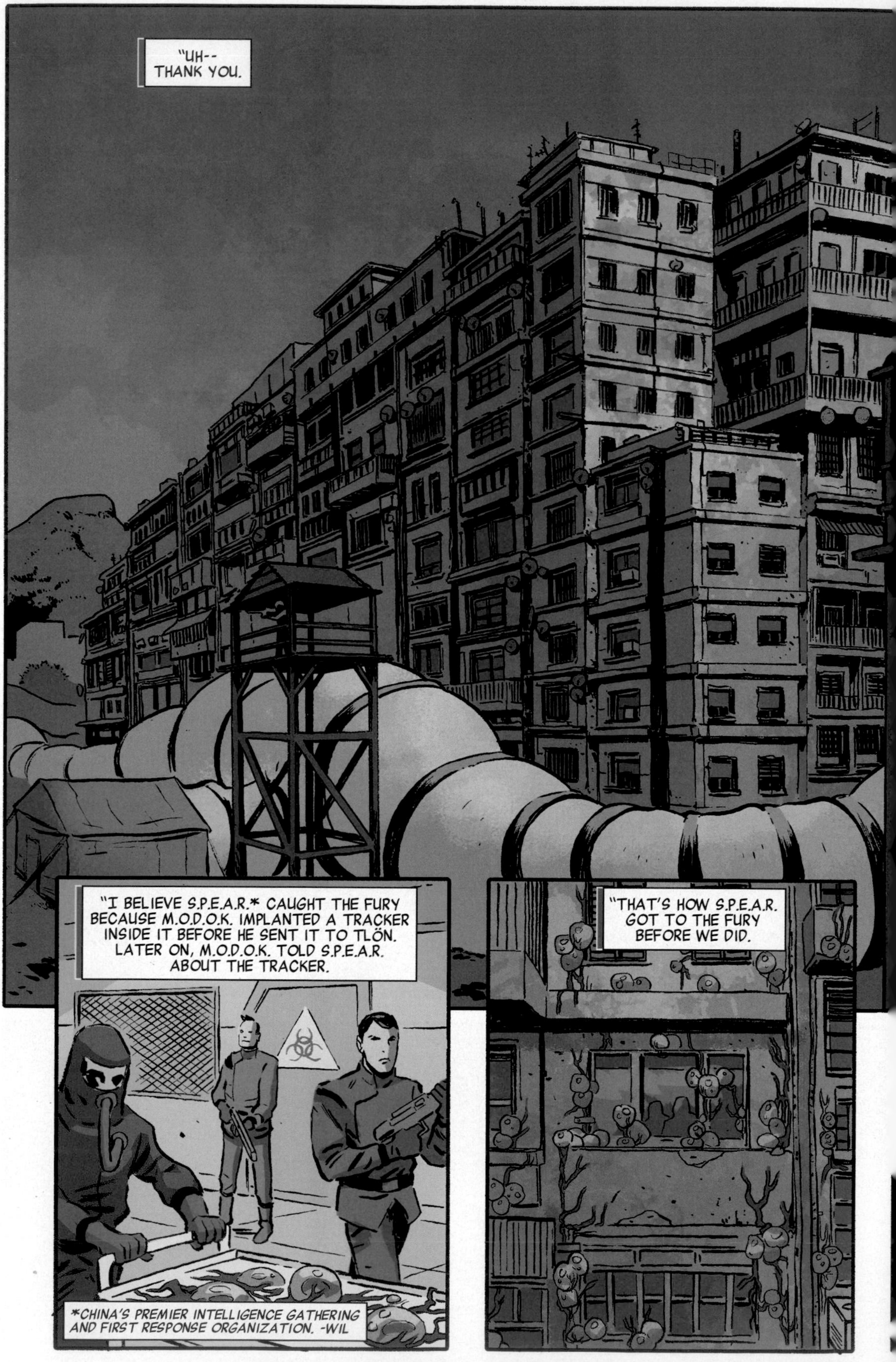
"UH--
THANK YOU.
"I BELIEVE S.P.E.A.R.* CAUGHT THE FURY BECAUSE M.O.D.O.K. IMPLANTED A TRACKER INSIDE IT BEFORE HE SENT IT TO TLÖN. LATER ON, M.O.D.O.K. TOLD S.P.E.A.R. ABOUT THE TRACKER.
*CHINA'S PREMIER INTELLIGENCE GATHERING AND FIRST RESPONSE ORGANIZATION. -WIL
"THAT'S HOW S.P.E.A.R. GOT TO THE FURY BEFORE WE DID.

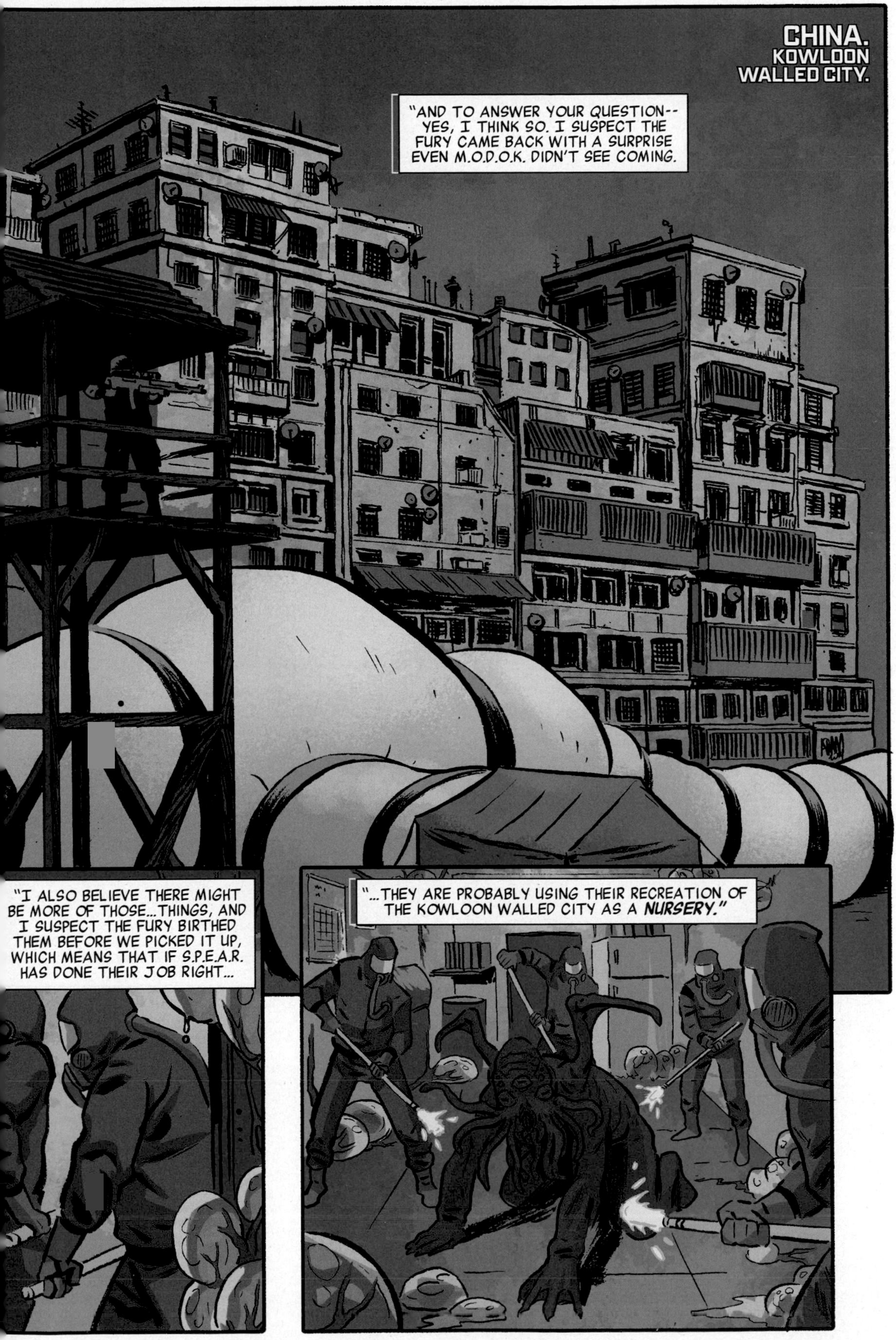
CHINA. KOWLOON WALLED CITY.
"AND TO ANSWER YOUR QUESTION-- YES, I THINK SO. I SUSPECT THE FURY CAME BACK WITH A SURPRISE EVEN M.O.D.O.K. DIDN'T SEE COMING.
"I ALSO BELIEVE THERE MIGHT BE MORE OF THOSE...THINGS, AND I SUSPECT THE FURY BIRTHED THEM BEFORE WE PICKED IT UP, WHICH MEANS THAT IF S.P.E.A.R. HAS DONE THEIR JOB RIGHT...
"...THEY ARE PROBABLY USING THEIR RECREATION OF THE KOWLOON WALLED CITY AS A NURSERY."

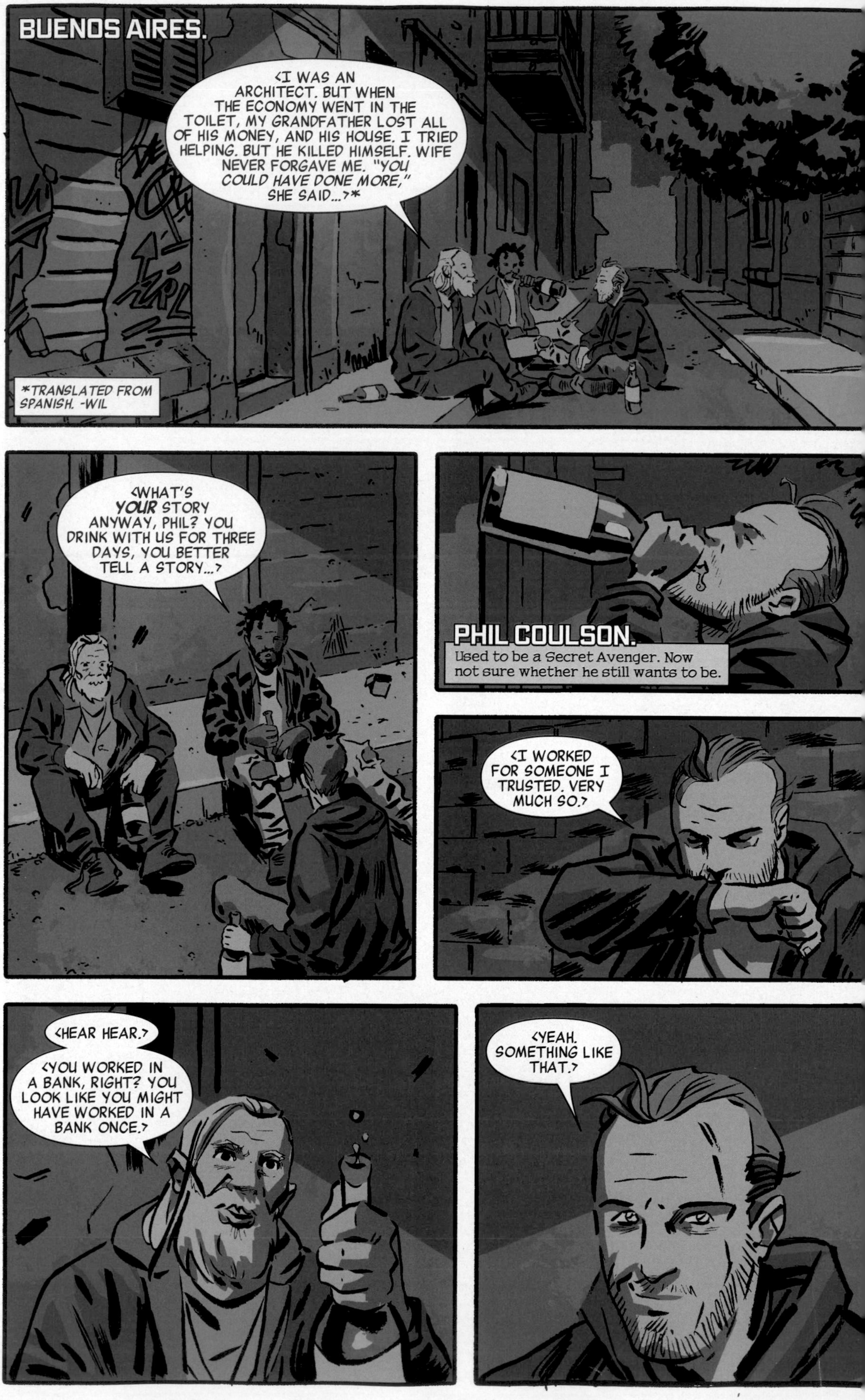
BUENOS AIRES.
<I WAS AN ARCHITECT. BUT WHEN THE ECONOMY WENT IN THE TOILET, MY GRANDFATHER LOST ALL OF HIS MONEY, AND HIS HOUSE. I TRIED HELPING. BUT HE KILLED HIMSELF. WIFE NEVER FORGAVE ME. "YOU COULD HAVE DONE MORE," SHE SAID...>*
*TRANSLATED FROM SPANISH. -WIL
<WHAT'S YOUR STORY ANYWAY, PHIL? YOU DRINK WITH US FOR THREE DAYS, YOU BETTER TELL A STORY...>
PHIL COULSON.
Used to be a Secret Avenger. Now not sure whether he still wants to be.
<I WORKED FOR SOMEONE I TRUSTED. VERY MUCH SO.>
<HEAR HEAR.>
<YOU WORKED IN A BANK, RIGHT? YOU LOOK LIKE YOU MIGHT HAVE WORKED IN A BANK ONCE.>
<YEAH. SOMETHING LIKE THAT.>

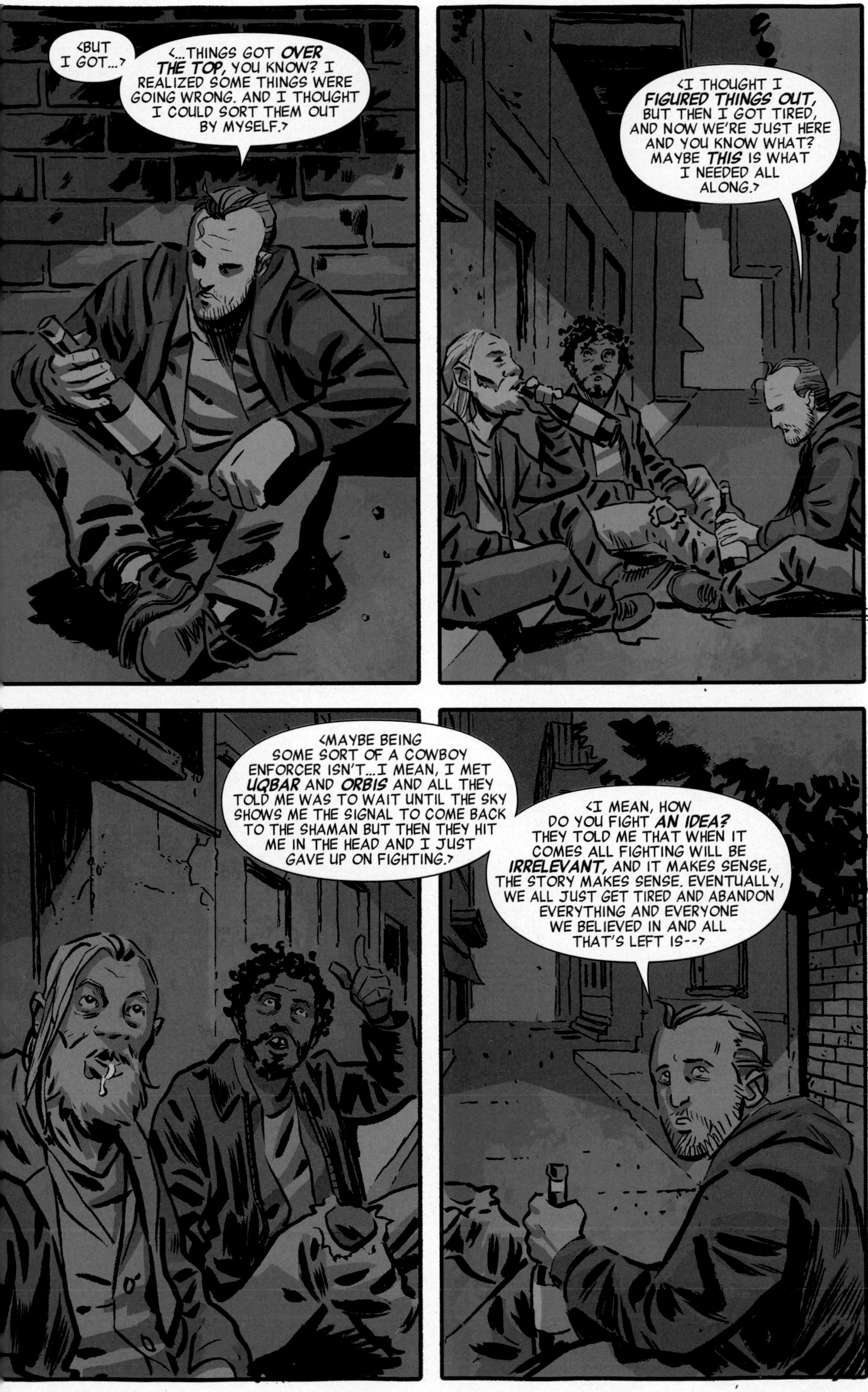
<BUT I GOT...>
<...THINGS GOT OVER THE TOP, YOU KNOW? I REALIZED SOME THINGS WERE GOING WRONG. AND I THOUGHT I COULD SORT THEM OUT BY MYSELF.>
<I THOUGHT I FIGURED THINGS OUT, BUT THEN I GOT TIRED, AND NOW WE'RE JUST HERE AND YOU KNOW WHAT? MAYBE THIS IS WHAT I NEEDED ALL ALONG.>
<MAYBE BEING SOME SORT OF A COWBOY ENFORCER ISN'T...I MEAN, I MET UQBAR AND ORBIS AND ALL THEY TOLD ME WAS TO WAIT UNTIL THE SKY SHOWS ME THE SIGNAL TO COME BACK TO THE SHAMAN BUT THEN THEY HIT ME IN THE HEAD AND I JUST GAVE UP ON FIGHTING.>
<I MEAN, HOW DO YOU FIGHT AN IDEA? THEY TOLD ME THAT WHEN IT COMES ALL FIGHTING WILL BE IRRELEVANT, AND IT MAKES SENSE, THE STORY MAKES SENSE. EVENTUALLY, WE ALL JUST GET TIRED AND ABANDON EVERYTHING AND EVERYONE WE BELIEVED IN AND ALL THAT'S LEFT IS-->

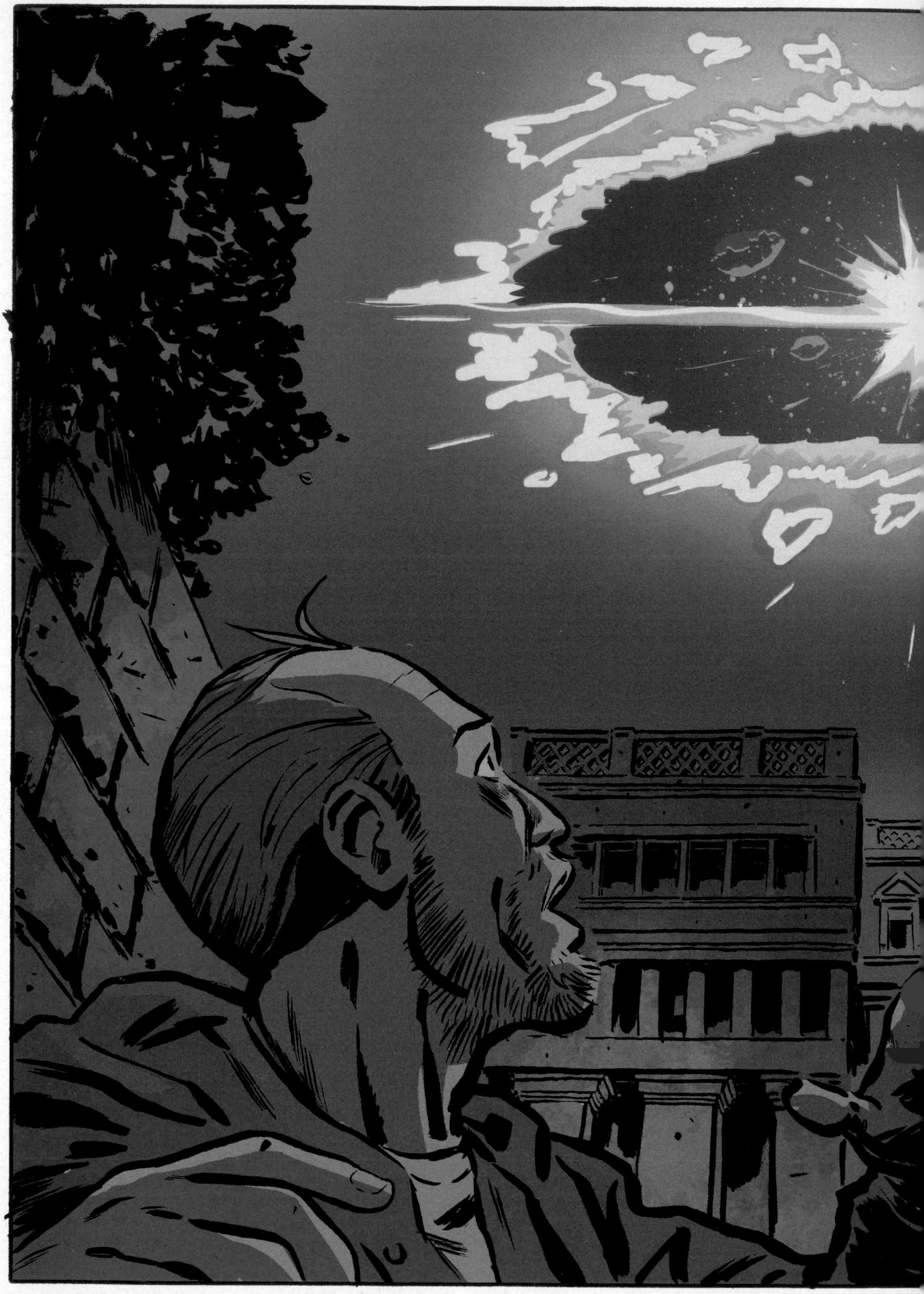

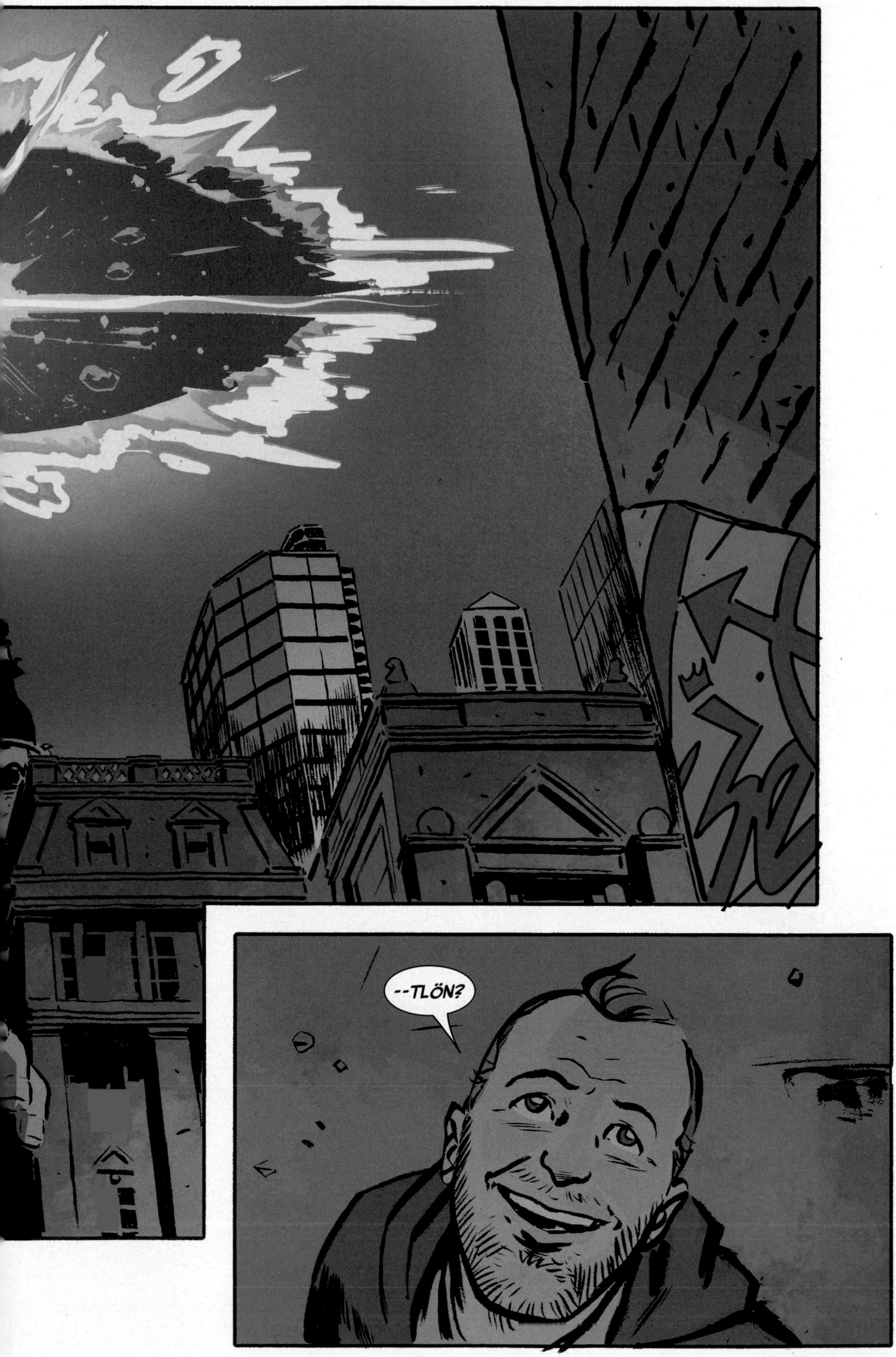
--TLÖN?

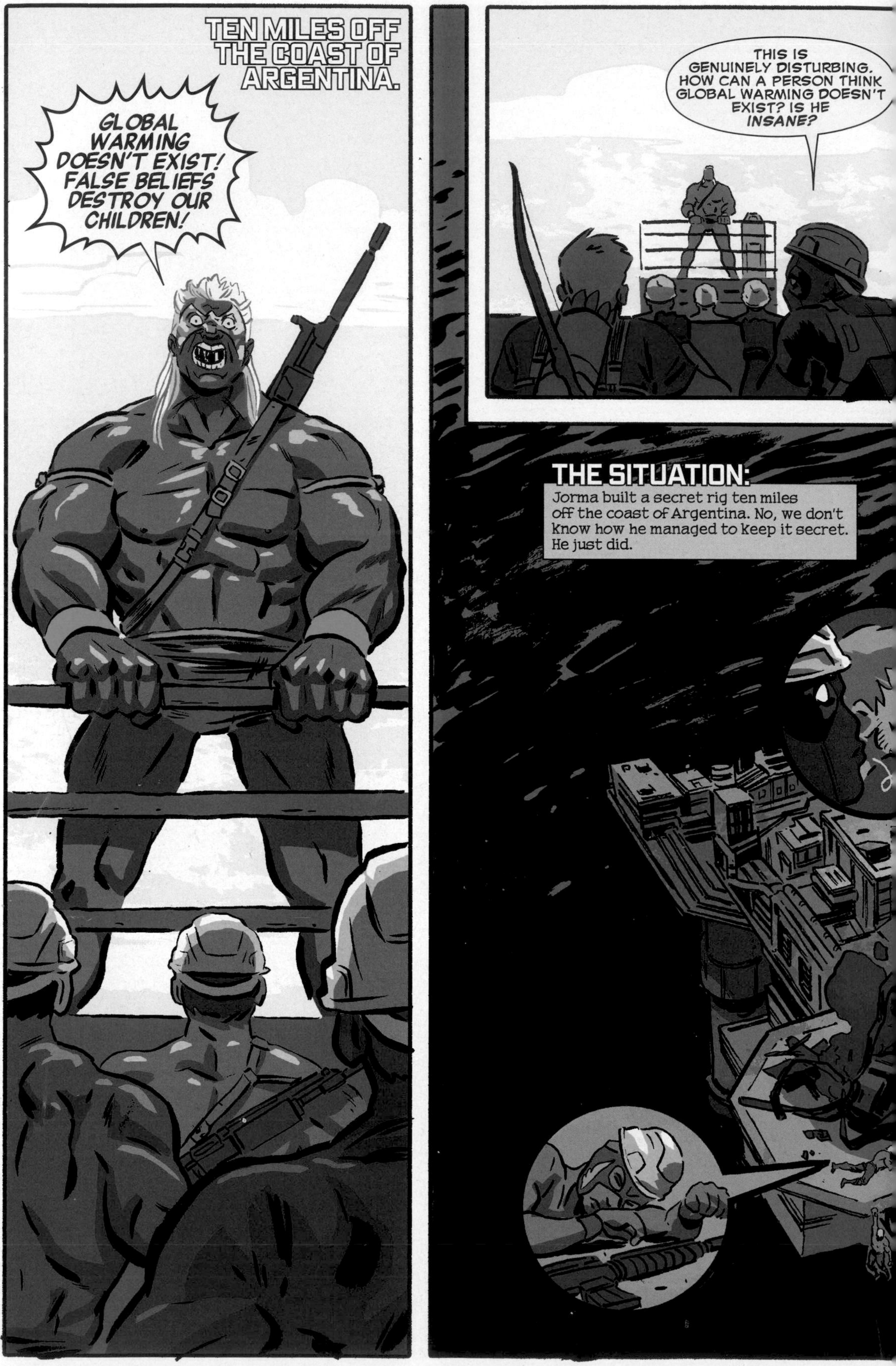
TEN MILES OFF THE COAST OF ARGENTINA.
GLOBAL WARMING DOESN'T EXIST! FALSE BELIEFS DESTROY OUR CHILDREN!
THIS IS GENUINELY DISTURBING. HOW CAN A PERSON THINK GLOBAL WARMING DOESN'T EXIST? IS HE *INSANE?*
THE SITUATION:
Jorma built a secret rig ten miles off the coast of Argentina. No, we don't know how he managed to keep it secret. He just did.

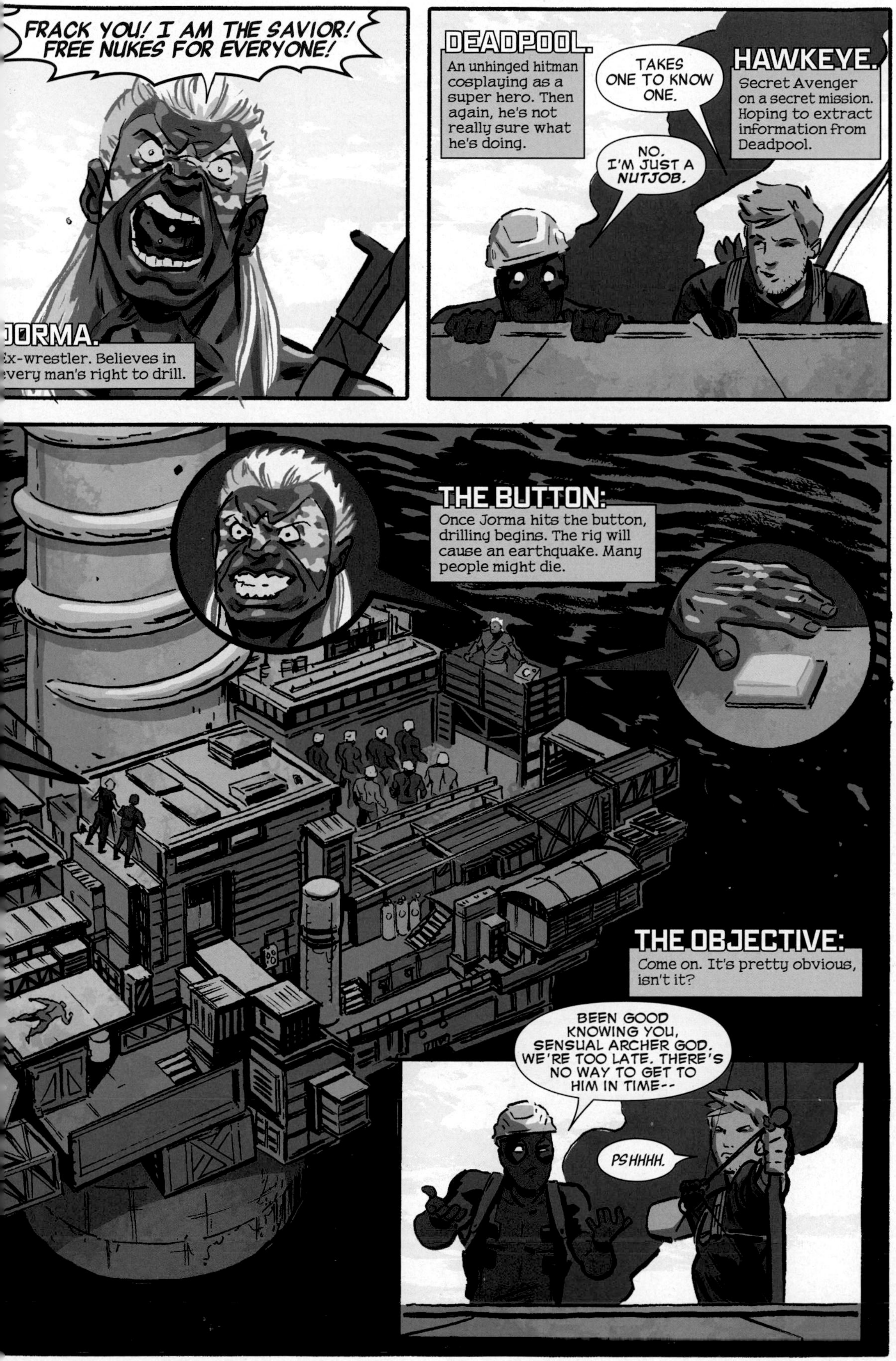
FRACK YOU! I AM THE SAVIOR! FREE NUKES FOR EVERYONE!
JORMA.
Ex-wrestler. Believes in every man's right to drill.
DEADPOOL.
An unhinged hitman cosplaying as a super hero. Then again, he's not really sure what he's doing.
TAKES ONE TO KNOW ONE.
HAWKEYE.
Secret Avenger on a secret mission. Hoping to extract information from Deadpool.
NO. I'M JUST A NUTJOB.
THE BUTTON:
Once Jorma hits the button, drilling begins. The rig will cause an earthquake. Many people might die.
THE OBJECTIVE:
Come on. It's pretty obvious, isn't it?
BEEN GOOD KNOWING YOU, SENSUAL ARCHER GOD. WE'RE TOO LATE. THERE'S NO WAY TO GET TO HIM IN TIME--
PSHHHH.

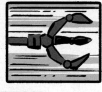

MAGIC. TRAINING.

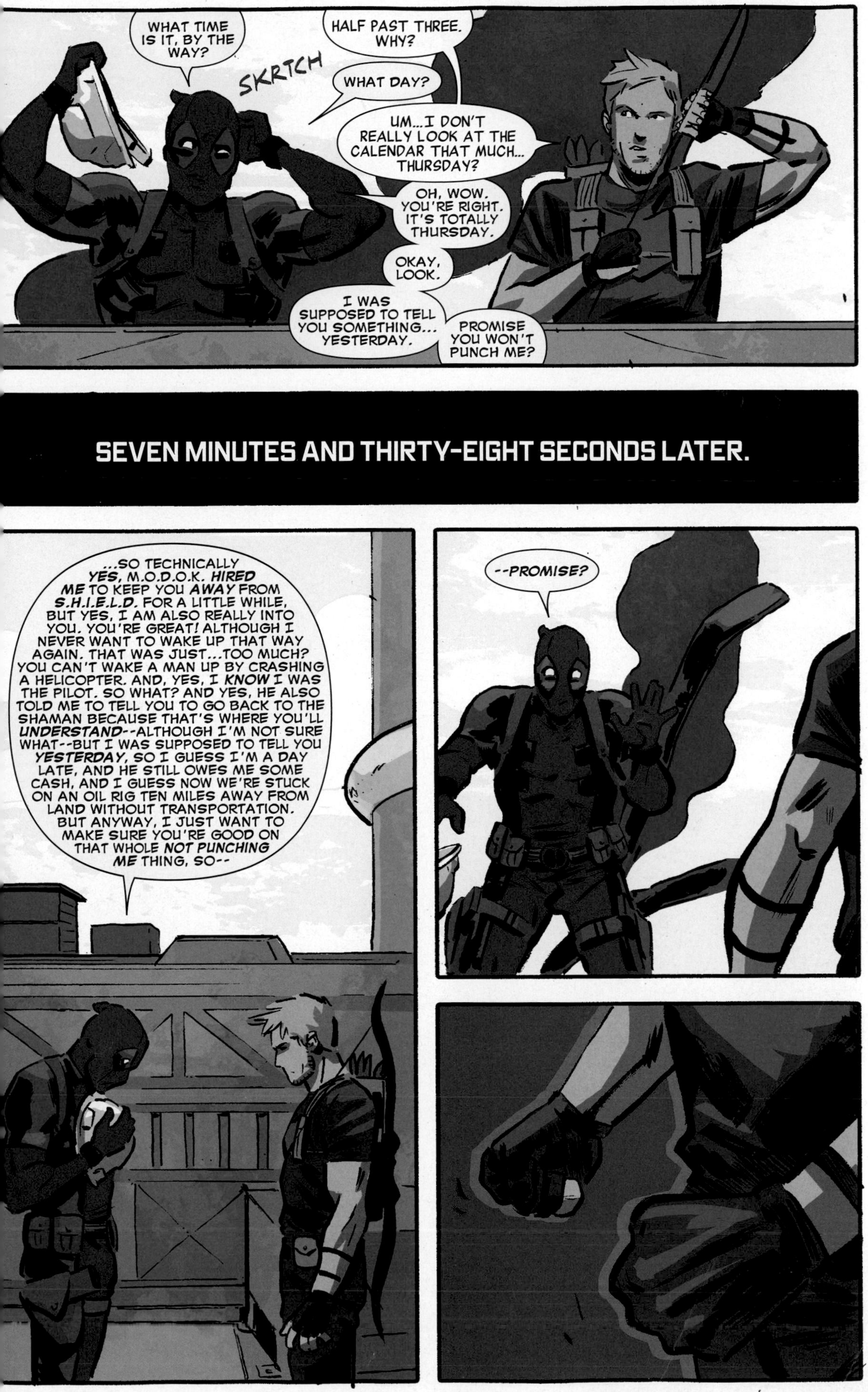
WHAT TIME IS IT, BY THE WAY?
SKRTCH
HALF PAST THREE. WHY?
WHAT DAY?
UM...I DON'T REALLY LOOK AT THE CALENDAR THAT MUCH... THURSDAY?
OH, WOW. YOU'RE RIGHT. IT'S TOTALLY THURSDAY.
OKAY, LOOK.
I WAS SUPPOSED TO TELL YOU SOMETHING... YESTERDAY.
PROMISE YOU WON'T PUNCH ME?
SEVEN MINUTES AND THIRTY-EIGHT SECONDS LATER.
...SO TECHNICALLY YES, M.O.D.O.K. HIRED ME TO KEEP YOU AWAY FROM S.H.I.E.L.D. FOR A LITTLE WHILE, BUT YES, I AM ALSO REALLY INTO YOU. YOU'RE GREAT! ALTHOUGH I NEVER WANT TO WAKE UP THAT WAY AGAIN. THAT WAS JUST...TOO MUCH? YOU CAN'T WAKE A MAN UP BY CRASHING A HELICOPTER. AND, YES, I KNOW I WAS THE PILOT. SO WHAT? AND YES, HE ALSO TOLD ME TO TELL YOU TO GO BACK TO THE SHAMAN BECAUSE THAT'S WHERE YOU'LL UNDERSTAND--ALTHOUGH I'M NOT SURE WHAT--BUT I WAS SUPPOSED TO TELL YOU YESTERDAY, SO I GUESS I'M A DAY LATE, AND HE STILL OWES ME SOME CASH, AND I GUESS NOW WE'RE STUCK ON AN OIL RIG TEN MILES AWAY FROM LAND WITHOUT TRANSPORTATION. BUT ANYWAY, I JUST WANT TO MAKE SURE YOU'RE GOOD ON THAT WHOLE NOT PUNCHING ME THING, SO--
--PROMISE?

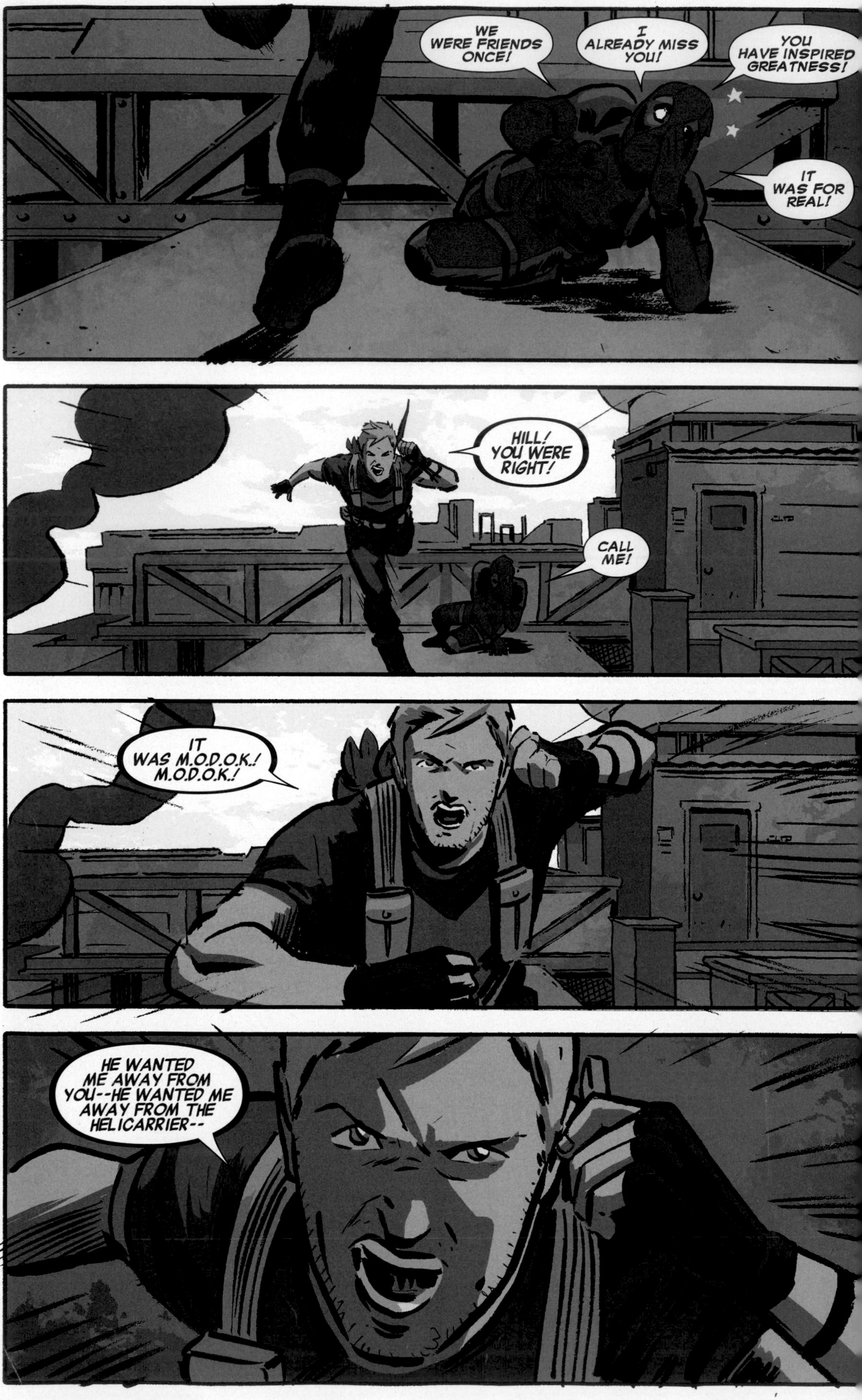

WE WERE FRIENDS ONCE!
I ALREADY MISS YOU!
YOU HAVE INSPIRED GREATNESS!
IT WAS FOR REAL!
HILL! YOU WERE RIGHT!
CALL ME!
IT WAS M.O.D.O.K.! M.O.D.O.K.!
HE WANTED ME AWAY FROM YOU--HE WANTED ME AWAY FROM THE HELICARRIER--

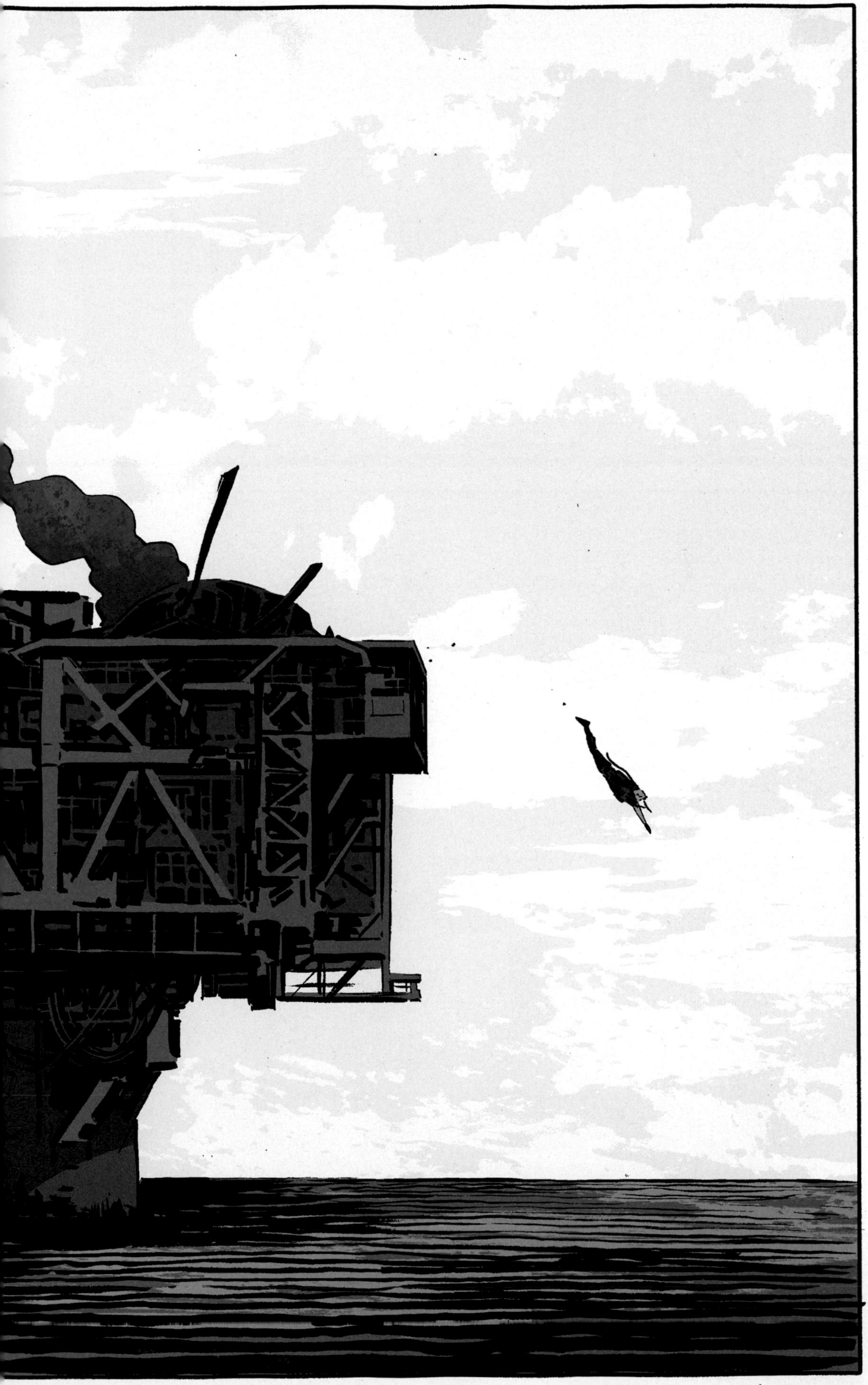

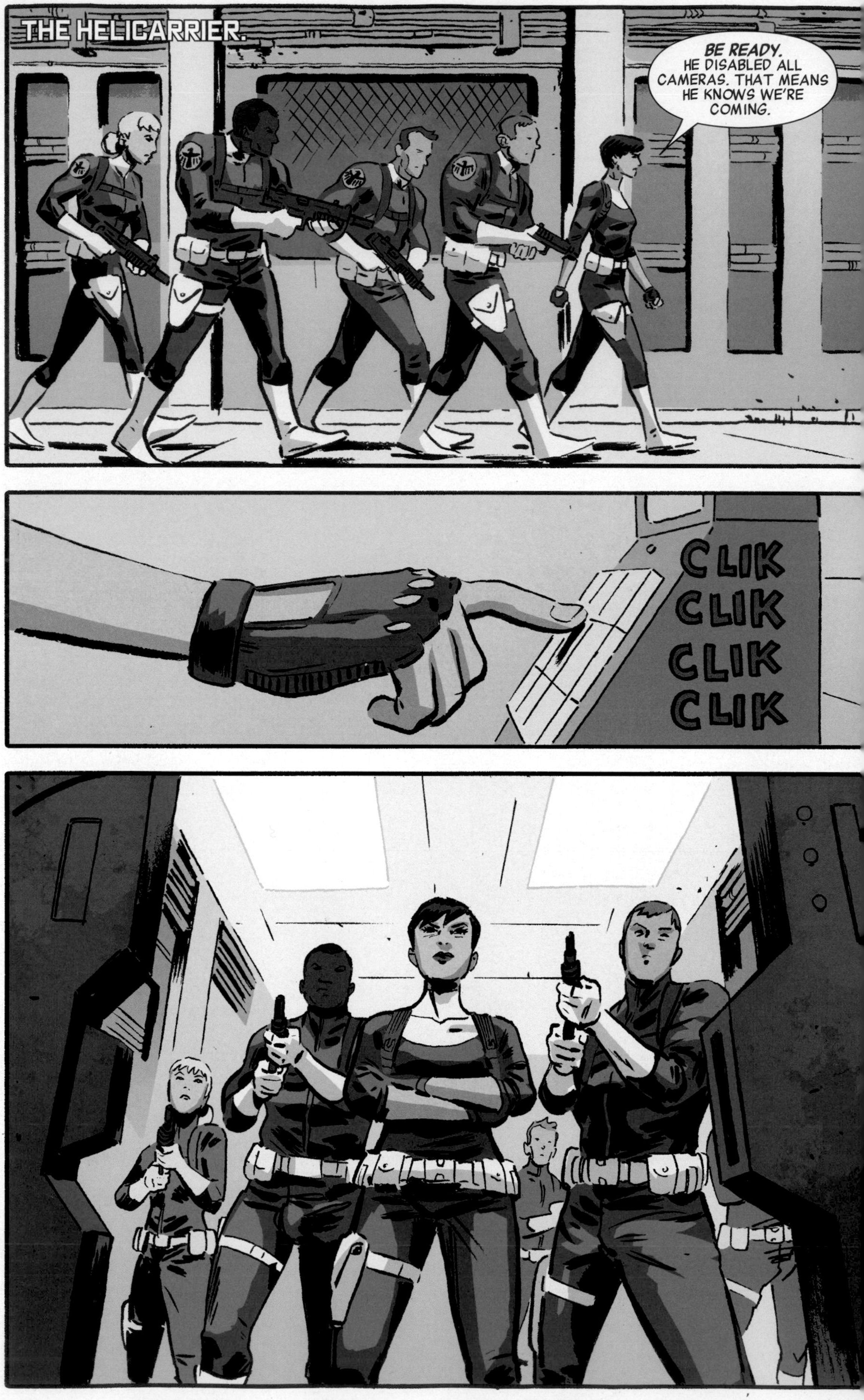
THE HELICARRIER.
BE READY. HE DISABLED ALL CAMERAS. THAT MEANS HE KNOWS WE'RE COMING.
CLIK
CLIK
CLIK
CLIK

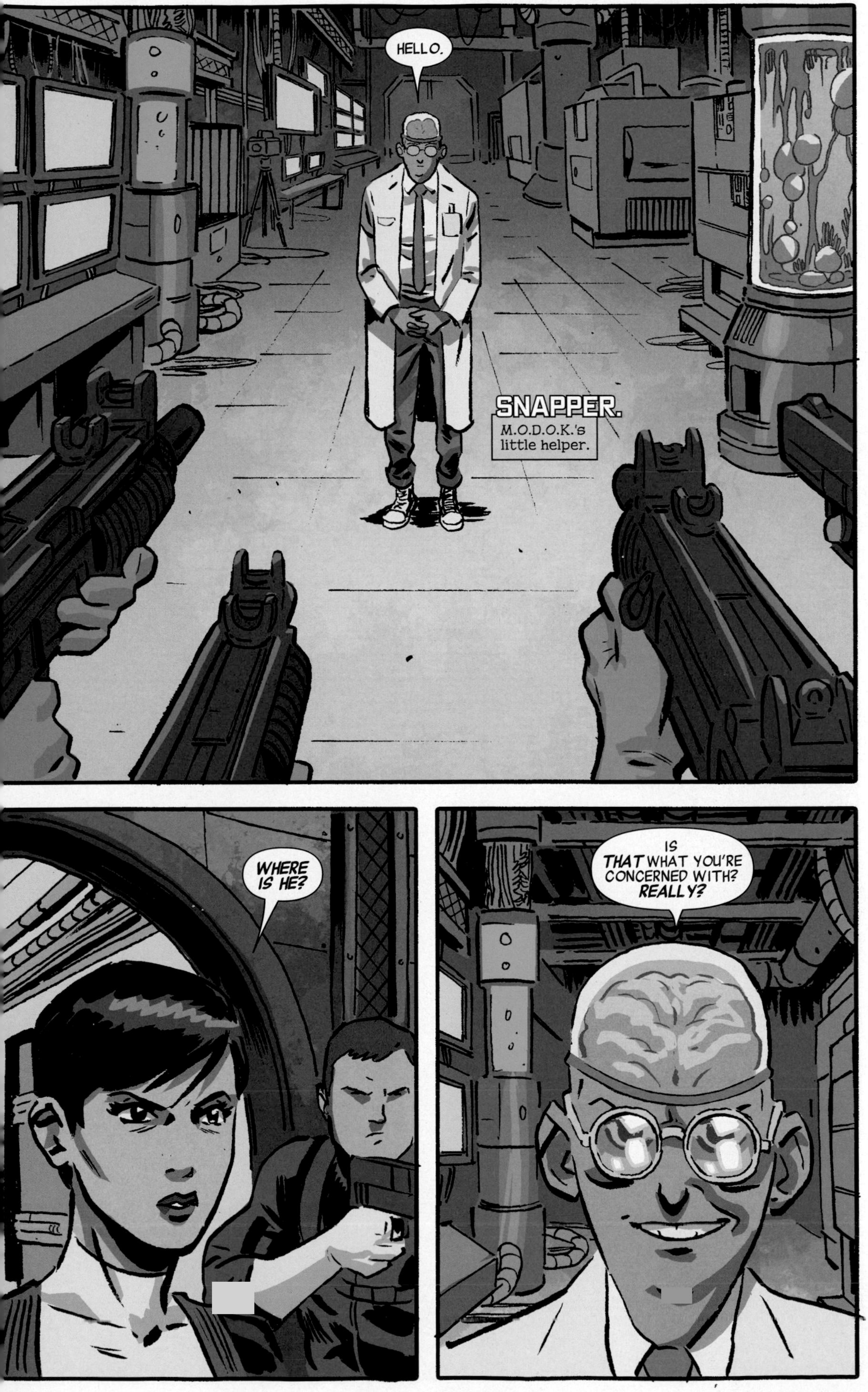
HELLO.
SNAPPER.
M.O.D.O.K.'s little helper.
WHERE IS HE?
IS *THAT* WHAT YOU'RE CONCERNED WITH? *REALLY?*

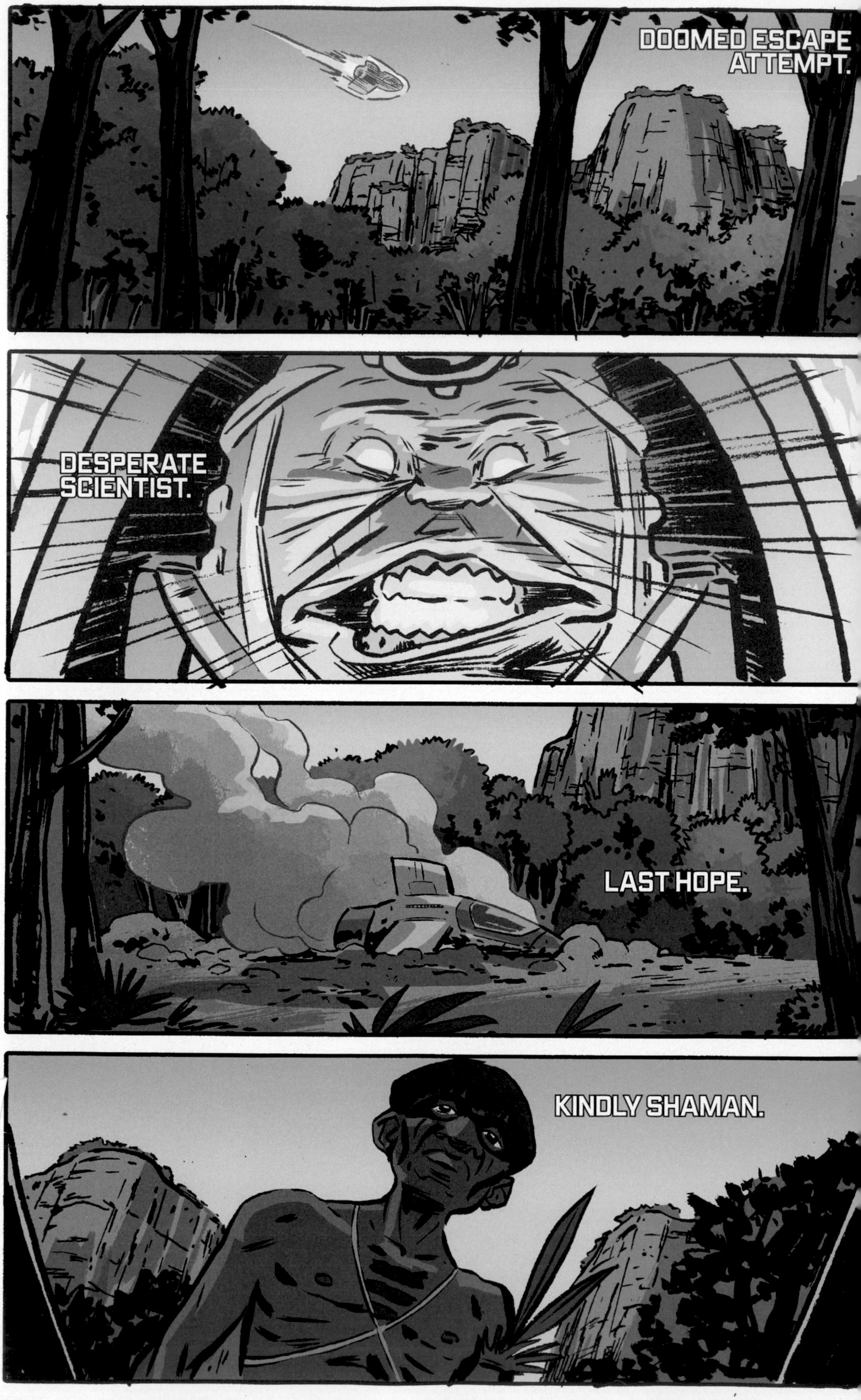
DOOMED ESCAPE ATTEMPT.
DESPERATE SCIENTIST.
LAST HOPE.
KINDLY SHAMAN.

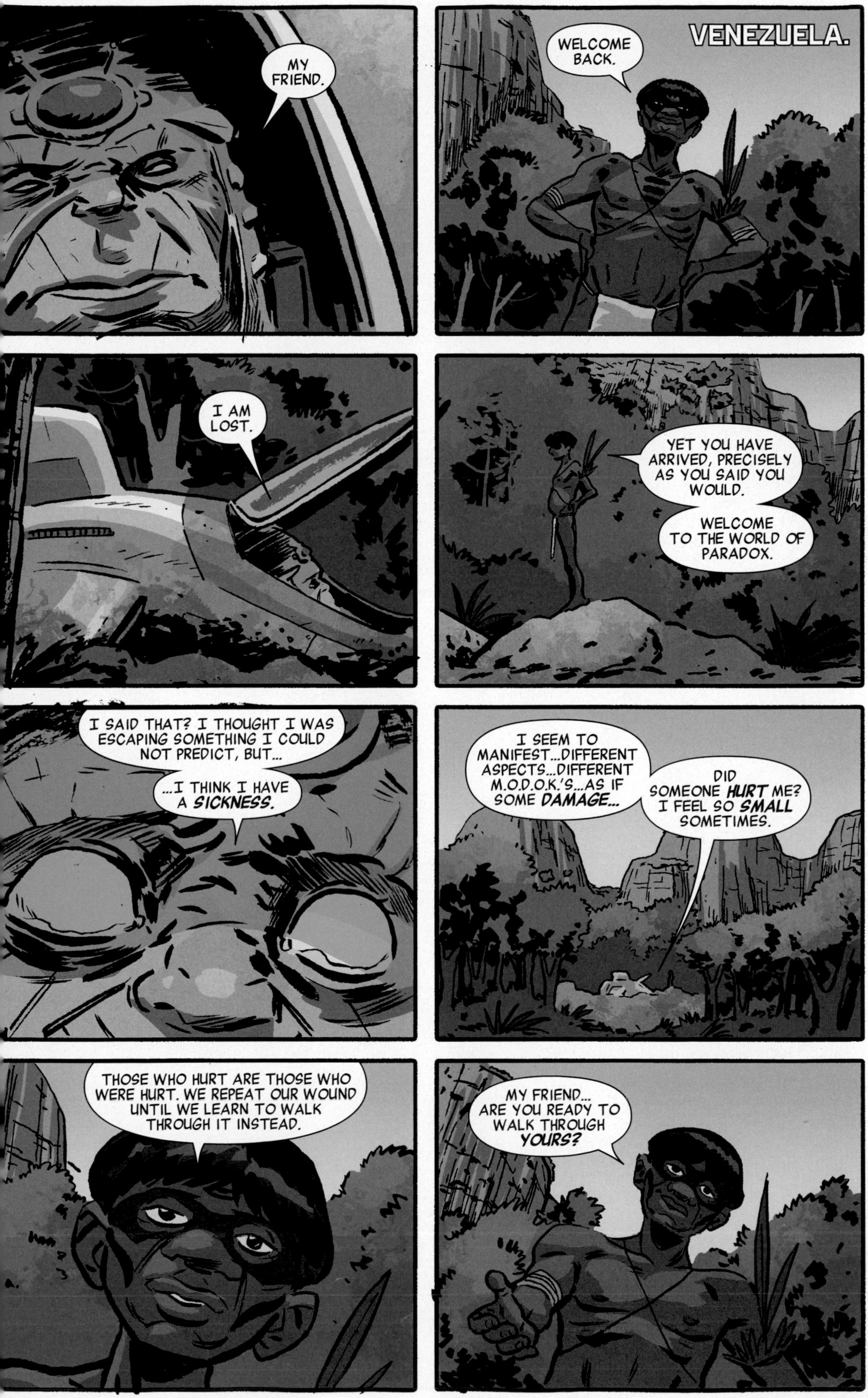
MY FRIEND.
VENEZUELA.
WELCOME BACK.
I AM LOST.
YET YOU HAVE ARRIVED, PRECISELY AS YOU SAID YOU WOULD.
WELCOME TO THE WORLD OF PARADOX.
I SAID THAT? I THOUGHT I WAS ESCAPING SOMETHING I COULD NOT PREDICT, BUT...
...I THINK I HAVE A SICKNESS.
I SEEM TO MANIFEST...DIFFERENT ASPECTS...DIFFERENT M.O.D.O.K.'S...AS IF SOME DAMAGE...
DID SOMEONE HURT ME? I FEEL SO SMALL SOMETIMES.
THOSE WHO HURT ARE THOSE WHO WERE HURT. WE REPEAT OUR WOUND UNTIL WE LEARN TO WALK THROUGH IT INSTEAD.
MY FRIEND... ARE YOU READY TO WALK THROUGH YOURS?

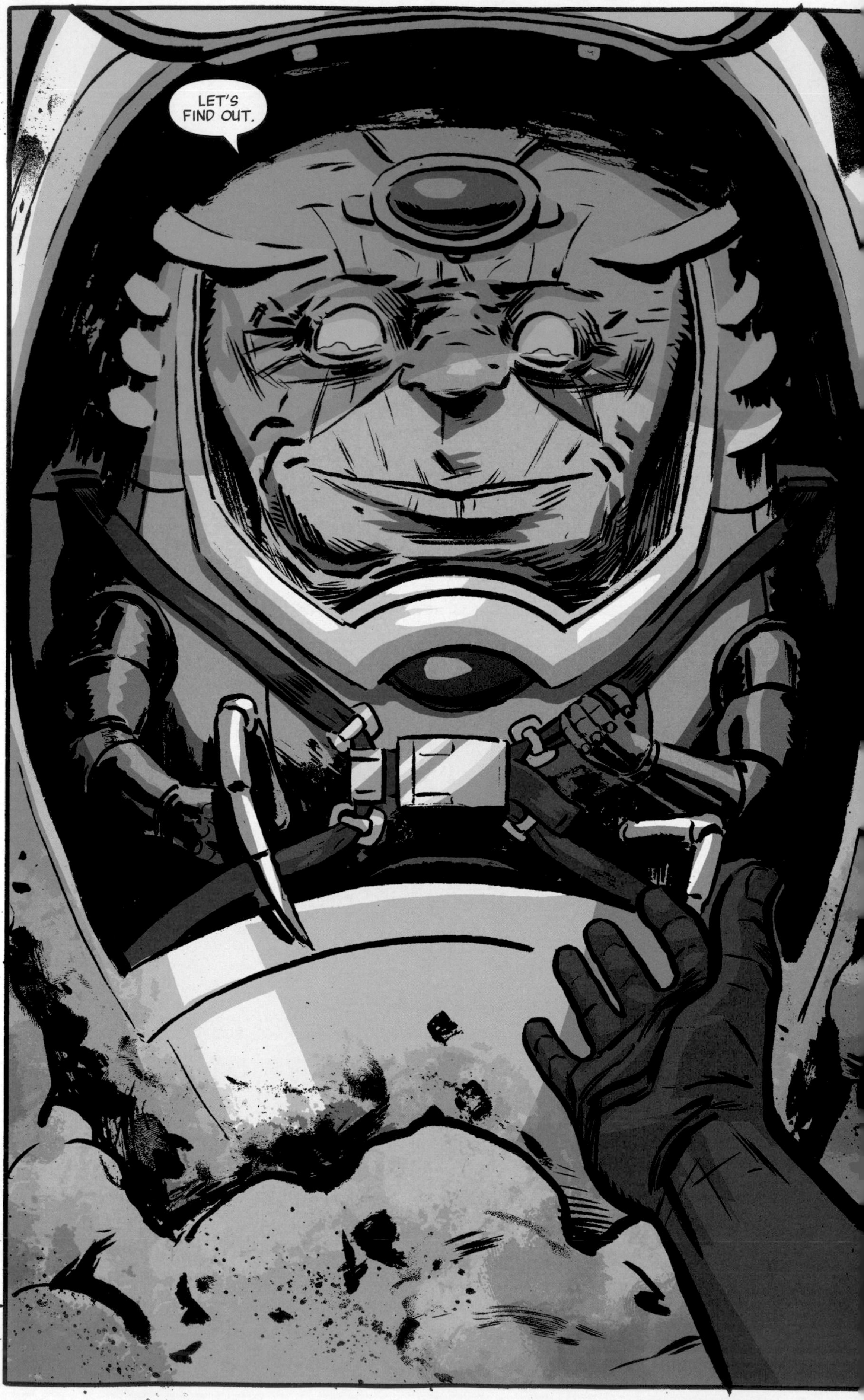
LET'S FIND OUT.

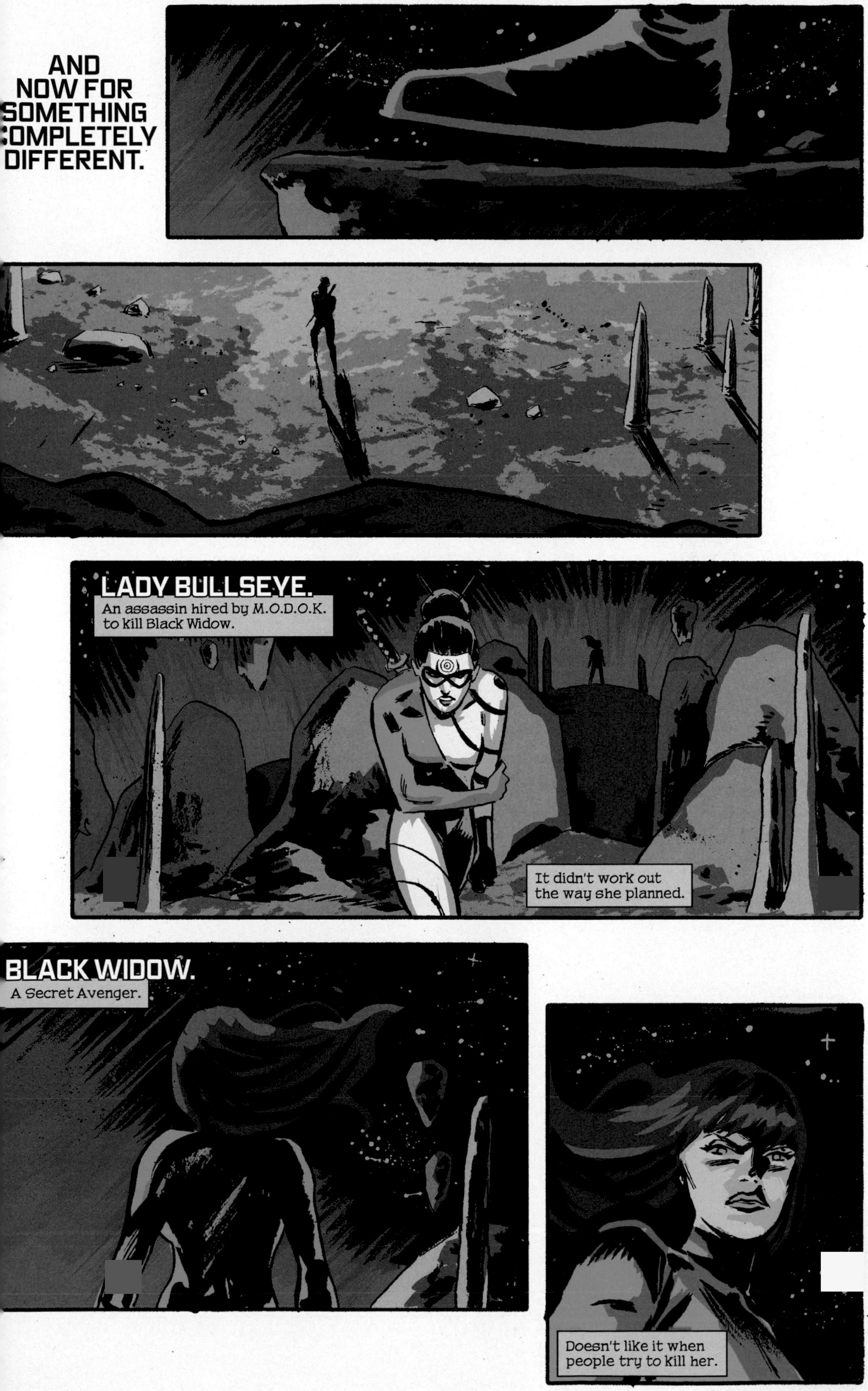
AND NOW FOR SOMETHING COMPLETELY DIFFERENT.
LADY BULLSEYE.
An assassin hired by M.O.D.O.K. to kill Black Widow.
It didn't work out the way she planned.
BLACK WIDOW.
A Secret Avenger.
Doesn't like it when people try to kill her.

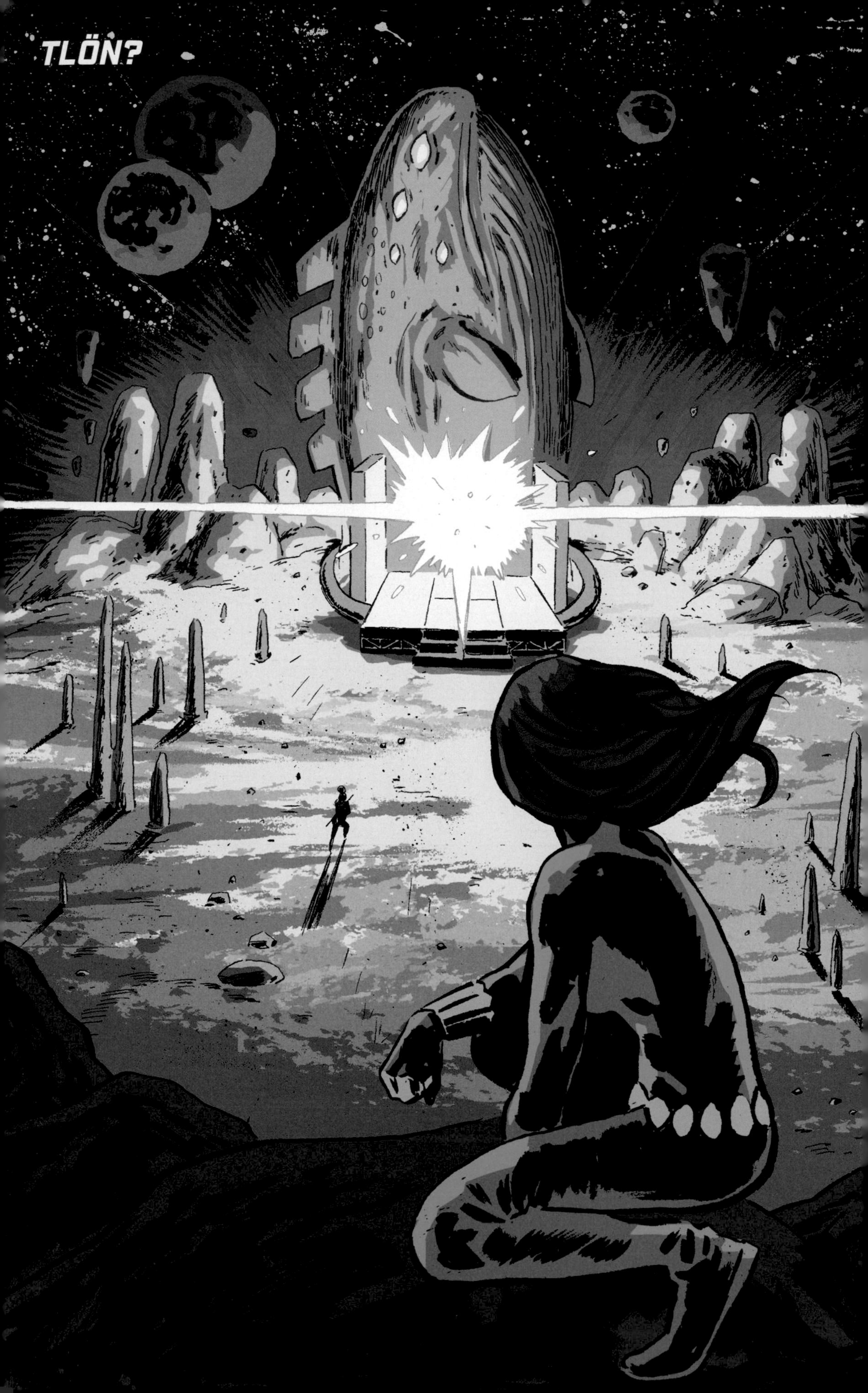
TLÖN?

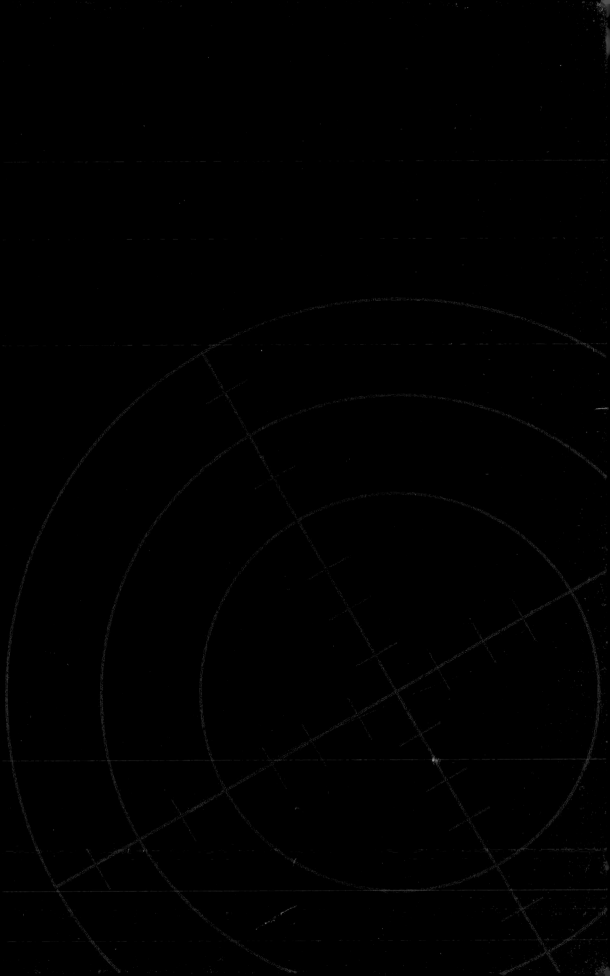

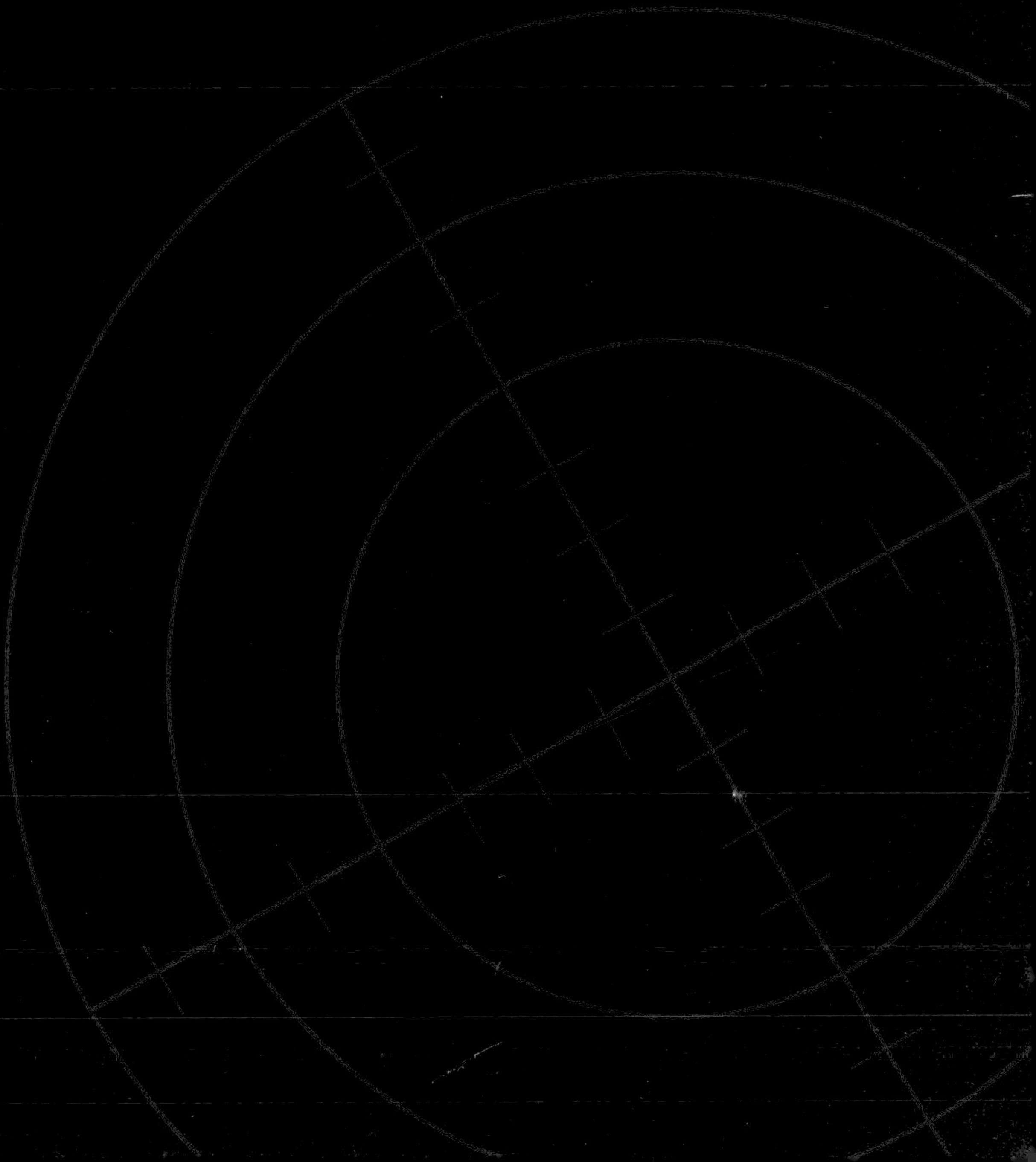

10

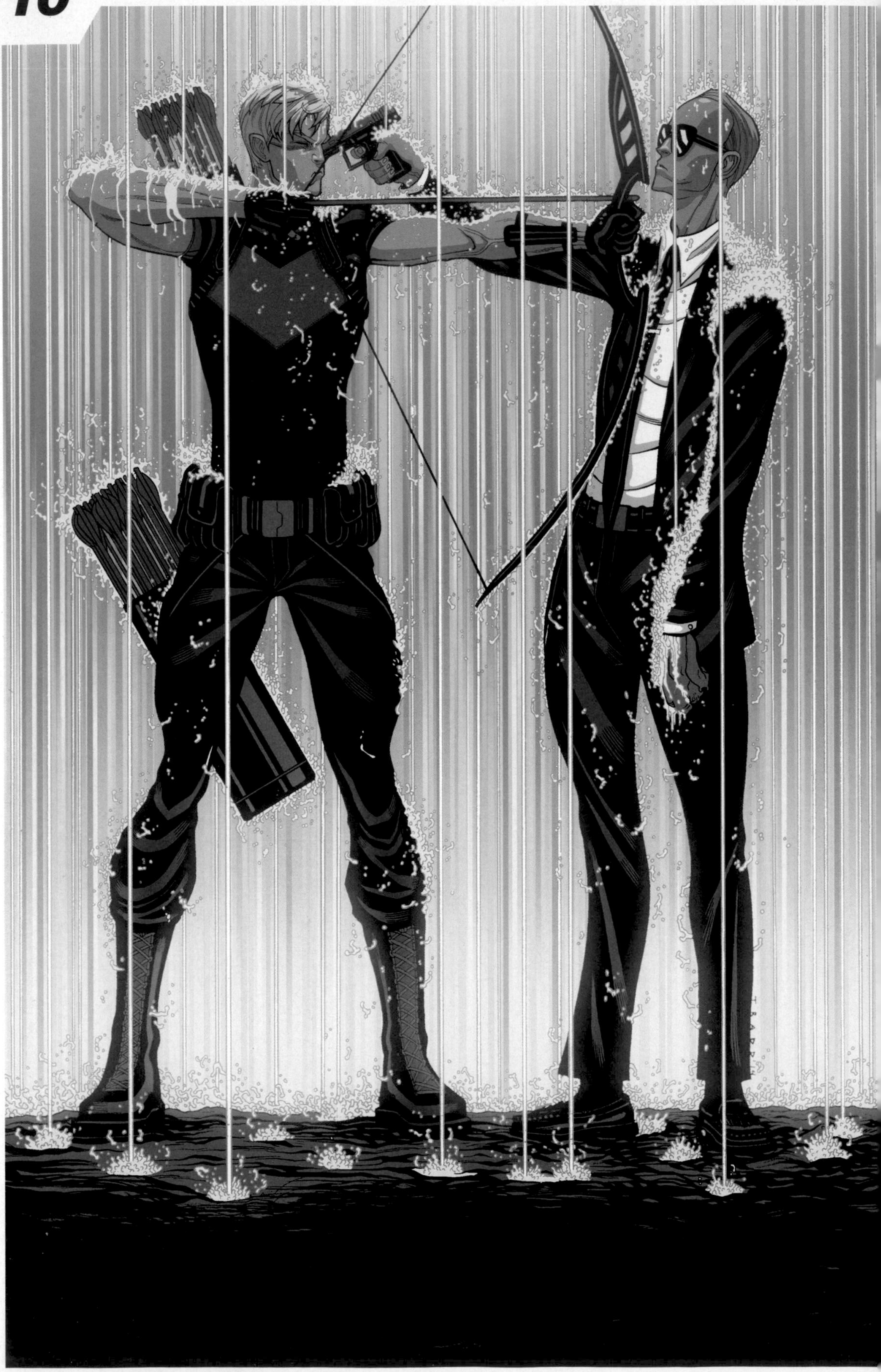

ROAD TO NOWHERE

S.H.I.E.L.D. HELICARRIER *ILIAD.*

SOMETHING TELLS ME HILL SHOULD KNOW ABOUT THIS.

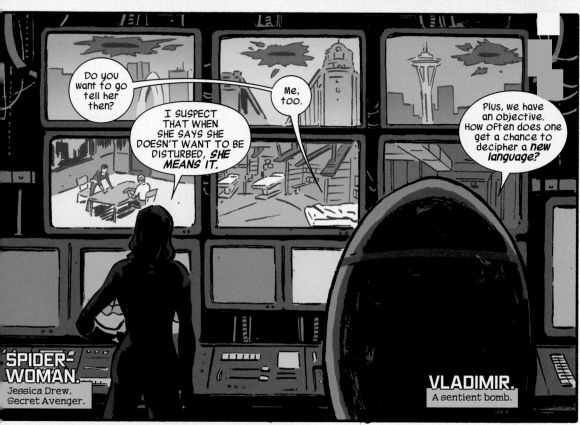

DO YOU WANT TO GO TELL HER THEN?

ME, TOO.

I SUSPECT THAT WHEN SHE SAYS SHE DOESN'T WANT TO BE DISTURBED, *SHE MEANS IT.*

PLUS, WE HAVE AN OBJECTIVE. HOW OFTEN DOES ONE GET A CHANCE TO DECIPHER A *NEW* LANGUAGE?

SPIDER-WOMAN.
Jessica Drew. Secret Avenger.

VLADIMIR.
A sentient bomb.

IN THIS UNIVERSE? PRETTY OFTEN.

TOUCHÉ.

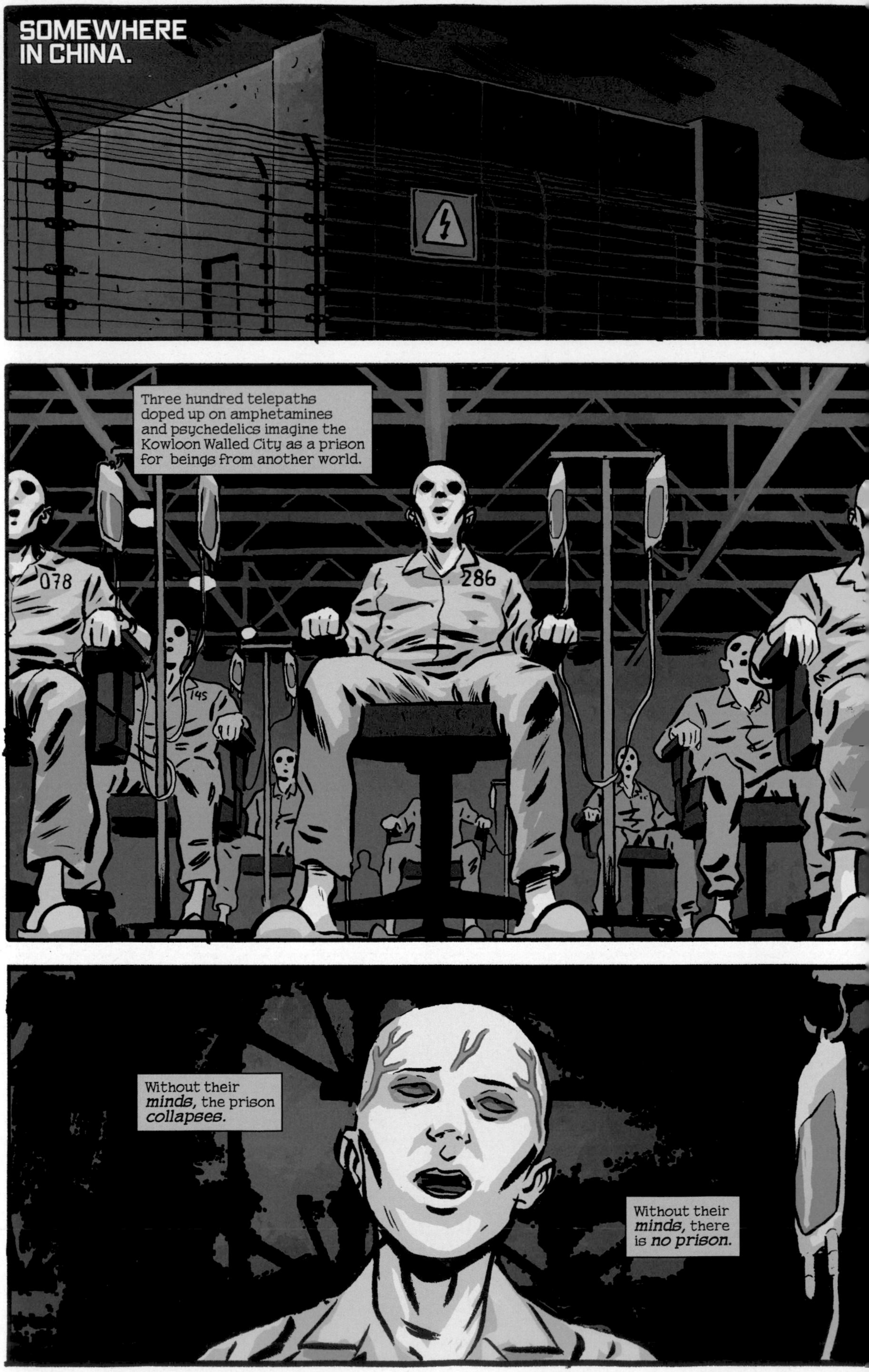

SOMEWHERE IN CHINA.
Three hundred telepaths doped up on amphetamines and psychedelics imagine the Kowloon Walled City as a prison for beings from another world.
078
286
145
Without their *minds*, the prison *collapses*.
Without their *minds*, there is *no prison*.

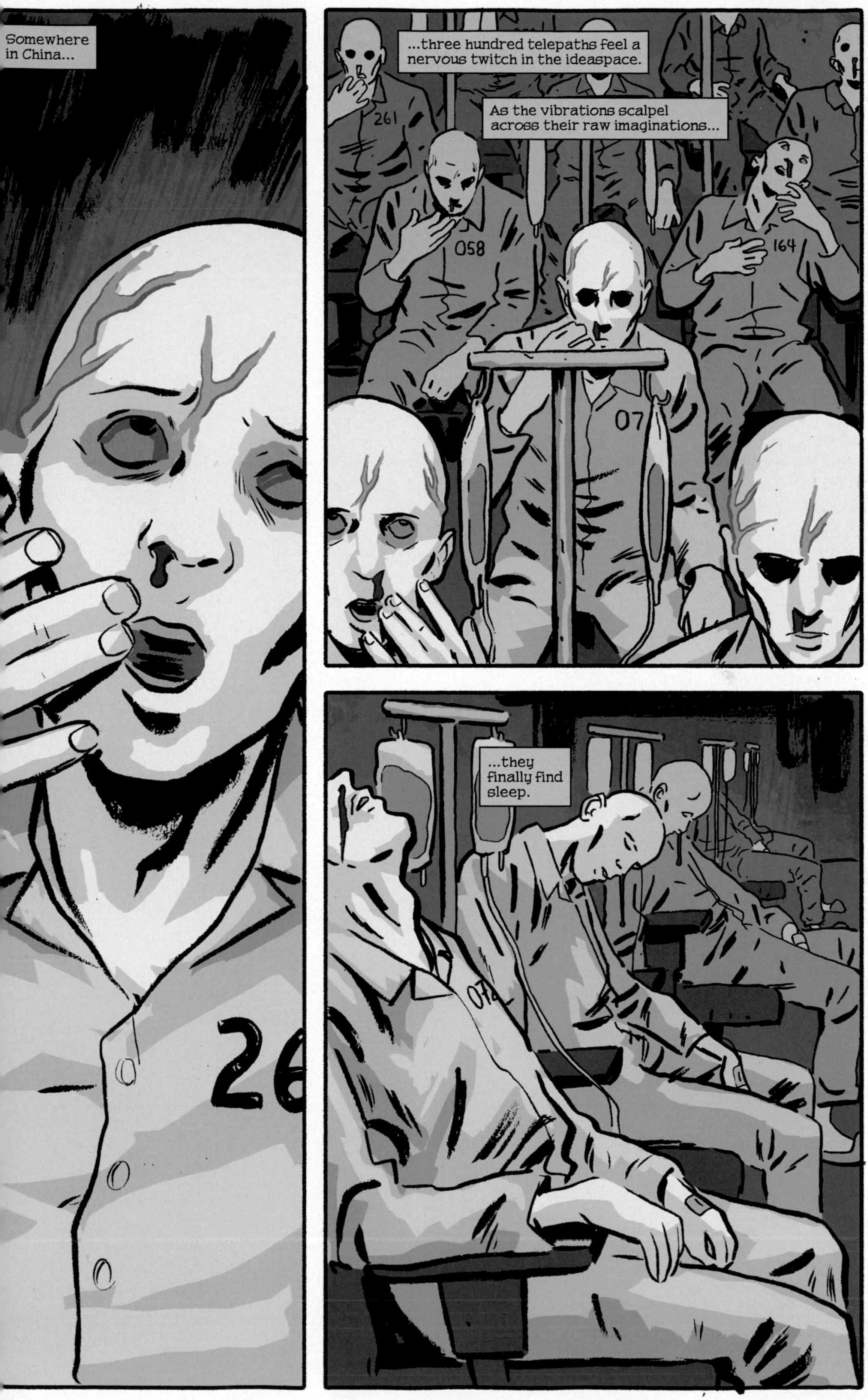

Somewhere in China...
...three hundred telepaths feel a nervous twitch in the ideaspace.
As the vibrations scalpel across their raw imaginations...
261
058
164
07
...they finally find sleep.
26

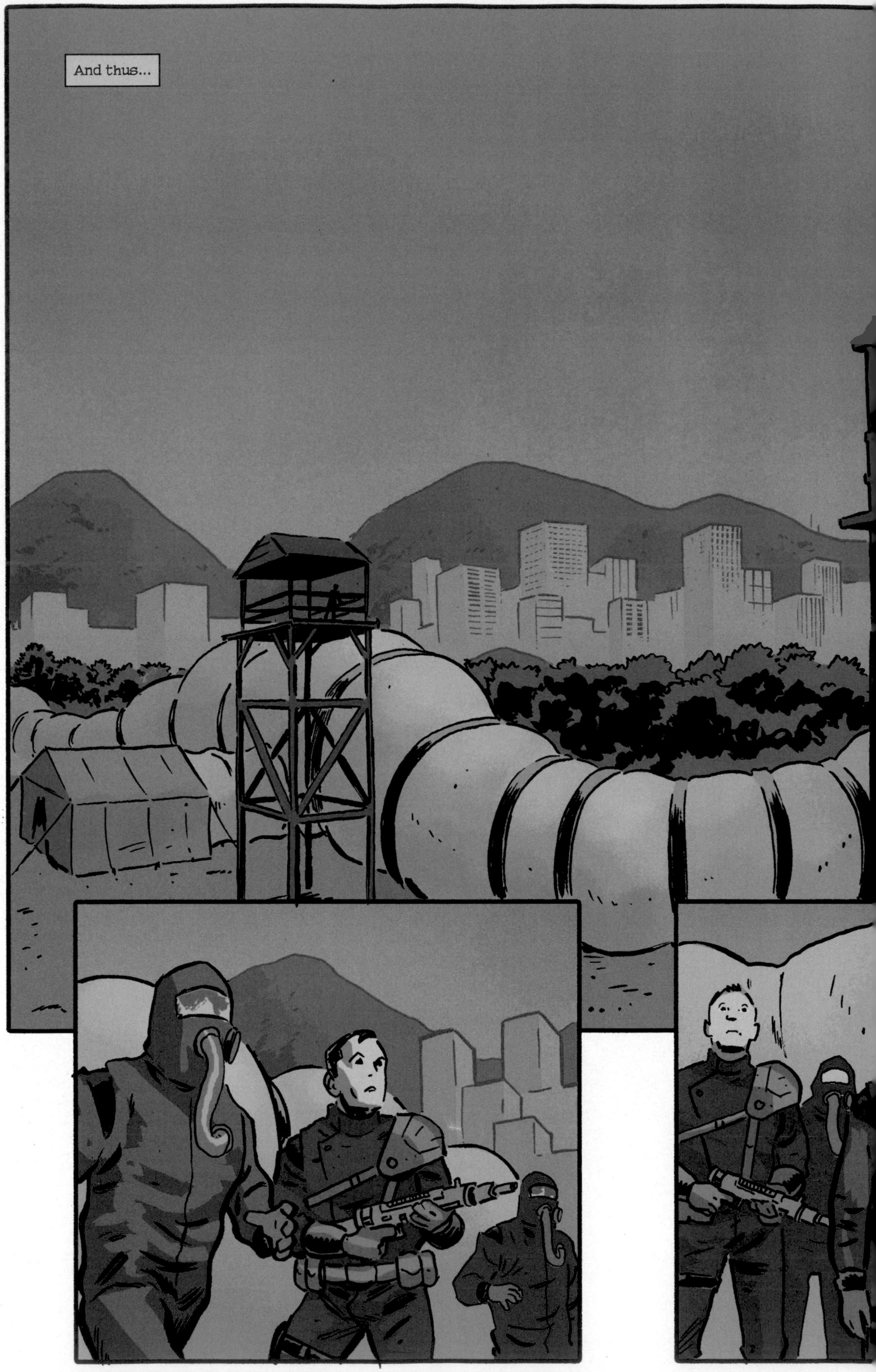
And thus...

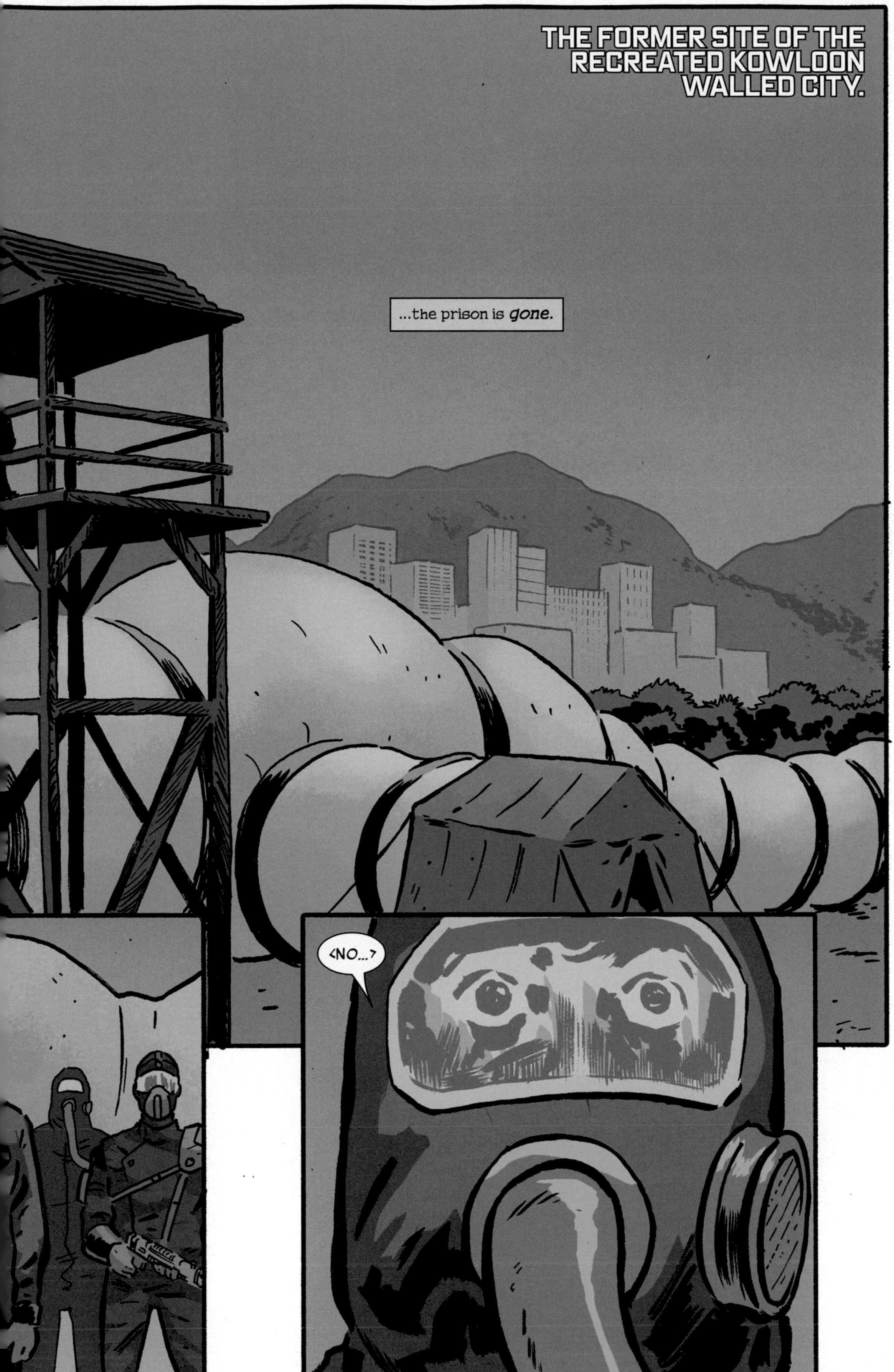
THE FORMER SITE OF THE RECREATED KOWLOON WALLED CITY.
...the prison is *gone.*
<NO...>

MEANWHILE, IN ARGENTINA...

PHIL COULSON.
Ready to change the world. Secret Avenger.

HAWKEYE.
Clint Barton. Ready to catch Phil and find out what he's up to. Secret Avenger.

...AND AWAY FROM IT...

...AND DEEP INTO THE VENEZUELAN JUNGLE...

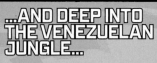

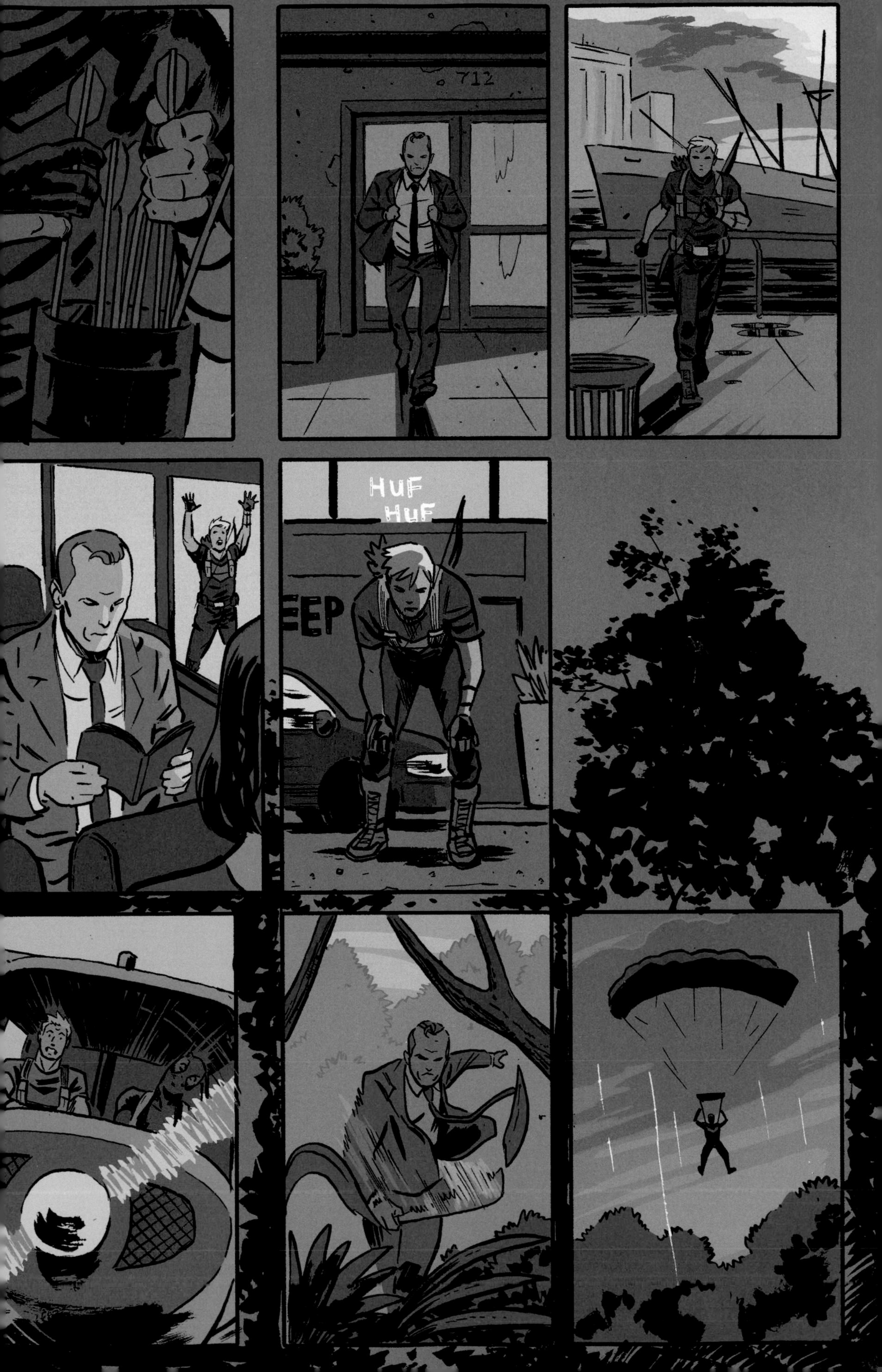
712
HUF
HUF
EEP

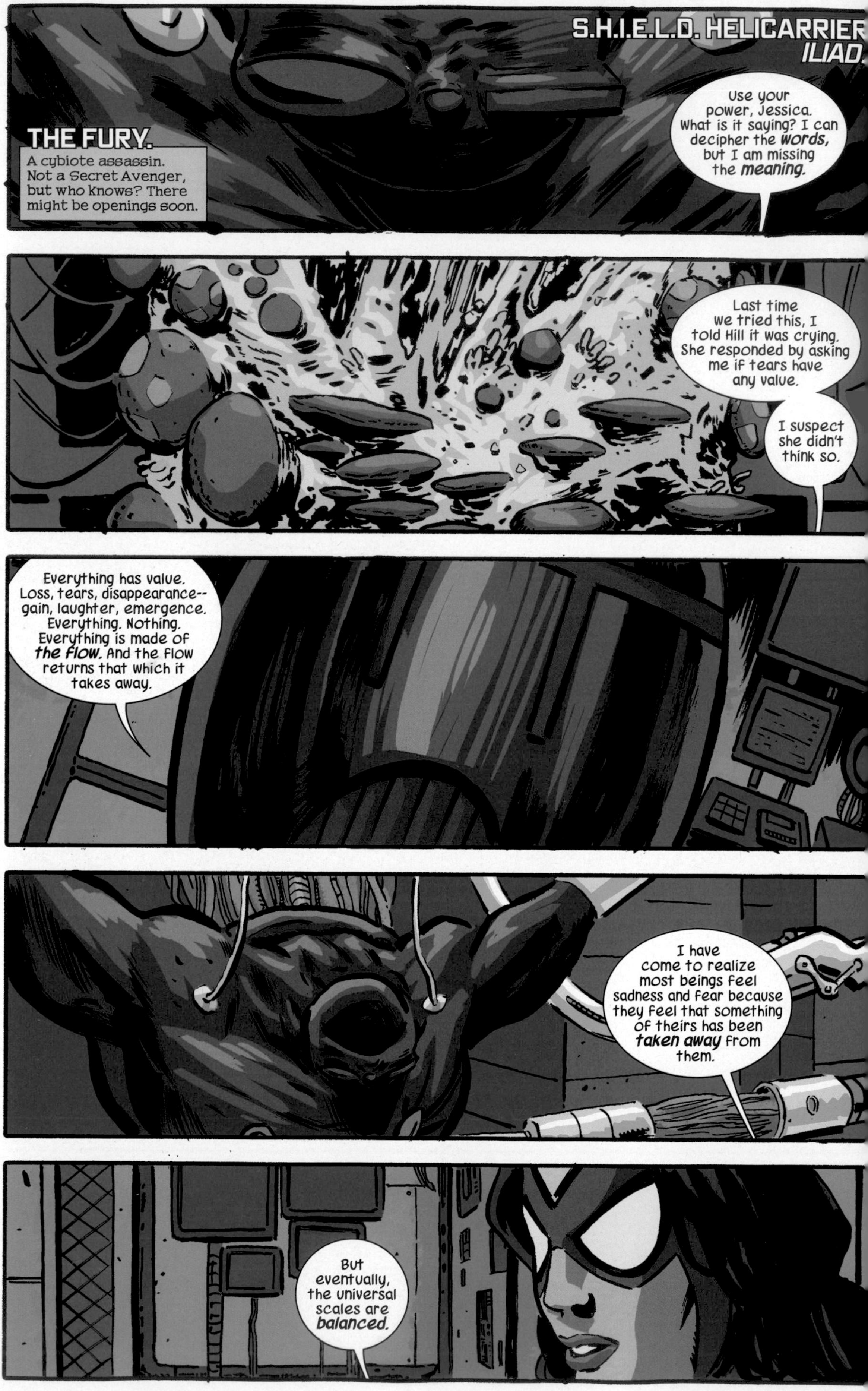
S.H.I.E.L.D. HELICARRIER ILIAD.
THE FURY.
A cybiote assassin. Not a Secret Avenger, but who knows? There might be openings soon.
Use your power, Jessica. What is it saying? I can decipher the words, but I am missing the meaning.
Last time we tried this, I told Hill it was crying. She responded by asking me if tears have any value.
I suspect she didn't think so.
Everything has value. Loss, tears, disappearance--gain, laughter, emergence. Everything. Nothing. Everything is made of the flow. And the flow returns that which it takes away.
I have come to realize most beings feel sadness and fear because they feel that something of theirs has been taken away from them.
But eventually, the universal scales are balanced.

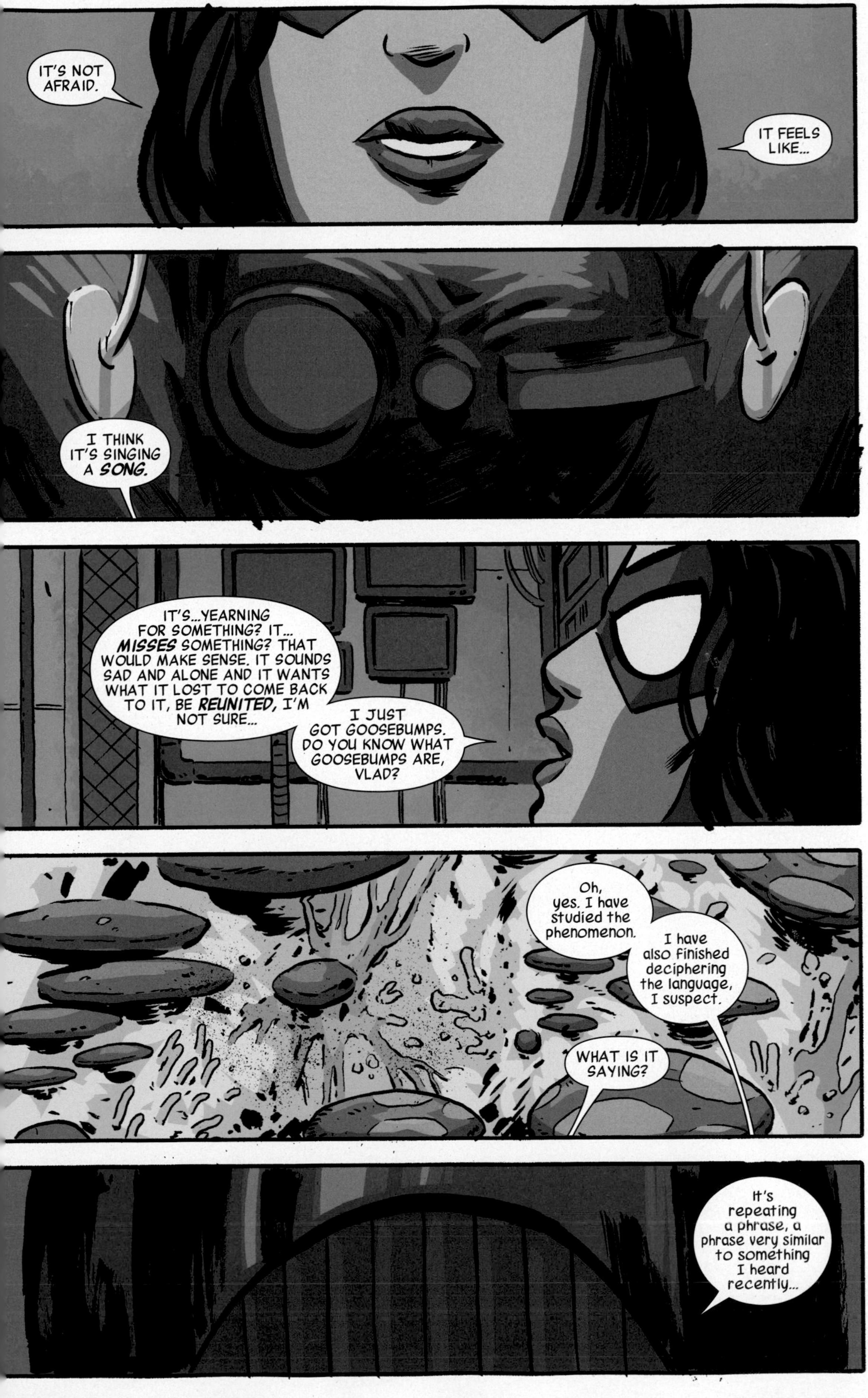
IT'S NOT AFRAID.
IT FEELS LIKE...
I THINK IT'S SINGING A SONG.
IT'S...YEARNING FOR SOMETHING? IT... MISSES SOMETHING? THAT WOULD MAKE SENSE. IT SOUNDS SAD AND ALONE AND IT WANTS WHAT IT LOST TO COME BACK TO IT, BE REUNITED, I'M NOT SURE...
I JUST GOT GOOSEBUMPS. DO YOU KNOW WHAT GOOSEBUMPS ARE, VLAD?
Oh, yes. I have studied the phenomenon.
I have also finished deciphering the language, I suspect.
WHAT IS IT SAYING?
It's repeating a phrase, a phrase very similar to something I heard recently...

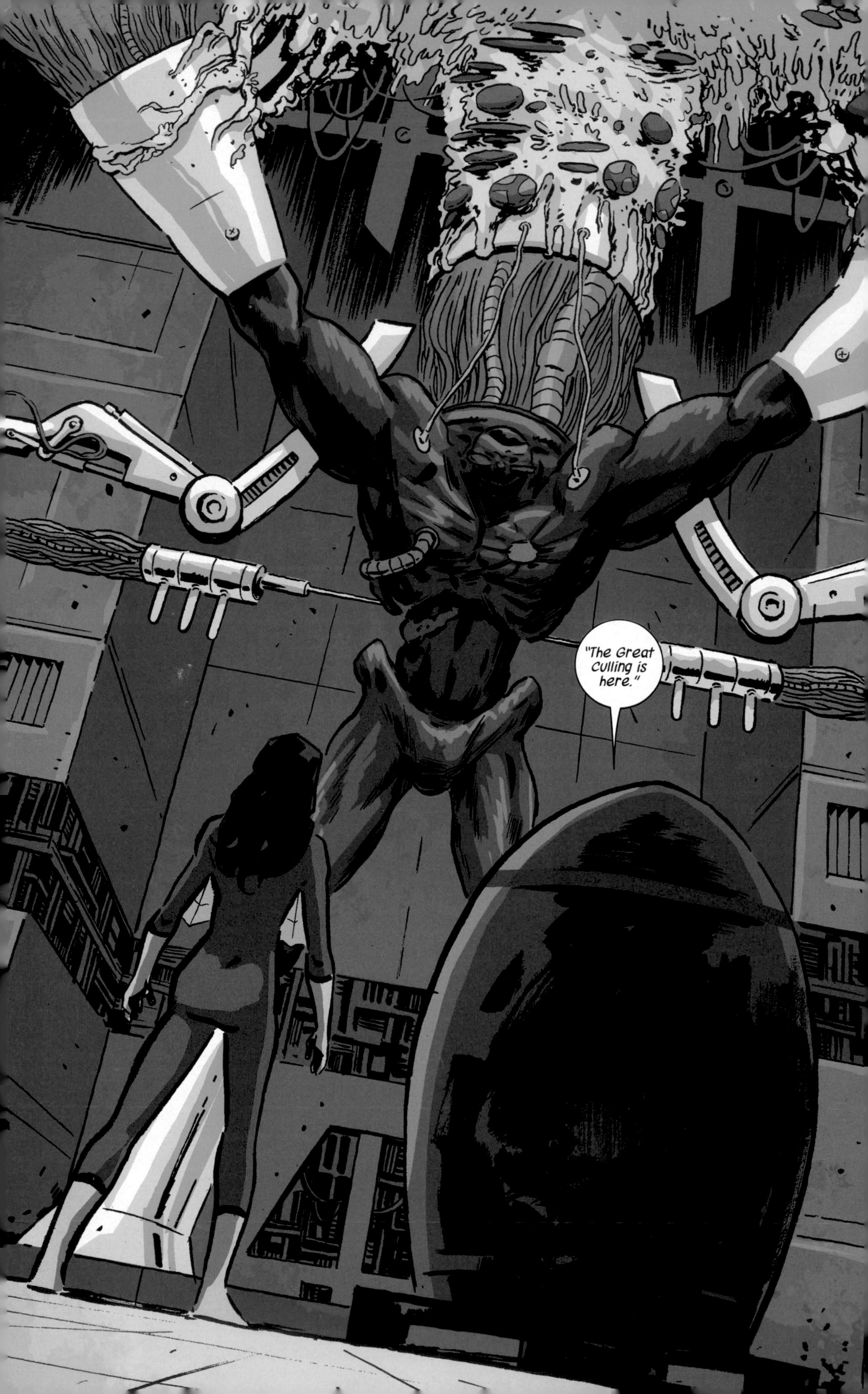
"The Great Culling is here."

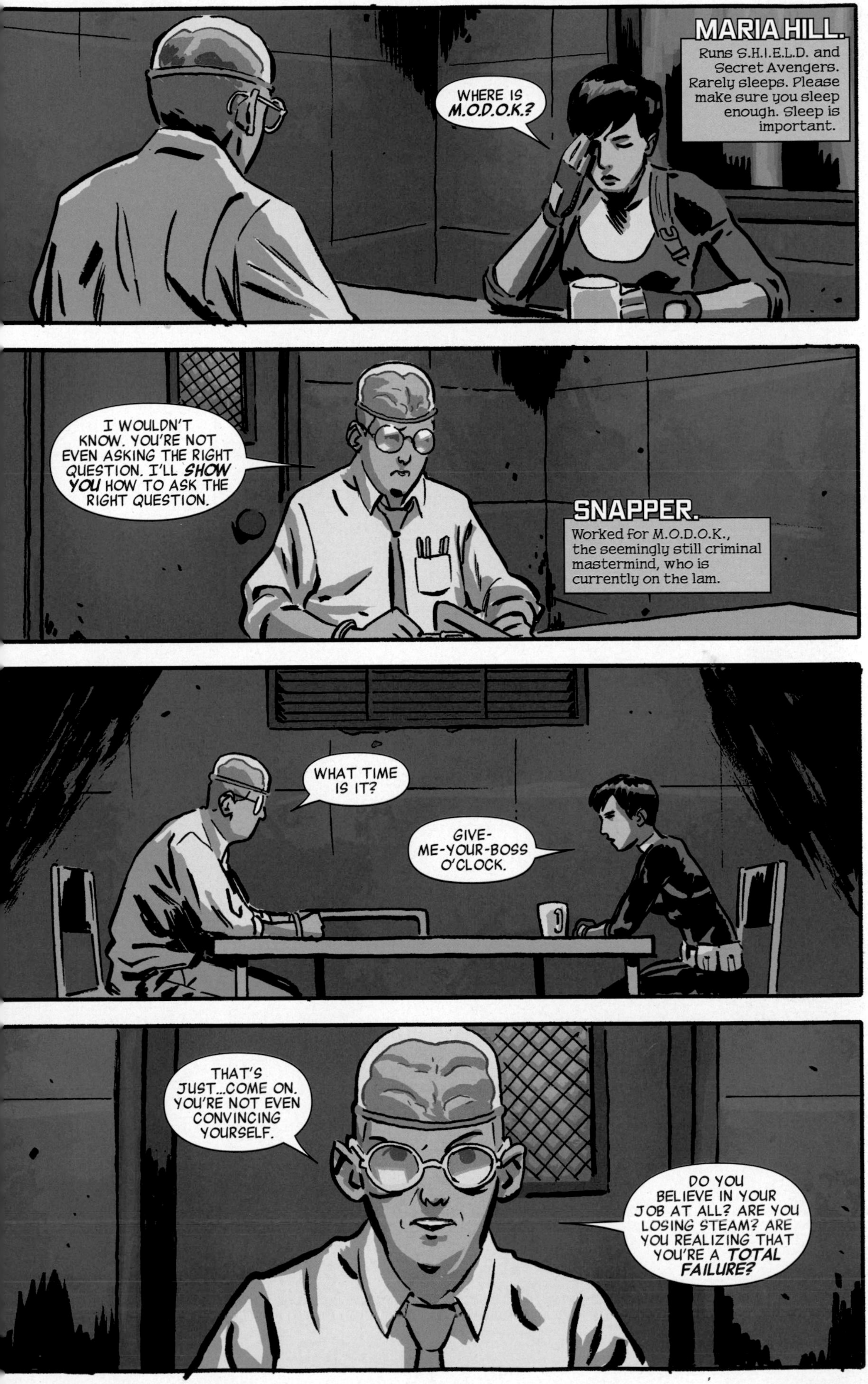
MARIA HILL.
Runs S.H.I.E.L.D. and Secret Avengers. Rarely sleeps. Please make sure you sleep enough. Sleep is important.
WHERE IS M.O.D.O.K.?
I WOULDN'T KNOW. YOU'RE NOT EVEN ASKING THE RIGHT QUESTION. I'LL SHOW YOU HOW TO ASK THE RIGHT QUESTION.
SNAPPER.
Worked for M.O.D.O.K., the seemingly still criminal mastermind, who is currently on the lam.
WHAT TIME IS IT?
GIVE-ME-YOUR-BOSS O'CLOCK.
THAT'S JUST...COME ON. YOU'RE NOT EVEN CONVINCING YOURSELF.
DO YOU BELIEVE IN YOUR JOB AT ALL? ARE YOU LOSING STEAM? ARE YOU REALIZING THAT YOU'RE A TOTAL FAILURE?

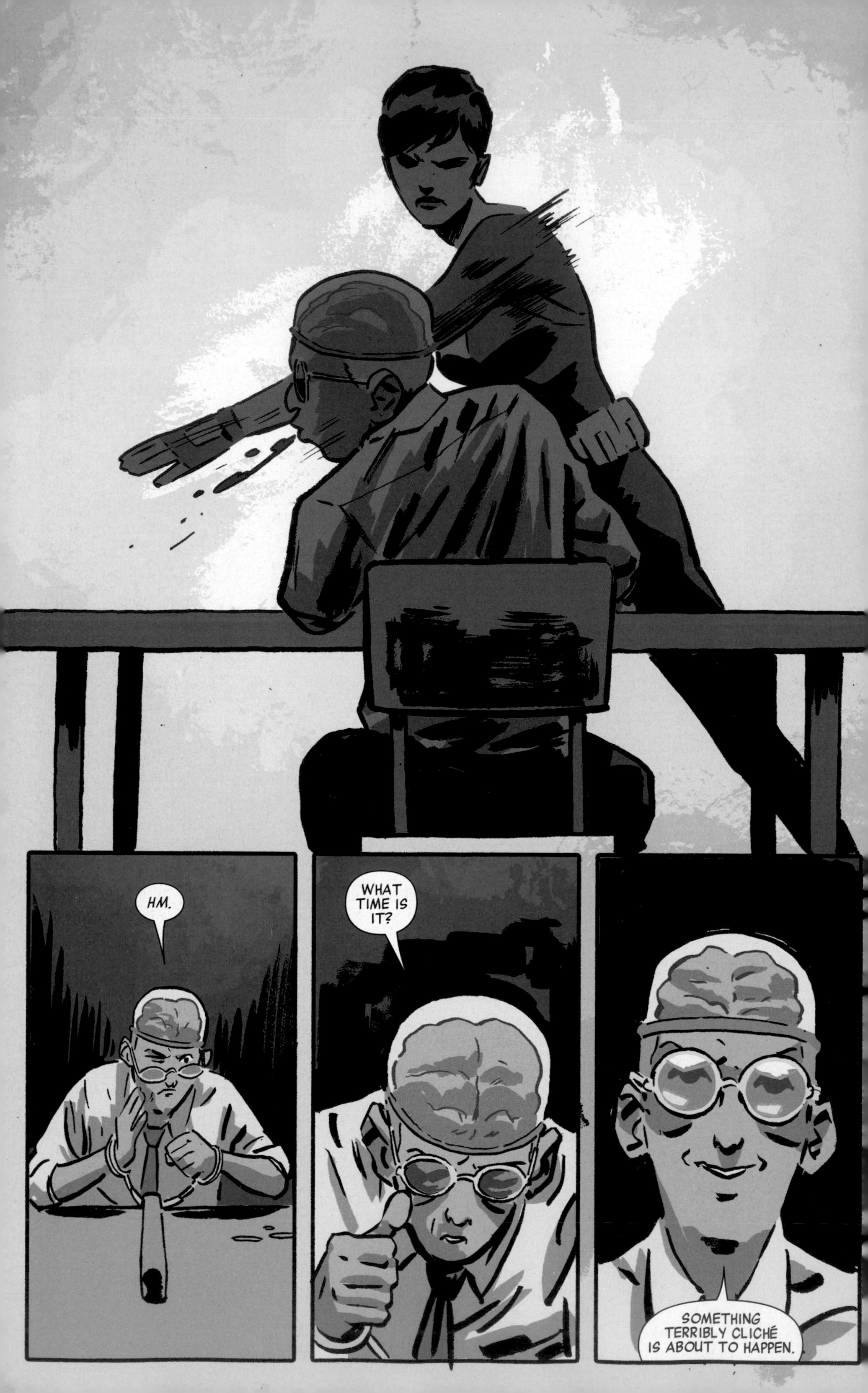
HM.
WHAT TIME IS IT?
SOMETHING TERRIBLY CLICHÉ IS ABOUT TO HAPPEN.

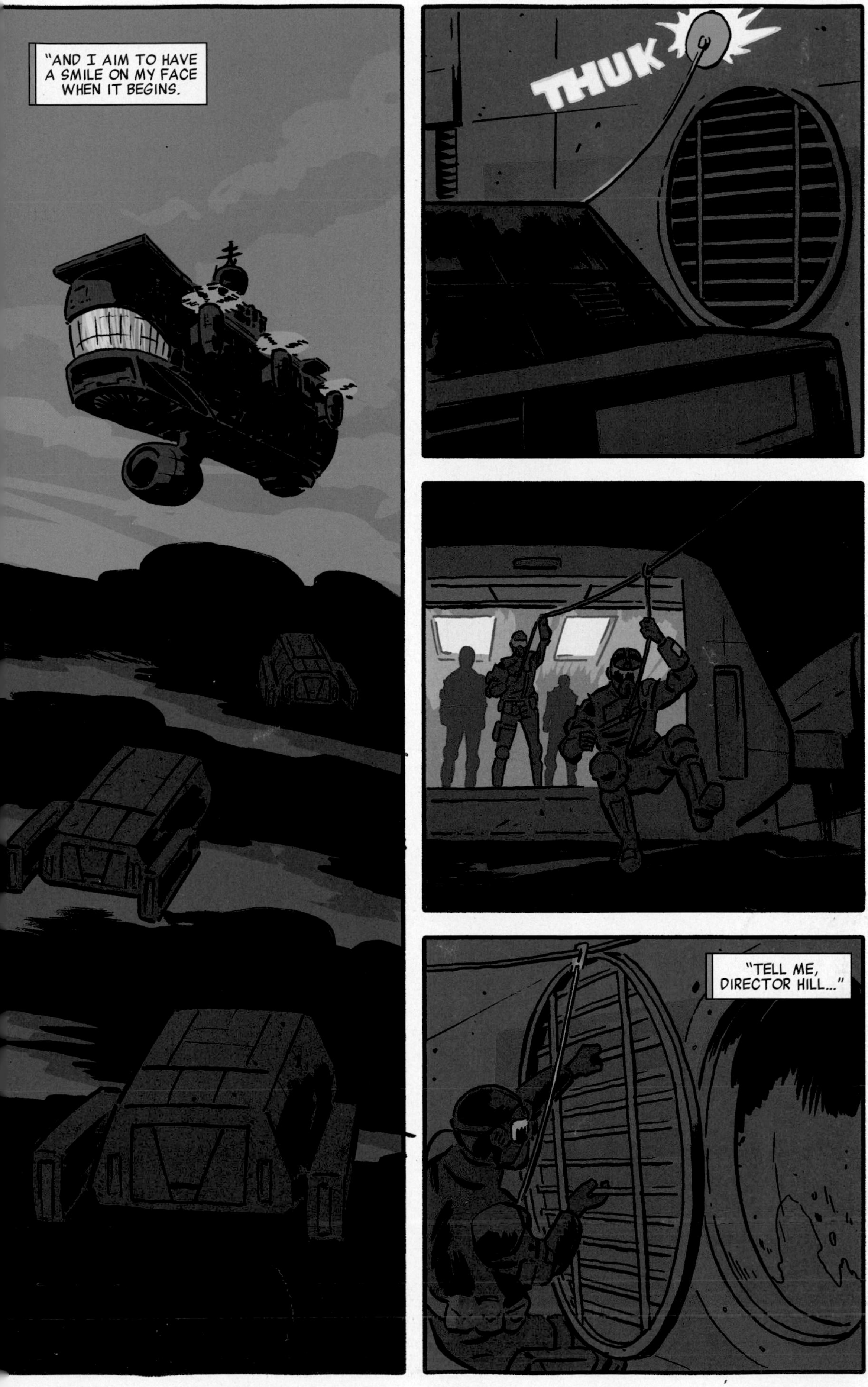
"AND I AIM TO HAVE A SMILE ON MY FACE WHEN IT BEGINS.
THUK
"TELL ME, DIRECTOR HILL..."

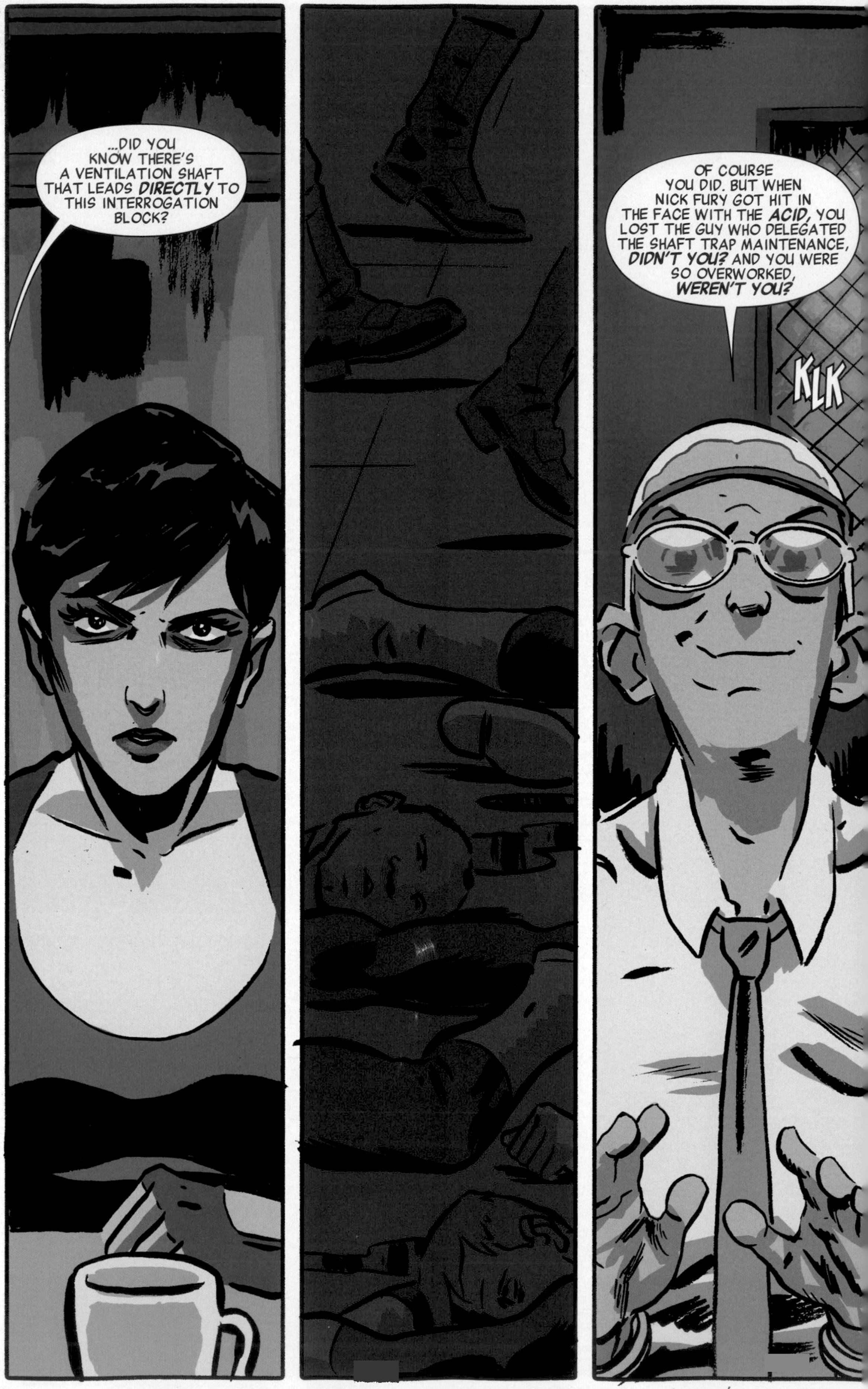
...DID YOU KNOW THERE'S A VENTILATION SHAFT THAT LEADS **DIRECTLY** TO THIS INTERROGATION BLOCK?
OF COURSE YOU DID. BUT WHEN NICK FURY GOT HIT IN THE FACE WITH THE **ACID,** YOU LOST THE GUY WHO DELEGATED THE SHAFT TRAP MAINTENANCE, **DIDN'T YOU?** AND YOU WERE SO OVERWORKED, **WEREN'T YOU?**
KLK

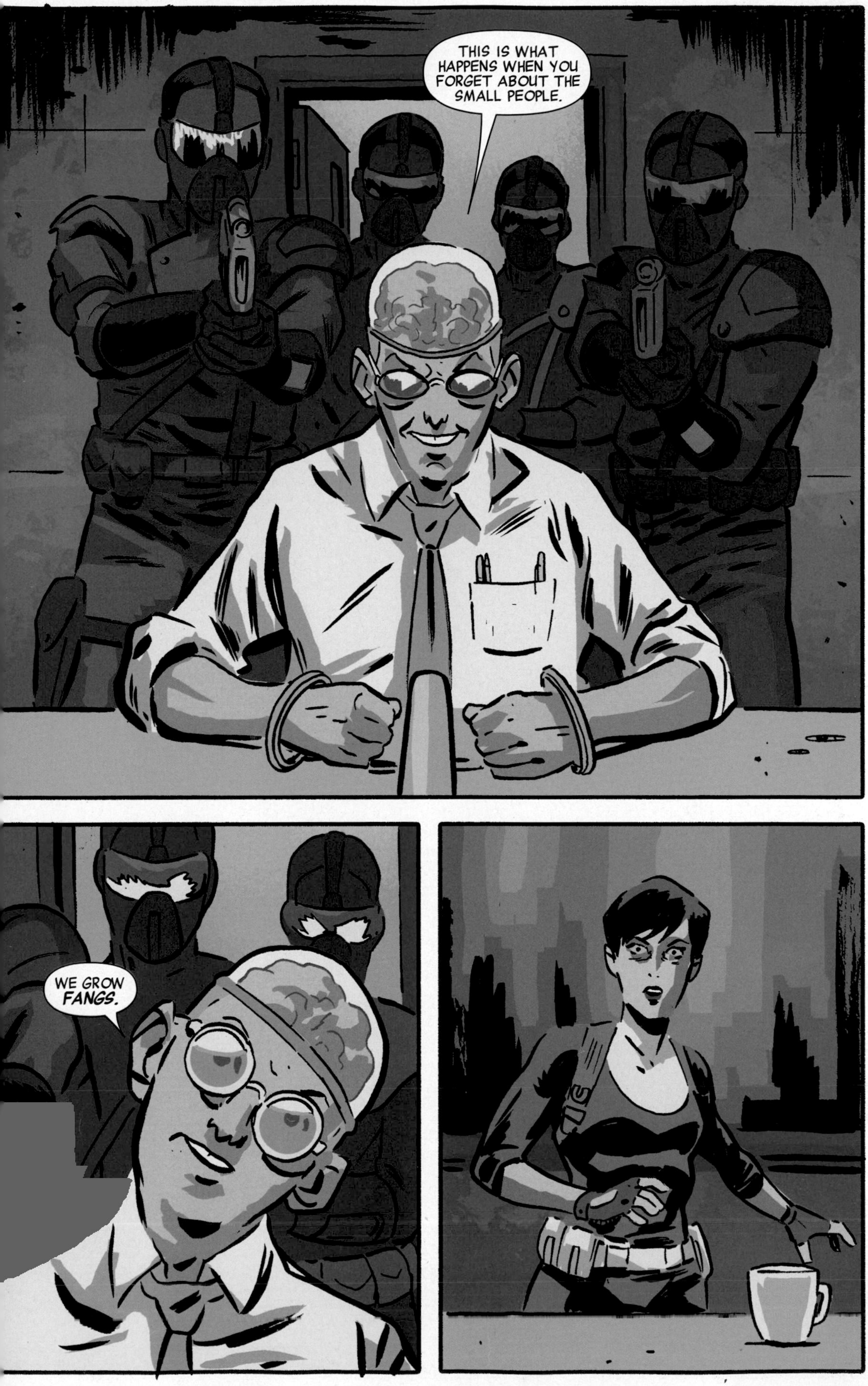
THIS IS WHAT HAPPENS WHEN YOU FORGET ABOUT THE SMALL PEOPLE.
WE GROW FANGS.

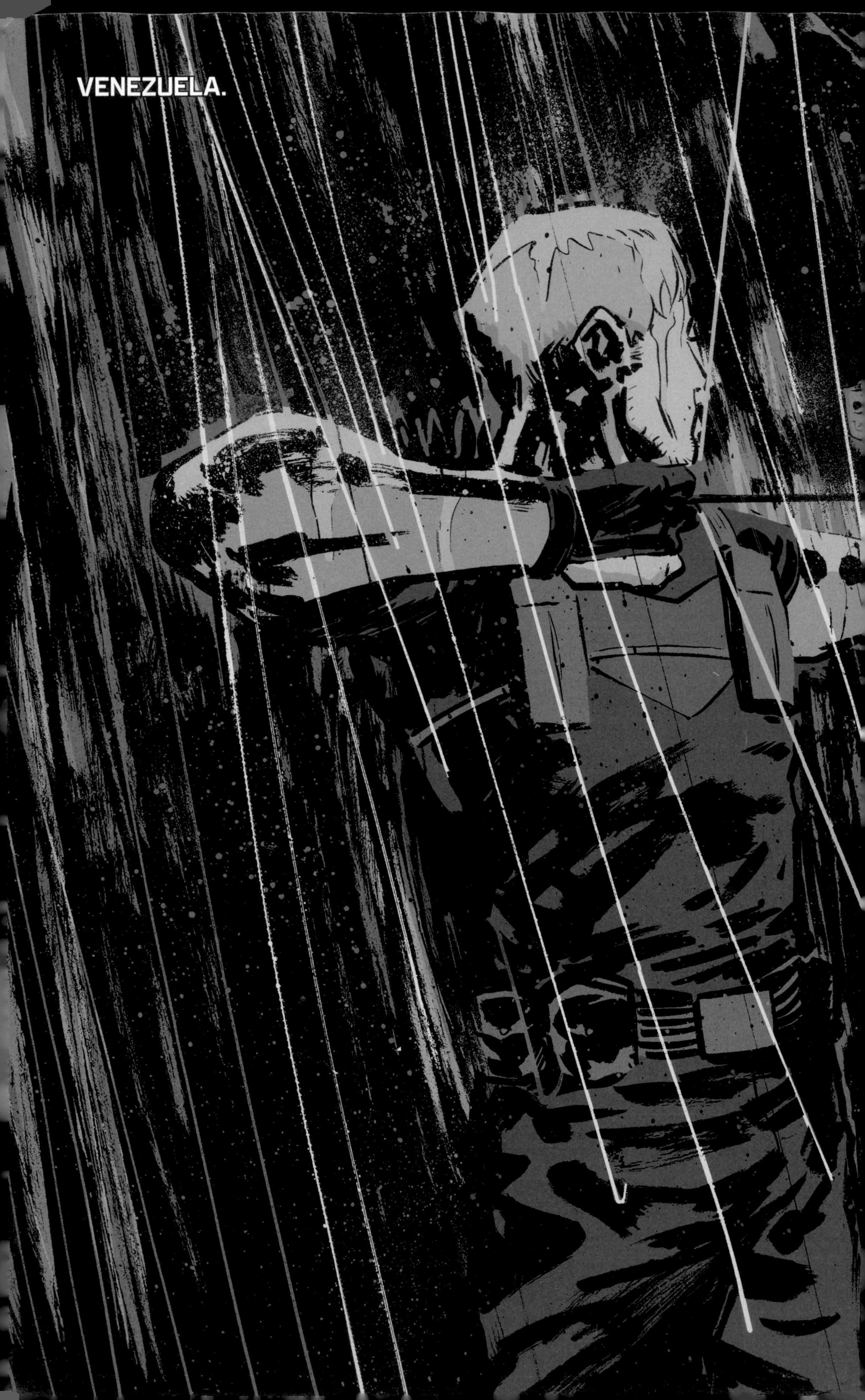
VENEZUELA.

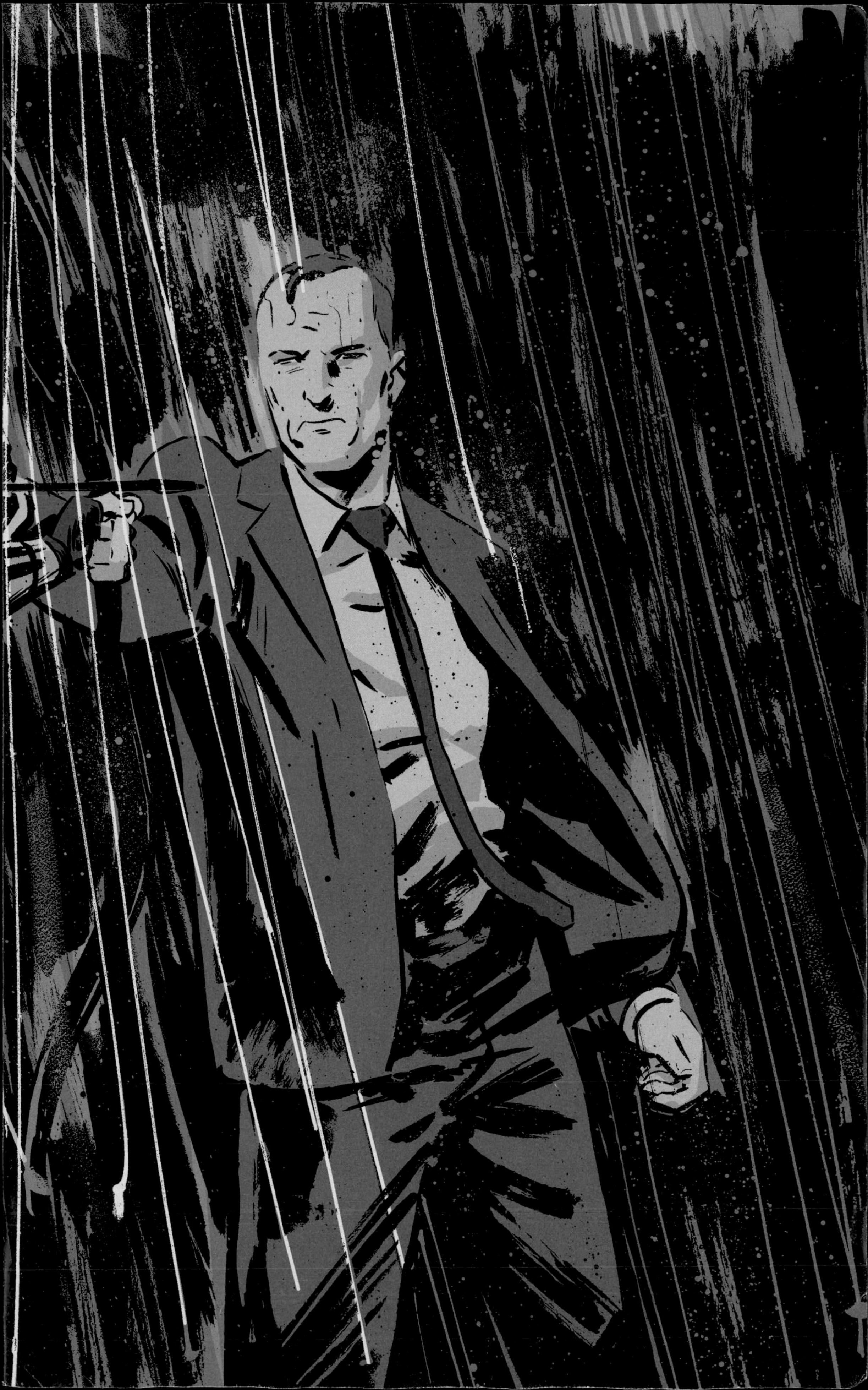

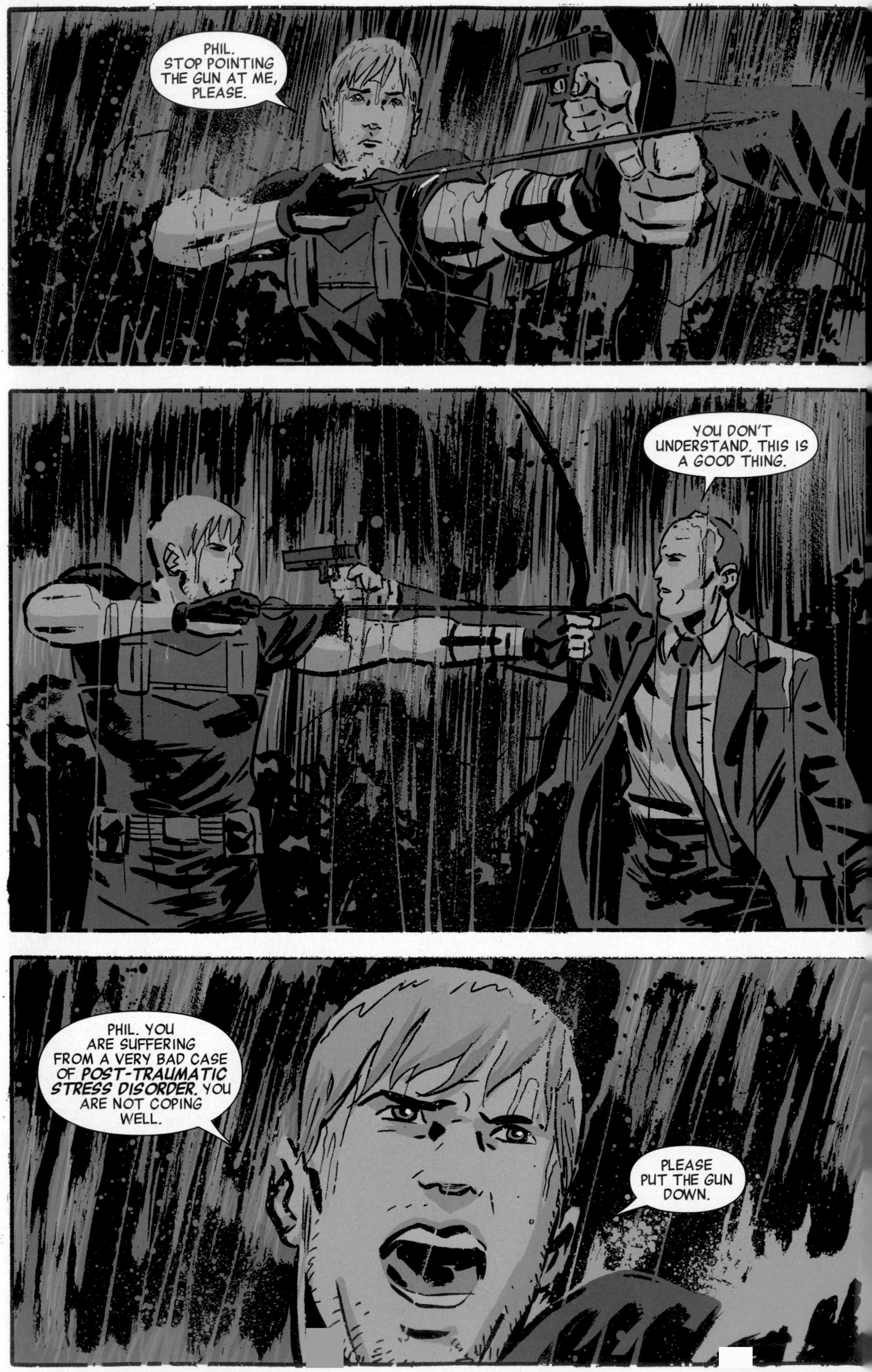
PHIL. STOP POINTING THE GUN AT ME, PLEASE.
YOU DON'T UNDERSTAND. THIS IS A GOOD THING.
PHIL. YOU ARE SUFFERING FROM A VERY BAD CASE OF ***POST-TRAUMATIC STRESS DISORDER.*** YOU ARE NOT COPING WELL.
PLEASE PUT THE GUN DOWN.

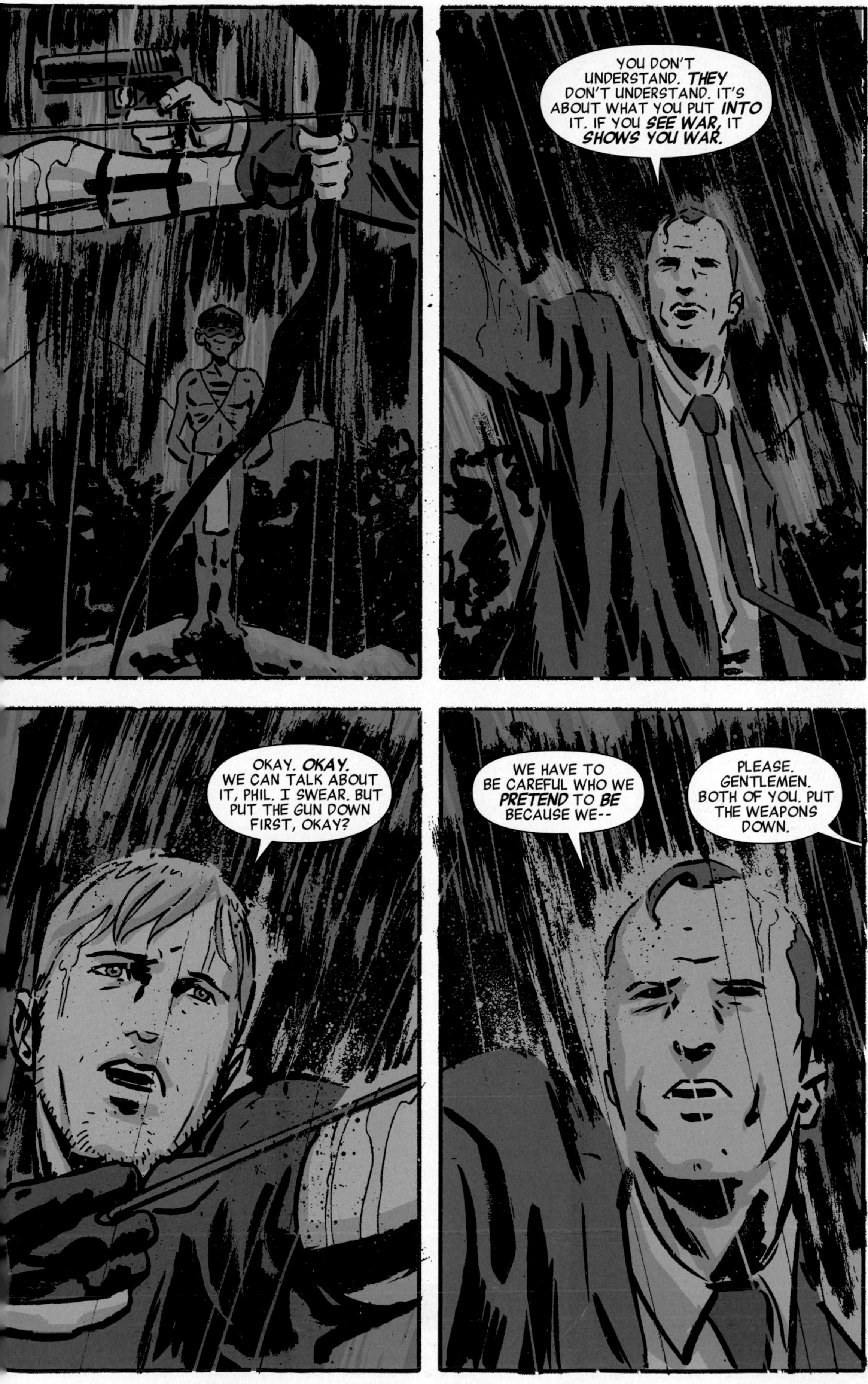

YOU DON'T UNDERSTAND. THEY DON'T UNDERSTAND. IT'S ABOUT WHAT YOU PUT INTO IT. IF YOU SEE WAR, IT SHOWS YOU WAR.
OKAY. OKAY. WE CAN TALK ABOUT IT, PHIL. I SWEAR. BUT PUT THE GUN DOWN FIRST, OKAY?
WE HAVE TO BE CAREFUL WHO WE PRETEND TO BE BECAUSE WE--
PLEASE. GENTLEMEN. BOTH OF YOU. PUT THE WEAPONS DOWN.

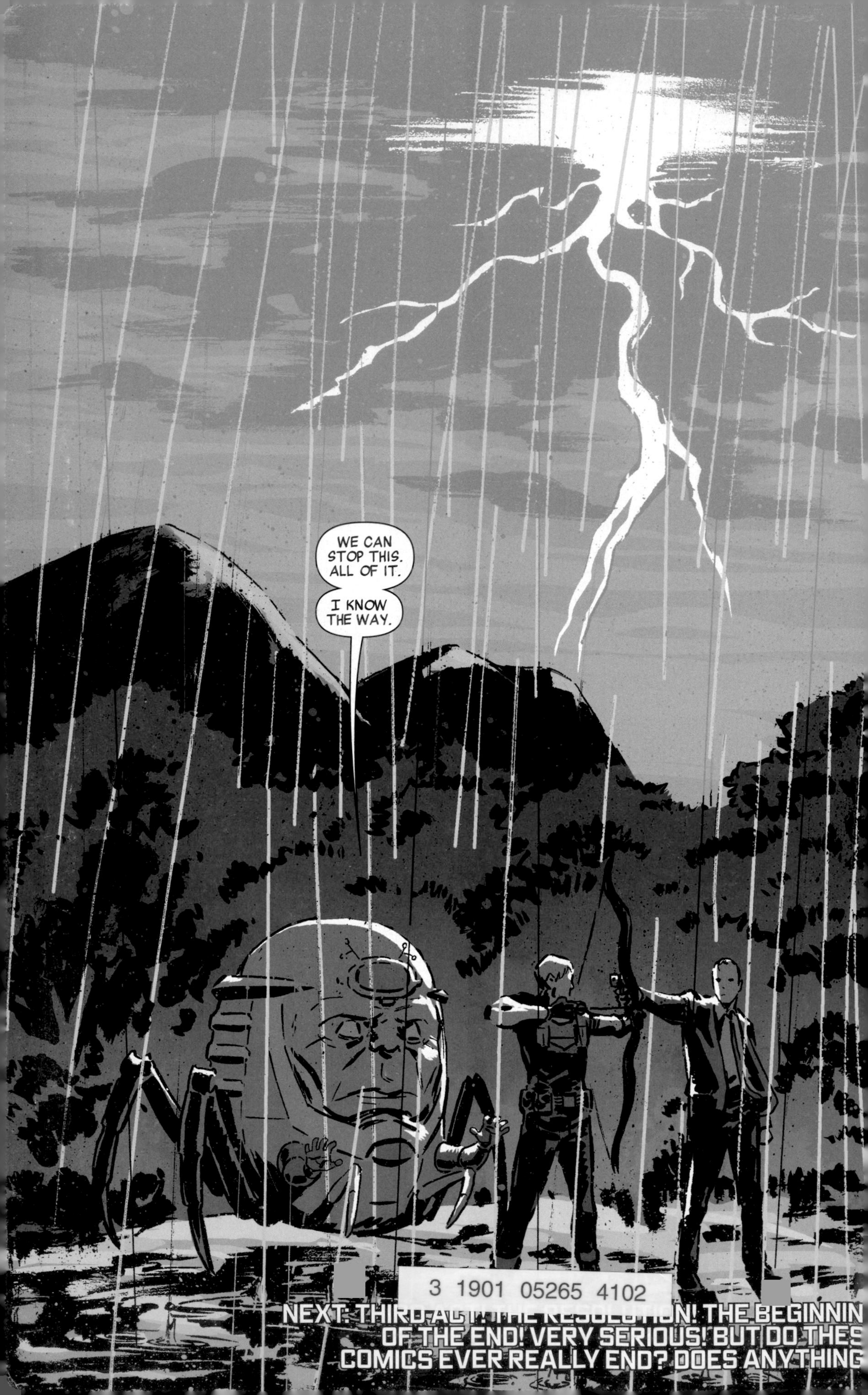
WE CAN STOP THIS. ALL OF IT.
I KNOW THE WAY.
NEXT: THIRD ACT! THE RESOLUTION! THE BEGINNIN
OF THE END! VERY SERIOUS! BUT DO THES
COMICS EVER REALLY END? DOES ANYTHING